MOMENTUM
IS YOUR
FRIEND

MOMENTUM IS YOUR FRIEND

THE METAL COWBOY
AND HIS PINT-SIZED POSSE
TAKE ON AMERICA

Joe Kurmaskie

BREAKAWAY BOOKS
HALCOTTSVILLE, NEW YORK
2006

Momentum Is Your Friend: The Metal Cowboy and His Pint-Sized Posse Take on America
Copyright 2006 by Joe Kurmaskie

ISBN: 1-891369-65-2
ISBN-13: 978-1-891369-65-0
Library of Congress Control Number: 2006926643

Published by Breakaway Books
P. O. Box 24
Halcottsville, NY 12438
www.breakawaybooks.com

FIRST EDITION

For Quinn and Enzo,
my Princes of the Pacific,
my Kings of the Coast

It's never enough until your heart stops beating.
—New Order

Prologue

A few things you should know about me: I'm involved in a rather unhealthy relationship with caffeine; it's been going on for years, and I have no intention of breaking things off. Also, by my twenty-first birthday I'd quit more jobs than you'll ever have, leaving me free to follow the only path left for a strapping young man of questionable aptitude and work ethic: I became a writer. When folks ask me what that's like, I tell them to picture a super-hero with no special powers. You're all Clark Kent, all the time. Worse, someone along the way, probably my mother, convinced me that I did possess god-like abilities. This will turn out to be in my imagination.

What else? I don't know when to say quit, especially around certain flavors of pie, or after I've climbed onto a bicycle. Often, combining my suspect intellect with my stubborn resolve makes for lively entertainment. Case in point: I once raced a greyhound on foot along uneven New Mexico sand teeming with barrel cacti. This, while an entire deck of partygoers looked on. I was not drunk or running for my life, nor was this a high-stakes wager. I just thought it might be fun, and part of me actually believed I could beat this graceful animal (see Mom, and the special powers ruse), and because someone needed to wipe that cocky grin off its streamlined face.

I would learn too late that centuries of breeding are responsible for its loopy smile, not to mention its incredible speed out of the blocks. Also, that there is no margin of error when running between barrel cacti.

One more thing. I have what teachers euphemistically referred to on progress reports as socially excessive verbal proficiency. I'm chatty; my mouth runneth over.

Let's review. What we have is a jittery, unemployable scribe, a tenacious bastard to be sure, but lacking a certain intellectual curiosity, who wants nothing more than to ride his bicycle . . . and won't shut up.

I'm as surprised as you that it's worked out this well.

Part 1

How Momentum Works

"The aim of life is to live, and to live means to be aware, joyously, drunkenly, serenely, divinely aware." —Henry Miller

"Know thyself? If I knew myself, I'd run away." —Goethe

1

"He did every single thing as if he did nothing else."
—Charles Dickens

Climbing a healthy series of switchbacks through the chill of a Colorado dawn, I don't feel tired. I don't feel the miles I pedaled yesterday or the weight I'm carrying now. Pockets of warm air hug the corners of the road. I spot wildflowers, rebels against the altitude, clinging to washes as I clear the treeline. When I look over my shoulder there's another cyclist, some industrious insomniac out for an early morning ride. He's determined to catch me before the top, but it doesn't happen. We rest beside a sign marking Cottonwood Pass, at more than 12,000 feet above sea level.

It's every man's secret desire to raise a middle finger to the approach of midlife. High time to stick it to the Reaper while I still have the lung capacity. I want to humiliate that cloaked coward. Put Death in polyester bell-bottoms, gaudy gold medallions, cue the DJ and make him do "The Hustle" for the viewers at home.

After that maybe we'll dress life's little party crasher in tight Lycra, ride him hard, then drop Death like a wet bag of dirt on some slow rise in the Midwest. Who's with me?!

"You're coming from where?!" Insomniac asks a second time, looking over fourteen feet of loaded rig: my two boys and the tagalong bike and trailer I've been towing for 1,576 miles. He nods reverently. "And here I thought I was doing something this morning."

We let that hang there for a few moments. In an uncharacteristic show of modesty, I try to shrug it off. The cycling equivalent of Jack LaLanne pretending he hasn't just crawl-stroked the English Channel pulling a hundred speed boats by his teeth.

"Don't kid yourself." Insomniac spreads his arms wide, in an effort to take in the whole monstrosity, before he gives up. "Oregon all the way to Washington, DC pulling that? My man, this is a *bold* statement."

I want to agree with him, but my perspective blurred beyond repair somewhere back in Idaho. These days, unless I'm in well over my head, it's not even interesting.

I should probably have that checked.

When it comes to needing a competent mental health professional, Insomniac could certainly give me a run for my money. It turns out bold statements backed up by equally derelict actions are his operating instructions.

He has to be pushing thirty, but when the helmet comes off a spectacular abundance of piercings, ten in one ear alone, and a little metal pipe, glowing cobalt blue in the predawn light, runs the width of his pinched and punctured forehead. It's an unsettling marriage of tribal art to a pack of angry teens. You know, the ones who loiter, smoke, curse, and nod with no enthusiasm from the steps of the public library; maybe a tribal leader failing community college who's stopped speaking to his parents.

"I lost my sweetest trick bike into Blue Mesa Reservoir last weekend," Insomniac announces.

A promising way to open an anecdote. It brings my second-grader, Quinn, back from whatever reverie he's lost in across the horizon. Five-year-old Enzo pops up through the top flap of the bicycle carrier, a prairie dog emerging at the first whiff of excitement on the breeze.

"It wasn't a road bike." As if this explains everything. We wait him out.

"I do BMX most weekends. Trick riding, extreme jumps. People know about me . . . I mean people outside the Colorado aggro biker community."

We nod encouragingly.

"Dudes, I'm awesome."

I recognize this behavior. To back up bold statements, a certain amount of grandstanding is required. Not always pretty, but absolutely necessary if one wants to complete the motion.

"On weekends, we toss up a plywood ramp on the railing of the bridge. It's sixty feet to the water. Crowd mushrooms by noon. Music, Frisbees, lots of vans, a real Dead show vibe."

But with more tattoos and Incubus music, is my guess.

"Never a question of 'if,' I'm just waiting until the crowd can't take any more tension."

Or they've run out of Ecstasy, perhaps?!

"Where was the other ramp?" Quinn asks. His question makes me proud and a bit melancholy, motivated as it is by a sense of safety and his misguided belief in self-preservation as a universal human trait.

You can tell Insomniac lives for moments like these. "The lake,

Big Guy. I'm over the top and landing in the lake . . . roll tape, news at 11. You want to catch huge air, nail a triple spin like you do this every day, then kick out from the bike before hitting the water. No one wants to be near their ride when it lands. Bonus for a quick resurfacing to snag your swag before it sinks to the bottom."

I watch Quinn's worldview shift before my eyes. As though he's studying the zoo orangoutangs hanging on high vines doing something foolish with fruit, a garden hose and their nostrils. The evolutionary connection has been made. I will need to watch my eldest son more closely the rest of the way to the Atlantic.

"Nailed the jump, but did it get ugly on the way down. Bike came back under me. I had to take evasive action or else . . ."

"Or else monsters would get you?" Enzo's into the story now, standing completely upright in the bike carrier, solar cover thrown back and bracing himself with the top bar . . . essentially turning his rig into a de facto Popemobile and himself into a mini Pontiff. We'll teach him the official Vatican wave later.

"Or else I'm impaled on my bike seat and they're dragging the res for my remains." Insomniac winks, playing to his audience. "But I'm not going down like that."

I interpret for the boys, complete with hand gestures. We should all have access to a diplomatic translator in Lycra.

"Speared, splattered . . . sunk."

A cliffhanger before breakfast . . . it just doesn't get any better for my kids.

"Bammo . . . I have to give the handlebars a roundhouse kick, then torque my back around like some circus performer, Dudes. Hit the water so wrong I forget everything until I'm pulled out and panting back on concrete."

The boys sigh at the same time and in the same pitch. The only thing more satisfying than Insomniac's ending would have been if it included a prize at the bottom of the box.

They might be done, but I have a few loose ends that need tying. Like how he has come to possess such a high-performance road bike.

"My brother took it in trade for a drywall job. He says I'll bury his best time by the end of the summer."

Replaying how Insomniac stalked me up the mountain like some sleek jungle cat leaves little doubt.

"You know, there's not a lot of crossover between trick riders and roadies," I say.

Insomniac looks back down the mountain. Its angle and the distance to the lake below are something out of a Dr. Seuss drawing. Then he eyes our bikes, the boys and the radical tilt of the Earth in the other direction.

"There ought to be," he says, not a trace of guile in his voice. "If this ain't extreme, I relinquish my membership."

We wait for sunrise at the top of the world—casual gods surveying an evergreen kingdom that spans for miles in every direction—then roll the summit and barrel into another day on the road.

2

"This is a perfect world, riding on an incline."
—Talking Heads

We're a few weeks and brutal headwinds beyond our triumphant cresting of 12,000-foot Cottonwood Pass.

"Come on, Dad," Quinn pokes at me with a bike pump in the same fashion I've seen him use on roadkill. "Get up! We're almost over the rainbow."

I'm lying yards from afternoon rush-hour traffic. The mercury tops 106 degrees, and Quinn's reference is to both the Judy Garland classic and the name of the steepest hill in Kansas City . . . probably less than five hundred feet, which I've failed to top.

To my left is a church, its spiral steeple penetrating the heights that man can reach. To the right, a hospital . . . which will come in handy if the spots at the edges of my vision continue to grow.

Since clearing the Colorado border, I've talked up Baum's Oz classic, even calling Kansas City its spiritual home. The boys are to be on the lookout for a horse of a different color. I'd give anything at this moment if they could locate a canister of oxygen.

It's on the humidity-stoked hill of Rainbow Boulevard, straddling Kansas and Missouri, caught between the cracks, that I wish there were "do-overs" in long distance cycling.

Wait a minute. Why not join me down here on the gravel? That's it, lie down in the road and let the burning asphalt blister your sweat-drenched skin, swallow back the tips of your lungs poking right through your throat and try to roll into the shade like some wounded Green Beret hunting for a depression on the battlefield, only to find that shade, like everything else inside the breadbasket of America, is a Heartland lie. Okay, that could be the heat stroke talking, but we are stretched across what most call a gutter, two hundred yards from the summit, seemingly incapable of forward progress, two kids counting on us and it's not getting any earlier—I'm allowed a little latitude.

And since you're down here, I'll tell you what we're looking for: Somewhere between the gravel pocking your soft spots and the glass shards boring into your back, the ants going about their business as if you don't exist and the hint of fresh-cut grass carrying memories of renewal . . . is our will to live. We'll need that, or, at the very least, faith enough to fake it.

One more thing: don't lie so close to me; I really should take in some air that no one's been breathing for a while.

We're nine blocks, less than two miles from our destination, but I don't know that. I can only recall it's something of an oasis, the home of close family friends, godparents more or less, and their beautiful daughters, one of whom broke my heart in all the right places years ago. Oh, and there's a pool, nestled under tall pines and lush flowering plants.

Still, Eden always comes with a price tag.

I can't beg or borrow the strength to do what is necessary on that bike. Eyeing the angle of our slope divided by the buildup of lactic acid in my muscles, then carrying the remainder of the day . . . nope. I'd better stay here a little longer, until my math improves or time and nature grind the hillside down to an acceptable size.

"Go Laaaannnce!" Followed by a few yips and yeehaws from the passenger side of a pickup truck. I'm too far gone to let its sarcastic undertone, or what may have been snickering from the back seat, touch me. Nothing's thrown in our direction, so there's that. Quinn wields the bike pump like an old man waving his cane at the neighborhood hooligans.

"Dad?" Lack of forward motion has interrupted my five-year-old's afternoon nap. Enzo emerges from the cave of his carrier holding a spray bottle of water. It sports a little fan attached to the nozzle.

"Do you have any chocolate?" He comes to a halt over me, stares for a moment, and shakes his head. My current state does not offer him much hope of obtaining cocoa product. I hear the little fan whirl into action. Enzo spritzes himself a few times, then, in an act of unprovoked kindness—what I choose to read as empathy—he turns the mist on his old man.

"No one's out of gas around here until I say so," Quinn barks, parroting one of my favorite self-help seminar lines. He gets in close, eyeing me with the disappointed glare of a high school football coach. "Get up. We're in the Emerald City."

I don't even make an attempt.

"Emerald City for you two, maybe," I say. My breathing is reminiscent of someone locked inside an iron lung. "For me, it's all tornados and flying monkeys right now."

Enzo turtles his neck a little and scans the skies for aerial chimps and twisters. I'm not trying to scare them, just buying some time.

It occurs to me that if I can still make fun of my situation, there might actually be something left in the tank.

"Another minute, boys, that's all I need. Quinn, get me some of that Clif recovery powder from the right pannier. It's in a Ziploc."

I manage a seated position without blacking out. Quinn has my water bottle in one hand and a bag of powder in the other.

"No, no . . . that bag's your grandpa. I'm talking about the other Ziploc, next to the gel packs and Band-Aids."

Did I mention we have three generations on board? After my dad's heart blew, Thanksgiving morning of 2000, his urn ended up in my home office. Not much of a final resting place. The man spends a lifetime grinding it out inside cubicles . . . it didn't seem right to keep him cooped up any longer. Deserving better in life, but when all that's left are gestures, go big. That was before every ounce mattered, back when rolling weight on a bicycle was just an abstract theory and a source of future bragging rights.

But when the road hits this hard, every item, even your long-suffering dad's remains, feel like a burden.

With Pop back in the bag, a few gallons of electrolyte therapy down my throat, and a pair of wobbly sea legs under me for support, we soldier on. It's asking too much to straddle the bike yet, but pushing it the short distance to the top is no picnic either, even with Quinn's help. Enzo has located the dregs of a lollipop along the floor of the trailer, silencing him for the moment.

The adventure hits rock bottom at what could be the highest point of Kansas or Missouri. In my bleary excitement to crest the rise, I surge the bike forward faster than we've been coaxing it up the hill. Not by much, but it's enough to catch Quinn in the calf with Enzo's trailer. I can only watch as he performs a slow motion stumble forward.

My stomach jumps into my throat.

I'm on the wrong side of the handlebars. I can do little more than witness him hit the sidewalk. Quinn's bike gloves and one of the knee pads work like a charm. Little consolation to the other knee, scuffed under the pad just enough to raise a light but crimson patch of blood.

Quinn's rage and recriminations are perfectly natural. The only surprising thing is why it hasn't happened before now. For a seven-year-old, more than two thousand miles into a bike adventure, he's been, with a few exceptions, Jedi-like in nature. Knocked down by the rig that has brought us all such joy, and by a father who, until now, has protected him from injury, not caused it; all this is too much of a betrayal to let stand. His outpouring of raw emotion is a Roger Clemens hardball to my head. Knowing it's coming doesn't make it hurt any less. Shame, exhaustion and this hapless feeling of failing my son nearly send me over the edge.

I pull him close, a bear hug he's both encouraging and resisting with physical violence. I take a deep breath, absorb the worst of the blows, and for once really question the wisdom of this wheeled endeavor. Am I giving them the time of their lives on two wheels, or making them do hard time in the saddle? We stay like that until his tears dry up and his breathing levels out. I'm not broken yet, but for the first time on our "Boys of Endless Summer Freedom Tour," you can see some cracks.

That's when he remembers the swimming pool.

"According to this sweat-stained freebee map of Kansas City's best BBQ joints, it's nine more blocks. Just nine," I say.

Helmet to helmet, we lock eyes. "Gonna take all my strength (and probably a blood transfusion) to get us there, son. I'll need to go radio silent . . . maybe you could count us down, block by block?!"

Enzo removes his lollipop. "I know you guys can do it."

And with that we have our momentum back.

How important is this underrated law of physics? Here's the thing about trying to push pounds of metal, gear, human cargo and two thin strips of Kevlar four thousand miles across America. At some point, no matter who you are, after the excitement and scheming, purchases and preparations are behind you, the full weight of your possessions will threaten to crush your deepest ambitions.

Narrow mountain roads focus your attention like finding religion or dating a supermodel, ancients navigating motor homes around blind curves send shivers down the small of your back, hills go on without end, windstorms blow, fatigue settles in, flash floods threaten, black flies bite, humidity, tornados, traffic and worse try to break you like balsa wood under a well-made work boot.

Momentum . . . is the only force on Earth that can possibly carry you through.

But if you want to come out the other side with more than miles, then you'll have to grab the brakes, get off the bike when your gut tells you or your legs force you, and have a good look around.

I decide we've seen enough of Rainbow Boulevard. It's time to take us to the water.

"56th Avenue!" Quinn calls out clear and strong, like he's a cadence jockey on the Tour de France Postal team. The miles have really worked him into quite a stoker, hollering "car back" and "on your left" as though he's been riding for years.

"One more block, boys." I've been stifling back cries of anguish, choosing instead to focus the pain into a meditation of little circles, suffering in silence while tears run the length of my cheeks. I burned the last of my fumes back on 57th Avenue, before searching around for the packaging it came in so I could torch that up, too. The top of each short but deadly rolling hill is achieved by digging deep into muscle memory, then letting the enthusiasm in Quinn's voice wash over me and push us along. Anyone witnessing our caravan barrel down that boulevard, looking good from tail to hood, has no idea, not a clue of the battle raging around inside.

It's that way with most of us.

"59th Avenue!" My son's screaming now, a half-mad third base coach waving me in. We round the corner and it all floods back. I know where I am. It's 1980. I'm fifteen years old, fueled by lust, Little Kings beer in the bottle and Black Sabbath concert tickets. The world and my hair know no boundaries. It was quite a summer.

The pedals crank on one last surge of energy. I dump our rolling whale on the front lawn and crumple in a happy heap. No ticker-tape parades, brass bands or medal ceremonies; the hum of cicadas in the high branches is our only soundtrack. Chain grease covers my calf, gratitude the rest of me. I'm on my feet before the boys can locate bike pumps and spritz bottles.

"Pool's out back."

Quinn hits me with a bear hug, Enzo whoop-whoops from the carrier. We've come halfway across America, and, for the moment, all the way home.

Part 2

Portland, Oregon
to
Kansas City, Missouri

"I don't want to sell anything, buy anything, or process anything
as a career. I don't want to sell anything bought or processed . . .
or buy anything sold or processed . . . or process anything sold,
bought, or processed . . . or repair anything sold, bought, or
processed. You know, as a career, I don't want to do that."
—Lloyd Dobler, *Say Anything*

3

"We all agree that your theory is crazy, but is it crazy enough?"
—Niels Bohr

JULY 1   0 MILES
Portland, Oregon

Neighbors stop weeding their flower beds and let hoses spill water down porch steps as we wobble by.

"Feels like a parade," Enzo calls from the trailer. I can barely hear him at this distance, but I'm glad he's enjoying himself.

"We are the parade," Quinn points out.

Big Steve, an engineer who is never without his smokes, bottled beer or his black convertible with suicide doors—the John F. Kennedy assassination car—stands at the curb shaking his head. He smiles at us through a prodigious cloud of smoke rings.

It's T minus two hours until liftoff and I still have a few bugs to work out, but even this minor victory tastes sweet. I imagine it's what the Wright Brothers savored high on that hill. Granted, we're going to have to stay aloft for more than a couple hundred feet, but considering that twenty-four hours earlier our engineering setbacks had reached an Apollo-13-rescue-scramble, with not a rocket scientist in sight, I feel pretty damn good.

"Your arms look like Popeye," Quinn says. It really is taking some muscle to steady the rig and soldier forward on our pancake-flat boulevard. I try to ignore the fact that we aren't even fully loaded yet. Pannier ballast will trim the wobble and straighten the ride, but add to the overall rolling weight. I'm vindicated regarding a winter regimen of free weights and hours spent wrestling with the basement Bowflex machine—Spanish Inquisition style.

I wave to the white haired woman on the corner who wears nothing but brown tunics or billowing pastel mumus no matter the season. This innocent action almost takes us to the ground. Adrenaline, angle, and dumb luck avert a pre-trip disaster.

Speed seems to level out our ride, so I increase it. More reactions from front porches and other pedestrians. A blind man could read their expressions.

"Would you look at that! He thinks we haven't daydreamed about some foolish jailbreak from the daily grind? But what sort of man acts upon such things? And with kids in the bargain?!"

I opt to nod instead of wave this time, hoping to hold off a call to Child Services. If there was more time, I'd stop and explain myself.

It's like this: I misspent the better part of my youth on a bicycle, with a career total of a hundred thousand miles and counting. That includes six coast-to-coast marathons, a two-thousand-mile epic across Australia's crimson-red Nullarbor Plain, and up-and-down rollers on both of New Zealand's islands. I've chased ice cream trucks around Baja and pedaled a surfboard to the breakwaters of Jaco, Costa Rica. If a twelve-step program for addicts of open-road adventure existed, friends would have tackled me to the ground years ago.

I was raised in a community of Tupperware pioneers making damn sure no one would want for anything they could order from a catalog. This left me insulated, parochial and restless. Who wouldn't wander into traffic? I did stop rolling long enough to find a full life. But a wife, two boys, three books, and one mortgage later, the dangerous notion that it doesn't have to end in one ZIP code keeps surfacing. Still, a meandering, unsupported, seventeen-state ride from Portland, Oregon, to Washington, DC, at the height of summer, my two sons in tow, Beth lost to us at grad school, and the big clock set at sixty-five days and counting?

Vegas bookies call this one a sucker's bet, throw open the window and try to mask their grins as they take my money clip. Close friends talk around me in hushed tones. Several have the backbone to come right out and predict I'll get the whole fiasco hooked together, realize my folly and call it off in the driveway.

Only my wife seems serene. Maybe it's the thought of all that peace and quiet, but it's more than that. We've witnessed enough of each other's lives to know real resolve.

"You need this," she says during a rare respite from the chaos around our homestead. "But if this is about our promise of always trying to stay awake, you do know we were young, foolish, and strung out on Springsteen at the time. Okay, and only because I know you'll be the same big-hearted safety freak of a dad no matter where you are. So, have fun storming the castle."

That went well, considering that my backup plan was nothing more than to say we were heading out for some Snapple, then keep going.

We're calling this the WWLDD tour. It stands for What Would Lloyd Dobler Do? For those who missed the 1980s, or VH1's "I Love The 80s," Dobler was the working teen's hero in *Say Anything*, a very smart film starring John Cusack that, despite a few hairstyling missteps, feels contemporary even today. It dealt with love, tax evasion, kickboxing as a career choice, and how to look cool holding up a forty-pound boombox. (Answer: make sure it's playing Peter Gabriel.) Dobler had it together even though it didn't look like it. He took chances on things that mattered, while wearing a trench coat right through August. He'll be our patron saint for the duration of the ride.

I've had T-shirts printed up with WWLDD on the front, and Dobler's four-line, star-making speech on the back. Along the way our shirts will elicit responses I expect: "Great flick!" plus catchphrases from the movie like "Keymaster!" and the pantomiming of someone holding a boombox while they shout out the chorus to Peter Gabriel's "In Your Eyes." Other reactions will catch me off guard. I never expected so many thumbs-up signs and Amens from folks throughout the Bible Belt. They mistake it for a variation on What Would Jesus Do? In this case, What Would the Lord Do, or Decide to Do? or What Would The Lord Do, Do?

A sweetheart of a gal behind the meat counter at a country store in southern Indiana went so far as to ask me, after reading the "I don't want to sell anything . . ." quote on the back, if Dobler was some holy man she hadn't made the acquaintance of yet. Maybe on Sunday morning TV?

"As I live and breathe," I said. "But these days, he's only on cable."

Most wannabe mavericks looking to instill a bit of rebel yell in their sons would do well to start each morning by teaching them the lyrics, plus hand motions, to songs such as Violent Femmes "Blister in the Sun," and read aloud from *Huck Finn* every night. I've taken this prescription a step further.

Instead of a raft, we're floating on five wheels and so much forged aluminum tubing. Standing in for the Muddy Mississippi is every blue highway, back road, and occasional farmer's frontage path ending abruptly in barbed wire and robust cursing.

While Tom and Huck had the ingenious if not quite literate Jim, Quinn and Enzo have to settle for Papa Joe, clever in a limited sort of parlor-game way, chatty to a fault and, for what it's worth, fully matriculated. Those Missouri lads fought racism and a return to share cropping serfdom. We will battle headwinds and the end of their summer vacation.

Lest you think I lack for loftier goals to leave as a legacy, our plan includes learning, to public-performance level if asked, a full catalog of songs, mostly Brit punk, Talking Heads and three-part harmony on Bob Marley's "No Woman No Cry," because there's nothing more satisfying than really putting your suburban, white-boy back into the line, "Oba, Oba serving the hypocrites, mingled with the good people we meet" in a faux-Jamaican accent. It's been known to help heal the hurt when the engine of injustice bears down on your rear wheel. A simple Trenchtown gift from Mr. Marley, which I want my boys to make their own; if only for singing in the shower, or in lieu of slugging a nasty coworker one Tuesday morning twenty years from now.

And while I doubt our tales of chain-ring rebellion will be banned in libraries and classrooms someday (couldn't find myself in better company, though), the audacity of our endeavor is obvious. You heard the body-pierced man of Colorado: He called us a bold statement. And if that impulse-free adrenaline jockey of a man defines me as a radical, I must be completely off the map and I just don't know it yet. Stupid is as Stupid pedals, Sir!

Regardless, our project doesn't want for wanderlust, a solid grab at independence, the head-clearing simplicity of graceful transportation and enough journalistic commitment to make the ghost of Twain tear up a little. Braving first light with my pint-sized posse in tow, shaking off the easy pleasures of inertia and the merits of good sense all summer, we're entering serious windmill-tilting territory.

On the face of it, blame falls squarely on an article deadline imposed by *Men's Journal,* but that would be taking the easy way out. I'm all about personal responsibility, sometimes. To that end, I've been up nights assembling a long list of reasons for doing the ride and for doing it now, but here's one that feels authentic: I've just hit forty, and there's no denying every man's fantasy—no, not that fantasy, the other one—to see if his body, tuned up to its current best, will stand or fall; stage a bloody mutiny at the bow of the boat or hold the lines.

In other words, do I still have "It"—the soaring finger-roll into the basket while two men guard me (almost had that once), the perfectly executed swan dive from the three-meter platform (never had that). But did I have "It"?

What we have, then, is an old-fashioned Texas cage match pitting myself against the easy athleticism I might have treated with arrogance in my twenties. This could get interesting.

I'll be pulling fourteen feet of traffic-stopping rig: my custom-made twenty-seven-gear Rodriguez touring bike, plus four expedition-size Arkel panniers loaded with everything from replacement parts to fishing poles to pots and pans. Quinn's my copilot, pedaling a Burley tagalong cycle attached to my rear rack; Enzo will lounge in his Chariot trailer, wedged between sleeping bags, bike pumps, and the occasional watermelon. Most days this 250-pound caravan will feel like I'm hauling a Hobie Cat behind me. I draw inspiration from the unsung Sherpas working Everest, and New World conquerors weighed down by armor and battle-axes. This brand of insanity always gets my blood going.

Returning safely from our "startle the neighbors" tune-up ride, we begin the tedious task of refolding map after map covering the hardwood floor of our living room. More of an accusation than a departure date, the red circle around July 1 stands out from the piles of papers. By pedaling Oregon, Idaho, Montana, a bit of Wyoming, high-country Utah, and the length of Colorado, we'll get heart-pounding scenery instead of choking heat; I simply pretend not to notice how many times our planned route crosses the Continental Divide. But highlighting every mile of a proposed route is akin to cartographic masturbation. Once beyond the Big Muddy we'll improvise our way to the White House.

"We're bringing the red light saber for you, Dad . . . 'cause that's Darth Vader's."

And they say you're always the hero in your children's eyes. Losing interstellar laser battles from here to the Atlantic doesn't bother me as much as what those light sabers weigh.

With a long holiday weekend ahead of her, Beth will pace us out of Oregon, but she's about the tough love, agreeing only to cart our front two panniers and some extra grub in the car.

"It'll be less of a blow that way," she notes from the front seat of the Forester, windows down, AC blasting enough to compete with the Coldplay CD. Beth appears to be enjoying my burdens a little too much. I'm reminded of every Florida highway patrolman who wrote me a traffic ticket from a cool, comfortable, reclined position, with the notable exception that I never slept with any of them.

When we finally take our starting positions, the day turns against us. Not by wrath-of-God thunderclaps and plague-of-frog proportions; it's more subtle and far worse. A thin, hazy summertime cloud cover traps heat and humidity across the length of the Willamette Valley. I soak through my first jersey standing in place. It's 2 P.M., our rig is a few pounds shy of a prairie schooner, and there's a slight breath of sticky wind coming out of the East.

"Ready, Dad?" Quinn adjusts his helmet.

Absolutely not. I'd look back but I wouldn't want to turn to salt or lose my resolve. "Let's do it, boys."

4

"And they ate Sir Robin's minstrels,
and there was much rejoicing."
—*Monty Python and the Holy Grail*

JULY 2   82 MILES
Columbia River Gorge, Oregon

We're only two days outside Portland and already I'm playing fast and loose with the pedal count: Dog Mountain, a towering hiker's haven, is 25 miles off course. I know better than to toss in a hefty side trip this early in the game, but any solid adventure has, at its core, a casual disregard for good sense. So we pedal across the Bridge of the Gods, into the state of Washington, park the bikes at the trailhead, and hoof it three and a half miles and nearly 3,000 vertical feet for a bit of impromptu cross-training . . . and one helluva view.

We share the trail with a number of unsuspecting canine lovers forcing their pets to the top, then moaning when these wet-nosed best friends resemble captives on the Bataan Death March. My cruel streak doesn't run deep enough yet to explain that this peak was named by pioneers who had to eat their trusted companions to survive the rest of the push to the Pacific. While I have no intention of consuming any collies or labs, members of my family, or the photographer who plans to join us in Colorado, I don't judge. It's a long way to the Atlantic.

"Dad, can we get a dog?" Quinn asks. This will not be the last time my sons make such a request. Like any good relay team, they'll use the length of the trip, the power of repetition and the captive nature of their audience to work in tandem, stereo, shifts and by any other means necessary. I'm traveling with the Black Panthers of pet acquisition.

All's fair in love and pet ownership, I suppose. Their hope is that I'll slip up and make a promise. Promises may have lost their impact in today's scandal-ridden world of reality TV and corporate executives; strategically placed sweet nothings meant to enhance ratings or quarterly profits. But in the realm of the child, a promise carries the day. Throw those commitments around casually at your own peril. Just ask the father who finds himself, after midnight, sitting cross-legged and cramped in his underwear, recreating the Battle of the Bulge from Lincoln Logs, Legos, and fusilli pasta; all because for an instant he lost his focus at the breakfast table.

Their efforts aren't limited to dogs; donkeys, chicks, horses, otters, golden eagles (protected, incidentally), ducks, rhinos (God help us), bears (you gotta be kidding), and the one that really flummoxes me, a heartfelt plea for an albino pygmy alligator. Their work pays homage to some of the nation's best jailhouse lawyers—those who bury the system in information without regard to logic.

Each new request has the potential for a teaching moment. We discuss the pros and cons of housing a black bear or a four-thousand-pound bison in a Craftsman Tudor on a standard city lot. Lively animal husbandry chats pop up at all hours of the day, suspect biology lessons (I hold no advanced degrees in science), and the always popular comparative poop workshops; but when I'm exceptionally tired their questions wear on me the way a perpetual game of duck-duck-goose might break the spirit of, say, a man with no legs.

Dog Mountain offers the boys short-term adoption opportunities and me a break from their barrage of requests.

"This one likes to lick my knees," Enzo says, wriggling around while stroking a lumbering, tired mutt. Another panting pooch, outfitted in a red bandanna, flops down at Quinn's feet.

The boys do better on this ascent than their temporary pets or actual pet owners. It's not that my sons are part of some superhuman research program for the next generation of athletes. It's because I've been hiking them up and down Oregon's backcountry for the better part of two years now; an occupational hazard of working for *Backpacker* magazine. Deadlines don't wait for dads to pawn their children off on someone else so they can go walk in the woods for money.

Besides, these lush trails, fishing holes, and waterfalls are the perfect playground for young boys. No matter how much Madison Avenue has tried to bolt them to the couch with colorful crack for the eyes. I've been partially successful in explaining that a TV is really just a flashy advertisement delivery system. Besides, Xboxes were no match once they wandered onto their first herd of elk or tracked bobcat scat to a water source. Ten-mile hikes become manageable when you stop to inspect for animal tracks, host epic rock-skipping contests or collect thimbleberries every twenty minutes. In the process, Enzo no longer whines about walks around town. It's the same operating model I've settled on for the ride.

Here's my hypothesis: with sixteen hours of summertime day-light, I can cover roughly eighty miles a day without a full-scale revolt, as long as we get off the rig and into good trouble—play-grounds, pools, river banks and light saber battles—every hour or two. If I'm wrong, they may have to send out the search dogs. I'll be the shell of a man weeping openly by the side of the road, young boys painting his face with chain grease and blueberries.

Even with our months of conditioning, the final push to the top of Dog Mountain is no cakewalk, but the payoff is worth it: Standing on that windblown summit, one of the region's highest wildflower meadows, with a bird's-eye view of the Columbia River Gorge, we look upriver toward massive Multnomah Falls and downstream to our home of Portland. Squinting hard, we try to peer beyond the dry patches of eastern Oregon, through Big Sky country, across the Rockies, past the Plains, over Kentucky's rolling hills, and straight up the Blue Ridge Parkway to the dome of our nation's Capitol.

When we get back on the bike it doesn't feel quite so heavy. I'm still doing my best imitation of Pa Ingalls driving the wagon train forward, but something's changed. The difference between starting a motion and continuing it, maybe. Or possibly, Quinn sold Laura and Mary Ingalls into white slavery when no one was looking.

Today we've been given a free pass, and I won't forget it. Beth awaits our arrival at Hood River's Full Sail Brewery. Given the dead calm conditions that almost never grace this section of the gorge (Hood River being the kiteboarding and windsurfing capital of the country, if not the world—they don't call it "nuclear wind" around here for nothing), we could actually be there by dinnertime.

Every cyclist wants to believe in the myth of West Coast tailwinds and the steady descent to the Atlantic. I've done this enough times to know better, but like a man released from indenture I need to run hard and savor everything—good, bad, and sublime—that the road puts in front of me.

5

"I would feel more optimistic about a bright future for man if he spent less time proving that he can outwit Nature and more time tasting her sweetness." —William Westmoreland

JULY 4 195 MILES
Hermiston, Oregon

"I ate a whole watermelon, once," Enzo announces. He's using his 'I dare you to say differently' voice. Quinn takes the bait.

"Have not." As if the particulars of his brother's caloric intake and any discrepancies therein are an affront to his future manhood.

It's the Fourth of July, on the back end of a scorching afternoon. We're in search of the most all-American food this side of apple pie. Hermiston, Oregon is ground zero for the mother of all gourds. The highway welcome sign is shaped like a juicy, red half-slice.

WATERMELON CAPITAL OF THE WORLD. It says so right on the sign. I live for these small-town proclamations. Later in our adventure we'll pedal through the world capital for bighorn sheep, the largest ball of twine, the home of the first television set, and the site of the inaugural helicopter ride. Everyone needs something to brag about. A reason to talk of home. But right now it's all about the gourd.

It's something of a mystery to me, then, that in a town that assuredly has seed-spitting days and a beauty pageant complete with a crowned Melon Queen, we've been pedaling the better part of a half hour and haven't spotted a single patch.

"I ate all of that watermelon Mommy brought home from New Seasons."

The boys like to engage each other in what I call verbal drive-bys.

"That?!" Quinn throws his hands up in exaggerated exasperation. He can only do this maneuver because the tagalong bike is attached to my rear rack. "I believe that was a cantaloupe disguised as a watermelon." PBS is to blame for some of his more eloquent retorts. Enzo is at a two-year developmental disadvantage, but he compensates by stonewalling his older brother. It's a cunning move.

And the only one Quinn can't tolerate. Arguing with someone who pretends not to be listening is more frustrating than boxing shadows or grabbing for lightning-fast lizards in a rock quarry.

Technically, Enzo's correct. But in Quinn's defense, it was one of those designer watermelons no bigger than a softball. As a rule, I stay well clear of their verbal sparring unless things reach DefCon 5.

"Since you both know what a watermelon is, we're looking for a big field of them," I say. I'm not above distraction to end a discussion that might head south of civility. For the record, any conversation between siblings has that potential. It's best to choose one's battles, though.

Pace yourself—the parent's prayer.

I often wonder whether I've fathered a pair of boys or a couple of Chihuahuas; yip, yip . . . bite . . . then yip some more.

It's the nature of the beast. Boys will wrestle with anything, even words when they can't make physical contact.

Quinn scans the sides of the road for vines and gourds. If for no other reason than to show his bro the significant difference between cantaloupes and old-school watermelons.

In my present state of fatigue, doubt creeps in.

My legs feel so soft I'm reminded of pit-cooked pulled pork ready to fall away from the bone. During our morning sunscreen ritual I missed a spot just below my eye, leaving me with a third-degree burn the size of a nickel. Rubbing it makes it worse.

I can't trust my Jeopardy game show skills when I feel beat up like this. Maybe watermelons are harvested earlier in Oregon?

"Over there, Dad."

And maybe, as a contestant, I wouldn't make it beyond the first commercial break.

The landscape erupts with ripe green bumps. For the first time, I decide to take our rig off-road.

"Let's see what she's made of, gentlemen."

We veer from blacktop to gravel to packed dirt without incident, but contact with sandy loam soil, that which makes Hermiston, Oregon, melon-growing nirvana causes our road tires to cry out "No mas."

I'm running with thin slicks to help inch our daily mileage up a notch, but these tires are an advantage only if we stay on the straight and narrow. Loose dirt and slicks are not a safe combination.

I do manage a clumsy stop without ditching the entire contraption into the tall weeds.

"All ashore who's going ashore," I say, delivered in my deepest dockmaster's baritone. It's these moments when my boys study me as I imagine anthropologists might gaze upon a half-horse, half-man creature, if the man part was, say, Fred Flintstone. I'm just trying to soften the blow for their teenage years.

"This is your captain speaking. You're free to move about gourd country." I slump against the trailer, And still the boys aren't certain of their next move.

"Go thump some melons, gentlemen. Find us supper."

They take off like I've cracked a whip.

Digging around the rear pannier for a big jug of water, one that might still be close to room temperature, I remember something. "But don't pick anything, boys, until I find out the house rules."

My sons are well acquainted with a cautionary tale I brought back from Mexico a few years ago. Most Americans cross the border with cheap curios, maybe a pair of cheesy-looking sombreros. I returned with The Cantaloupes of Wrath.

If I have an Achilles' heel it would have to be cantaloupe. More than nourishment, time and again that sweet melon has restored my faith in a higher force . . . for the simple reason that nothing so delicious could be produced without some sort of divine intervention. Certainly not much to hang a theological dissertation on, but it works for me. Think about it: For years, roving missionaries and Bible-toting doorbell ringers could have saved time, energy, risk of humiliation—not to mention printing costs—by delivering boxes of ripe cantaloupe with a note that reads, "There is a God. Enjoy my melons."

In my state of religious euphoria, it seems I misunderstood who owned the field of melons I was merrily sampling south of the border. It did not end well. I feel fortunate they still allow me to return to that fine country.

Beth's on a fact-finding mission to the Chamber of Commerce, dispatched on my vague recollection of a place called Six Mile House, or perhaps Six Story House, a building that once boarded Lewis and Clark, various prospectors and sundry pioneers.

Since this will be one of our last evenings together for a while, I want to splurge on something historic and folkloric . . . anything that doesn't sport the word "Motel" or the number 6 on its welcome sign. The irony is, I'm so beat at the end of these days that you could push me down into a cellar, offer up a sack of potatoes for a pillow and a burlap blanket and I'd be content. That's as much ambiance as I'm capable of appreciating during the early going of an epic adventure.

The first seven days of any long ride decide the cyclist's fate. And this one is shaping up to be as long and hard as they come.

My favorite uncle is fond of this saying, "Either the dog dies, or his master."

There are still three days until I find out which one I am. In the meantime, let them eat watermelon. I look around the field for my crew.

I find them in the company of a pimply faced high school student who appears to be interviewing fruit with a Toys "R" Us Mr. Microphone he has jerry-rigged to some sort of device one might acquire from the control center of a submarine. I'm not going to let them hang out with him until I find out more.

My initial impression of this man-child, who's more Adam's apple and home school haircut than muscle tone, is that the math team is missing one of its finest. But bonus points for dedication. I'm guessing even hard-core geeks bound for the toughest engineering summer camps are off blowing up loud, dangerous stuff on a day like today.

Not Ronnie.

"Dad, he's talking with the watermelons!" Enzo yells across the patch.

If you told Enzo we'd discovered oil, he'd be less excited than the talking-fruit find.

It does appear that the young man is huddling with succulent produce in what I can only hope is a bootstrap science experiment.

Enzo is also leaning over the gourd in question, quite open to the idea that, given a fighting chance, this melon will speak, perhaps do a few minutes of stand-up, even, or belt out a progressive rock ballad . . . something by Styx, Boston, or Genesis before Gabriel left the group.

I have my doubts. Nevertheless I move closer, to fulfill my parent responsibilities, of course, and to position myself in the event that a true agricultural miracle occurs.

"In one sense, your son is right," he says, as if I've just come in to audit his class. Ronnie engages not so much in light banter as he lectures in the style of a visiting professor from M.I.T. It's as disconcerting as hearing President Andrew Jackson's voice booming from one of those waxy robots in Disney's Hall of Presidents.

"I'm holding a dialog with these melons . . ." His smile reveals a set of braces, endearing him to me. Dental work means that somewhere he has parents who love him, hugged him now and again, almost certainly ruling out sociopath.

"Through sound waves, they'll answer the only question I put to them." He sets the microphone against one end of the gourd before turning to my boys.

"My question: 'Are you sweet enough to eat?'"

Then he thumps the fruit and watches his control board with the intensity of a symphony conductor eyeing his players before the first downbeat. I haven't ruled out strange . . . and socially retarded is coming up strong on the outside rail, but psycho killer, that's off the table.

We watch the screen, though for what we haven't a clue. I imagine it filling with type, then somehow being translating into sound, à la Hal 5000, the computer in *2001: A Space Odyssey.*

Instead, we witness a bunch of lines bounce across the screen, then nothing.

"Yes!" Ronnie does one of those fist-pumping, end zone dances reserved for overpaid athletes.

My boys would jump at the chance to share in his joy, any excuse to dance like banshees, but throw 'em a bone. Nothing blew up, bled, belched, or, in this case, uttered a peep.

"This one is a winner. It told us so right here." Ronnie points at a spot on a battered laptop computer screen connected by a rat's nest of frayed cords to an eBay-obtained oscilloscope.

It's not the fight against cancer, but Ronnie's quest to determine the ripeness of watermelons is a noble one. For all I know we're looking at the next Bill Gates of perfectly ripened produce; better living through radio waves. It's the not-so-glamorous side of the invention game, but then no one rolled out the red carpet for the genius who created the first coat hanger, or saw screaming groupies rush the barricades for the inventor of the Post-It note.

"It all boils down to waveform decay time—the time for the wave to decrease to nothing. This is the most accurate predictor of ripeness." Ronnie looks to his young students for some signs of academic life. Enzo bangs the microphone a few times and giggles.

I step in. "You're saying your contraption can tell how sweet a watermelon is by seeing where the noise bouncing through it lands on your computer chart?"

"That's putting it in layman's terms, simplifying it a lot, but yes."

Ronnie hasn't seen layman's anything yet.

"Boys, think Battleship. Sweetness is the target and Ronnie's machine sends out sound missiles. If it's a direct hit the machine will tell him where on that screen."

It's Ronnie's turn to be stunned. He's just witnessed parenting on a Ph.D. level. He tries to recover with "I like to think of it as a partnership between biology, chemistry, computer programming, and physics." Ronnie shrugs, conceding that round to me, before unclipping a machete from his belt loop. I bring the boys back a few steps while he halves the miked-up melon in one fluid stroke.

"I only wish I'd thought of the idea first," he adds.

While the boys taste-test the validity of Ronnie's machine, it's revealed that he's building on research by a group of high school students out of Salem with M.I.T. funding. They put in a year of solid research and continue to tweak the project with each class of students. Ronnie saw it work at a demonstration, took copious notes, then added the one piece that divides dreamers and school science fair projects from stockholders—making something cost-effective enough to reach the marketplace.

I think about Fulton's steamboat and Marconi's radio. Neither man originated these ideas. Inventions usually come from one mind, but the name that goes in the history books and on the checks is the pioneer who can bring it to the people in a big way.

"I don't just want to sell it to farmers and packagers. I want to get it down to the size of a calculator that grocery store clerks and even the general public can take down the produce aisle."

I shake my head.

"How old are you, Ronnie?"

"Fourteen, Sir."

"And how much money have you spent on this project so far?"

He runs the numbers while I taste his results. "Seventeen dollars."

I look over at my boys, covered in melon juice. I realize we're going to have to pay for these sun ripened test-subjects, but it doesn't matter.

"And how much grant money have the Salem students burned through?"

"Twelve grand."

"Gentlemen, take a good look at Ronnie here. You're peering at the future of this country, if it's to be a bright one: resourceful, independent, curious, practical, and streamlined."

What do I really know . . . but it sounds good and feels true. Quinn gives Ronnie a wet grin while Enzo offers an encouraging thumbs up. Dad's speechmaking again, but at least this one comes with decent snacks.

At the farmer's market register, I ask the clerk if he's met Ronnie and his watermelon ripeness tester.

He relates that he has not.

I think back over all the folklore and shade tree advice I've heard for picking the perfect melon. Look at the color on top, the contrast between the stripes, or press on it, touch the tendril. Come to think of it, all the advice I've ever received only shows me that watermelon selection is a rather inexact science—until now. Guesswork could be a thing of the past if the ripeness tester makes it to market. I take my change from the clerk and look him in the eye.

"You really should get to know Ronnie."

He smiles the way people do when faced with amiable nut jobs. In my defense, the flashy Lycra and fourteen feet of bicycle made him predisposed. We pedal away with two perfectly ripe melons.

Beth is located in the parking lot of a Motel 6-style accommodations. She thinks the historic hotel of our dreams was turned into a museum years ago. We share our perfect melons with Beth, who just shakes her head when we recount our encounter with the Doctor Doolittle of the Gourd World.

Nevertheless, Beth reaches for another piece of what she agrees are some of the sweetest melons of the summer.

6

/ "Every exit is an entry somewhere else." —Tom Stoppard

JULY 5   225 MILES
Oregon-Washington Border

I bring our beast of burden, all grease, gears, and vague expectations, to a stop on a slight hill. This is the cardinal sin of cycling: Never quit on an incline unless something immovable, say, a rock slide, tidal wave, or all-you-can-eat buffet blocks your way. Nor is it because of fatigue, hallucinations or being chased from the saddle by an angry swarm of wasps (trust me, it can, does, and will happen on this trip).

"Welcome to Washington," Quinn announces; his reading skills have made a quantum leap in six months' time.

We're not actually there yet. Rather, we're poised in a no man's land between the LEAVING OREGON: DRIVE SAFELY billboard and the Evergreen State's entry point sign. While I catch my breath, we try to recall what color line separates Oregon from Washington on their bedroom wall map of the United States.

"I'm thinking sea foam green," Quinn says. They've taken to reciting specific Crayola colors every chance they get. It must feel good inside their mouths.

Enzo votes for canary yellow, then awaits my selection, but all I can focus on is how breaking through this first state barrier puts our epic at the point of no return. It's a political division, an imaginary line only made real through a cartographer's rendering, but until this moment I've told myself we've only been tooling around in our backyard. I try to explain this to the boys.

"Like Frodo going beyond the border of the Shire," Quinn notes.

We all nod in agreement. We're such nerds.

On that subject, if you want to find out how Gandalf would fare against Gryffindor House in Quidditch, or hold spirited discussions on who would win in a battle between ogres and dementors, just try reading your children the Fellowship of the Ring trilogy, while your wife is three books into Harry Potter with them.

"It could be robin's egg blue." Enzo's back to the map question, like a dog with a sand-dollar-white bone.

I close my eyes and savor this unbearable lightness of being nowhere at all for a few more moments. As soon as we stroke into Washington I'll remember there are at least sixteen more state lines to cross, but for now, it's about a slice of sanctuary found in the spaces in between.

"Azure blue, Enzo." Quinn has settled on his answer. But whatever color is on the boy's bedroom wall, right now it's the perfect shading of fear and freedom to me.

"Color me ready, boys."

Now we've gone and done it. Now we've crossed the line.

7

"There are plenty of good reasons for fighting," I said, "but no good reason ever to have without reservation, to imagine that God Almighty Himself hates with you, too. Where's evil? It's that large part of every man that wants to hate without limit, that wants to hate with God on its side. It's that part of every man that finds all kinds of ugliness so attractive."
—Kurt Vonnegut, *Mother Night*

JULY 6   330 MILES
Near Lewiston, Idaho

Rabbits and full bladders bring us to a stop, in that order. The rest area along Highway 12 could double as the setting in the book *Watership Down*. A gnarled old tree takes center stage with a wetland blanketed by cattails crowding up the lowlands. Baby rabbits dot the rises and dart in and out of bushes. Other rabbits, these ones fat as raccoons, wait at the edges of the fence line trying their best to blend in with the brown of the posts. These are the elders, ready to bring their children to ground, down dusty holes on the other side of the wire if need be.

There are few things in this world more life-affirming than belief and being in the moment. For instance, a seven-year-old's belief that while the first nine rabbits he has attempted to sneak up to and grab with his bare hands have managed, with little effort, to evade him, bunny number ten has victory written all over it.

Every new moment is new.

Quinn recruits Enzo to the cause, sending him to flank the bitty rabbits with soundless hand signals. Their laughter with each failed attempt puts me in a festive frame of mind.

That's when I spot a fellow cyclist and move in for some fellowship. In truth, it's only the loaded bicycle I locate across the grass. The rider is nowhere to be found. Keeping the boys in sight, I approach the rig hoping for a few minutes of commiseration.

It's hard to work up a good whine while in the presence of professionals—like all grade schoolers, my sons will whine you under the table if you set the tone. It's like an arms race, and no one wants to get one of those started.

First things first: it's not a bicycle in the traditional sense, but a touring trike loaded down with a mishmash of possessions one would expect to find in a homeless man's shopping cart.

I register the POW sticker, American flag and a ZERO TOLERANCE, NO MERCY bumper sticker at the same instant a gray and black Australian border collie emerges from a hidden bunker between the picnic table and the trike. Snaps and snarling explode from the hole as this bobcat-sized beast takes up a guard position on top of the table.

Any rational person would get the hint. No welcome mat here. Call it what you will, overactive optimism or poor emotional eyesight, but I'm not easily deterred. If I were a dog, I'd be one of those bounding huskies, banging stuff about and knocking over scenery in an innocent attempt to play with just about everyone.

I step toward the dog with the understanding that my smile will disarm the mongrel or confuse it long enough to locate its owner who will call him off. Unfortunately, the animal is immune to the international sign for friendship, and the owner is still AWOL.

It turns out its owner is present and accounted for after all, emerging from the same hole as the dog. He's been seated on a low slung patio chair and is none too happy that I've disturbed him.

His scorched face—all loose skin and disappointment—actually has me longing for the dog's undivided attention again. As it stands, the dog does not let up his barking, so I must speak between its outbursts. Walking away at this point is not an option. The old vet's eyes are the double barrels of a shotgun. It's a look that says, "You rang the bell, mister, now you'd better have something revolutionary to sell me."

And I've got nothing; road stories, a set of cheap steak knives. So I play the only card that may stick. People love to talk about themselves. Or maybe that's just me.

"Where are you coming from on this rig?" I say, spreading my arms to show that I'm impressed with his rig, which, after a fashion, I am.

He fixes me with a stare that could cut through granite. His dog shifts from apoplectic barking to a low, seething growl, which is the only thing that seems to meet the ancient vet's approval. Apparently, I've found the one person in Washington who does not want to talk about himself.

I panic. What follows is blather about our expedition. It sounds substantial and even worthy in my ears, but eventually the vet, who is looking more through me than at me, cuts things off.

"This ain't no joy ride, Mister." If words could take on physical forms these would be built of bile.

The dog doesn't make a sound. Enzo steps out from behind me, reinforcements, sort of. His appearance catches the animal and its owner, completely focused on me in that moment, so off guard that there's no barking to drown out Enzo's conversational contribution.

"That's right," Enzo says, "This ain't no party, this ain't no disco, this ain't no fooling around."

Enzo's grin tells me he knows he's nailed the lyrics. With a stylish nod he sends things back across the net.

The vet, decades beyond what a little touch-up paint, sleeping indoors, and human contact might have helped, sizes up all three feet eleven inches of my rest-stop performance artist. Slowly, and with great effort, the sneer lines jutting away from his chapped lips at unnatural angles begin to loosen. It's a face that would need a full crew doing close-in work with hammer and vise to pry into a smile. But a few well placed words from Enzo, courtesy of David Byrne, do the trick.

"Damn straight, little man. Damn straight." His eyes, beads of weary rage moments earlier, clear, soften, and focus for a few seconds.

There's something to be said for cultural literacy. My five-year-old channeling David Byrne and the rest of the Talking Heads to my rescue on a Tuesday morning in rural Washington—I defy you to find such heady curriculum at any uptown preschool. You know, the ones with a thousand-year waiting list. Best they might manage would be a Raffi throwaway chorus or some nonsense from The Wiggles.

It would be disingenuous to call what follows a fluid and satisfying meeting of the minds. It's not an Algonquin round picnic table discussion; we do not address VA abuses, debate the reasoning behind elective wars, the merits of endless summer bike rides, the pain of survivor's guilt, or my generation's embarrassment of riches and privilege without sacrifice.

He does tell us that Boise is his destination. A vague reference or two about some VA program he might be able to get into there.

At ten to twenty miles per day, all he can manage, I calculate he might get to Boise about the time we cross over the Mississippi.

"I'll most likely die out here on the road."

That's the spirit.

He doesn't thank me for the coffee that I bring over from the welcome booth, or the twenty I wrap around a spare bike tube, but he doesn't refuse these things either.

"Raise those boys right," he snaps.

I nod, with a pretty good guess of what his idea of right would be.

As we watch my sons playing what amounts to war games with the rabbits and king of the castle on the rocks, I feel conflicted and crappy that I don't want to spend another second with this malcontent and his prickly dog. And I sure as hell don't want my children meeting his same fate, no matter how hard people in power might pimp the next cause.

What sort of citizen this makes me, is up for debate. As to what kind of father I am, that's never been in doubt.

We pedal away from the rabbits, all of them still safe and sound, at least for now, by their parents' side.

8

"The gods had condemned Sisyphus to ceaselessly rolling a rock
to the top of a mountain, whence the stone would fall back of its
own weight. They had thought with some reason that there is
no more dreadful punishment than futile and hopeless labor."
—*Albert Camus*

JULY 8   470 MILES
Idaho/Montana Border

Hemingway said that to learn the contours of a country best, one
must travel it by bicycle. He knew that a long-distance rider experiences every bend, every barely perceptible grade and pulse-quick-
ening descent. Pedal long enough and the road becomes an extension of one's body.

Now, I doubt that Papa left the great American cycling novel to

mildew under the floorboards of one of his famed Key West bunga-
lows, but clearly he'd been in the saddle at some point. Hemingway
did pen another little tome, though, and he called it *For Whom The
Bell Tolls.* Yesterday, right on schedule, during my seventh day working the chain-ring gang, somewhere short of 7,430-foot Lolo Pass,
my body and the contours of the country decided to reject each other.
Hear that ringing in my ears? The bell tolls for me.

Mile after mile of slow uphill death. I fixate on the memory of
Oregon's emerald gorges and the easy days of wheat-covered
flatirons across southern Washington. Anything to take my mind
off the river of asphalt I'm pushing against. My rig teeters when I
drop below 6 mph, snapping me to attention the way rumble strips
wake a punch-drunk trucker. The pavement heats with each passing mile. I lose my appetite, taste metal in the back of my throat,
and became serious and silent as I hug a shoulderless road and manage the pain and a crisis of confidence.

The boys sense my strain and curtail the breezy chatter about live
bait versus plastic worms begun during our morning fishing fun. Or
maybe they've grown so stoic because I just yelled out of nowhere to
knock off that constant carping in my sweat-stained ears.

"Can't you boys see that your father is caught up in the fight of
his life . . . and if he goes down it should be with some semblance
of dignity, not to the jib jab commentary about whether Darth
Vader would still be scary if he was the same height as Yoda."

Enough already!

Maybe that's why they're so quiet.

Since the pain seems to be affecting my short-term memory, I
really couldn't tell you. Whatever I've said, though, it's probably not
my proudest moment of parenting, but I can also attest that nothing else matters at this instant but the next pedal stroke . . . which
doesn't arrive.

And on the seventh day God rested . . . and enjoyed himself immensely by watching long-distance cyclists hit the delights of the one-week wall. It's when many cry like newborns and hightail it home on anything with a combustion engine and more than two wheels.

Pride has already left the building when I find myself lying in a heap a few hundred yards before Lolo Pass summit. Shame takes its place when my boys hover over my sweat-drenched body, trying to position the third plastic light saber in my gloved, unresponsive hand.

"That's good, Dad," Quinn says, looking the part of a prop master on a movie set. "You lie there just like that and we'll act out the scene where young Obi-wan beats a young Anakin and he almost burns to death on the lava planet."

I suppose I should be thankful that they don't have access to any lighter fluid.

The battle begins in earnest, dueling around in the grass beside me.

"Gentlemen, if I throw up, don't be alarmed. It's a perfectly natural part of the riding process."

Enzo pauses the battle, concern crossing his face for the first time. "Wait, Vader doesn't throw up in the movie, does he?" So now one son's a prop master and the other is head of script continuity. But no one seems appropriately worried about my welfare.

I'm testing the maxim that a father is invincible, in his boys' eyes. It appears to be true, for now . . . we'll revisit it come their puberty years.

I'll give them this: Their general lack of concern, commingled with their misplaced confidence in me, is just what I'll need to keep us pushing all the way to the coast. My nausea passes quickly enough, and as for the leg spasms . . . please. I've felt far worse. I root around the tall grass for my good pair of glasses, which I'd thrown to the ground in a fit of frustrated exhaustion.

You never forget your first bloody street fight to crest a summit. And let's not kid ourselves; the road only chewed on me a bit today, enough to make me bleed, but it lost interest before any vital organs were penetrated.

At least the scenery is five-star for my recovery: a carpet of forest giving way to subalpine meadows in soft, late-afternoon light. When I can breathe normally again, I host a light saber battle so epic it will become the stuff of legend, whispered about at Skywalker Ranch conventions someday. Then, when I can put it off no longer, we remount the dreaded device, top the monolithic hill, and head to a friend of a friend's remote Montana cabin.

Before I can continue through Big Sky country, some drastic measures must be taken. I have to drop significant ballast or suffer the consequences—Lolo Pass is not the last hill between here and the Atlantic.

Either you glide over the road or you wear it.

It's that simple. The beauty of bike touring is that most things get simple in a hurry.

Other inclines along the route will test my fortitude, a few even take me to the ground; it's an occupational hazard of not having a name that starts with Lance and ends in Armstrong, but I'm okay with that. I've made my peace.

There can be only one, Highlander.

But if I continue to let my equipment work against me as I've allowed it to do during opening week, then I deserve every mile of unnecessary pain. It's time to strip away luxury like at no other point in 100,000 miles of world touring. I'm about to get medieval on my possessions. You might want to look away.

With the kids tucked in the bunk beds of our remote mountain cabin for the night—a stark, rustic affair most likely brokered by

Unabomber Realty—I lay out every ounce of gear. I do this as a geisha might perform a tea ceremony ritual, touching each item with care and memorizing its volume, heft and purpose. In the half-lit halogen glow washing across the deck, it's an impressive haul, madness really.

What arrogant bastard thought he could pull all this *and* two growing boys to the end of the block, much less to the Atlantic seaboard? In my twisted fantasies I've considered having the boys take up smoking, just for the summer, to stunt their growth a little. Maybe I could find some of those rubber suits, the ones we used to wear when we'd try to make weight for the wrestling team. Hard as it is to admit, my boys are going to keep putting on pounds. So I need to lose some in a hurry.

Backup batteries? Duplicate swim trunks and enough protein bars to sustain a season of Everest expeditions?

Gone.

The first pass is actually liberating. As the pile builds behind me I get a little giddy. Hair gel? What was I, insane?

The second round proves more difficult. I'm cutting into my comfort zone by sending home my sleeping pad and opting to ball up a spare fleece instead of carrying a light but cumbersome camp pillow. Doesn't matter; I'm so tired at the end of each day I could lose consciousness across a pile of rocks or a brambly nest of thorn-berry bushes.

Things move from traffic jam-level discomfort on the next pass to dental-chair pain on the fourth go-round, until, by the last weight-shaving session, I have a hostage negotiation situation on my hands. Unfortunately, I'm both the hostage and the negotiator. It's like playing Russian roulette by oneself. Someone's getting hurt.

The problem is I'm no longer working with my possessions, but placing my boys' treasures on the chopping block. The mother bear in me rises up on her hind legs. This bloodletting runs deep into the evening. Temperatures usually drop drastically when you're so high in the mountains, but lucky me, it's a heat wave. I sweat into the wee hours, fighting myself for every inch and ounce.

It goes round and round; a fully grown white man, naked except for some swim trunks, ranting under Montana backcountry moonlight. You'd expect to find a cache of weapons and a manifesto nearby, but you'd have to settle for a spare canister of camp fuel, which I keep moving back and forth from one pile to the other.

"We can all eat out of the same pot, okay, and I'll give up their box of crayons on the strength of the melting-heat argument, but their backup socks are simply not on the table. I'm the only one who has to live in a small tent with rancid feet in my face and sweaty, smelly shoes just the other side of the mesh. Socks are frontline defense. Socks stay."

My only out is that Beth will rejoin the expedition for a guest appearance across Colorado. If I've made a crucial rationing error, we'll have to hold on, à la the Donner Party, until Gunnison, Colorado.

When it's over, I've accumulated what feels like an ulcer and two full panniers worth of gear, plus some spillover items.

Rick Reynolds, a comedian of the highest order, more of a truth-teller working magic through funny monologues, did this thing on shopping and consumerism. He said he likes to stumble around Costco trying to spot the people with real problems. It's easy: "The more crap in your heart, the more stuff in your cart."

Feeling purified and pilgrim-like, not to mention lean as a gazelle before the summer monsoons, I cook up one last bit of late-night inspiration: Why not banish the actual panniers home, not just the stuff inside them? Less cart, less crap.

Without the front bags stabilizing my rig I'll need to adjust for the wobble, but on the upside, one cannot add weight if there's nowhere to put it, Grasshopper. Psychologically, it can't hurt either. Putting all the rolling weight behind me streamlines the equation while framing it only in terms of pulling. Whereas right now I'm pushing, pulling, dragging, mule training, laboring and cursing in every direction—so much stuff hanging off the front and sides—generally resembling a drunken frat boy moving off campus mid-semester. If nothing else, it will add a little feng shui to the mix.

In the harsh light of morning I nearly lose my nerve, snap the bulging panniers back on the racks and consider starting a special fund for future knee surgeries.

I want to roll by UPS without stopping, but since getting back on the bike it's not been unlike, I imagine, torture devices of the Dark Ages.

We mail the bags without ceremony. I feel naked. I comfort myself with the notion that in the 1970s TV series "Kung Fu," David Carradine wandered the length of the Old West carrying only a flute, some gluten-free bread, and mediocre slow-motion martial arts skills, and he was just fine, blissful even; but that could have been on account of the actor's sizable drinking problem.

The front bags created something of a skirt around the bike, so I do feel exposed, but as soon as I hit the unflinching gravity of the first hill, I know I've made the right choice. Whether I pull us all the way to the edge of America is still up for grabs, but this new, sleeker machine gives us better odds. It's day eight and inexplicably I'm still in the hunt. That greyhound hasn't caught me yet, and could that be the faint cheers of a deck of drunken partygoers? I pedal on.

"Boys, you're killing me."

It's been less than an hour since we shipped off all that weight. Now, my demon seeds are gathering shirtloads of rocks from a dry creek bed and depositing them inside one compartment of the trailer. They've formed a fire line and are passing off rocks like seasoned professionals.

"We're building a habitat, Dad," Quinn explains.

These are not pebbles, mind you, or skipping stones even, but substantial rocks one might use to fashion a home improvement project; a patio or a pizza oven.

"For what, may I ask?" I really don't want the answer.

Enzo reaches into another compartment. He comes out with something long and rope-like. It takes my brain a moment.

"Snake," he yells gleefully.

All men, somewhere deep in our DNA, are hunters and gatherers. Without mammoths around every rock these days and Safeway open twenty-four hours, we do more in the way of gathering. Thus begins a running battle of item removal: "treasures" the boys have brought back to the bike carrier are cast out: live, dead, animal, mineral, vegetable and a completely unidentifiable category we'll call the "yuck" pile. Enzo must have some David Copperfield in his blood. I never saw the sleight of hand he used back at the Unabomber cabin to slip that garter snake into the trailer. It's a three-ring circus out here on the asphalt and we haven't even covered ten miles this morning.

Here's a little sampling of roadside flotsam and jetsam that I will unearth from our bags over the next two months:

1. A menagerie of soda twist-top game caps (all of which read "Sorry, LOSER, try again").

2. A full-color brochure for an Assisted Living Community in Scottsdale, Arizona, weighing in the neighborhood of a small phone book.

3. A bag of marbles coated in leaky "to-go" packets of McDonald's pancake syrup.

4. Barbie doll torso, no arms, no legs, but a Jack in the Box ping-pong-ball head where Barbie's movie star mug used to be. I find it an improvement.

5. The universal remote control to a hotel television set. I live in fear that I will receive a bill for it at some future date.

6. Ziploc bag of congealing grasshoppers. All deceased; hard to determine if death was caused by suffocation or blunt force trauma from a five-year-old's sweaty bottom or the sole of his shoe.

7. Sticks—lots of sticks, too many sticks, stop collecting sticks, Enzo! Various lengths, degrees of sharpness and plant varieties, any of which could poke Enzo's eyes out, and then where would I be with the missus?

8. A Speak & Spell toy suffering technical difficulties, possibly run over by a semi truck or just run down to a point where it speaks in the manner of a drunken sailor and spells on par with an unmotivated foreign exchange student. This we keep on board for entertainment value.

9. The bottom half of a basketball trading card. Could be Michael Jordan, based on the color of the shorts, angle of his legs in flight and brand of shoes. We'll never know, but Quinn holds to

it as though it were the only evidence of a long lost twin he's hoping to be reunited with one day.

10. An exploded fireworks ordnance the size of a Quaker Oats container labeled Fat Cat Flamer. The feline pictured on the packaging resembles Garfield . . . if he'd done hard time at Folsom. I located this one afternoon because the trailer reeked of sulfur and smoke and for an instant I feared my five-year-old had set the carrier on fire.

"We have to be able to collect stuff," Quinn says. There's something close to panic in his voice.

"Tell you what, boys."

They wait patiently while I blow some morning phlegm off the starboard bow using the patented single-nostril, gloved Jersey salute before returning to negotiations.

"I'm not without a heart. Whenever you want to bring stowaways on board, show the item to me. Most of the time I'll have you just take a picture of it—"

Wails of protest to rival Israelites at the Wailing Wall threaten to end the bargaining session right there. They pull themselves together when I look away and rub my temples. Much as the horned lizard arches its back before it spits blood out of its eyes, this is my warning signal that things are about to get ugly.

We return to the negotiation table.

"But . . . but items I do let aboard only have safe passage until we can ship them home in one of those flat-rate envelopes."

I'm fairly certain I've opened Pandora's box, or in this case her panniers, but when parenting from the seat of a Brooks saddle at 15 mph, concessions must be made. It's ten in the morning. I need food, a lot more sleep and even five minutes of adult conversation.

Enzo raises an eyebrow. "Can you send a snake through the mail?"

Once all rocks and reptiles have been returned to the river, I put our leaner, meaner machine back in motion.

"And one last thing, boys. For the love of God, stop picking up all these yellow SUPPORT THE TROOPS magnets. They don't stick to the bikes."

In Montana, they don't stick anywhere. It seems some penny-pinching entrepreneur sold everyone in the state a yellow ribbon magnet that lacked the proper amount of magnetism to stay on their cars. The roads are littered with them now, not unlike the way the roads in Iraq are littered with the bodies of the people these were meant for.

"On second thought, keep picking them up." Least we can do is give 'em a proper burial. Later in the ride, I will see another yellow ribbon magnet on the back of a car that cuts to the truth with harsh gallows humor. The magnet reads: SUPPORT THE MAGNET INDUSTRY.

I pedal on. But the gods must be very angry with me, because the very next breakfast cafe we roll up to features mimosas on its sidewalk sign. Who starts a Wednesday morning with a round of mimosas? And where can I party with these people?

I keep my head down and try like hell to center myself for the road ahead.

9

"If wishes were horses, beggars would ride." —James Halliwell

JULY 10   611 MILES
Colorado Gulch, Montana

Every touring cyclist knows the cheap thrill of causing a controlled stampede. Bulls, horses, cattle, or bison huddled along fenced pastures near a road will take to the hoof in spooked unison with nothing more than the backspin of a freewheel and a few yelps and yee-haws. The herd will give chase in a clamor of sound, dust, and fury, posts and barbed wire keeping you safe from the mindless mob.

It's every kid's deepest cowboy fantasy, and it ends in the same glorious way each time: with the herd pulling up short at the final fence line of a rancher's property while you emerge from this hoof-pounding stampede through billows of rising dust . . . a certified badass hero of your own little action-packed Western.

One day beyond MacDonald Pass we're riding a stretch of national forest service road—so remote even telephone poles haven't taken root along its edges yet—when a herd of wild horses appears behind us from over a rise.

"It's Spirit," Quinn yells.

"Stallion of the Cimmaron," adds Enzo.

Even this far from civilization there's no escaping the reach of Disney references.

Our jaws drop in unison. If the world were measured in terms of wonder, ours just grew exponentially. The horses keep coming. Imagine the longest train, but this one is running on several dozen invisible tracks, no conductor in sight, but somehow each animal knows where to go. Their pace quickens; the sound of pounding hooves is heroic as it grows louder, comes closer. I swallow back fear. No fences this time, and while Spirit is a stylized cartoon Mustang from a Disney production, these are made of bone-crushing flesh and blood.

It's hard to believe that wild horses still exist in such numbers. What's easier to wrap my head around is what will happen to us if we get caught in their path.

"Keep pedaling. And whatever you do, don't spin your free-wheel," I caution Quinn, remembering a second too late that you don't tell a kid not to do something in pressure situations.

We want to believe that these are Mustangs. What I know for sure is it's humbling to be so close to graceful power in fluid motion.

We pedal at full speed in labored silence for several glorious miles, the 'stangs matching our pace in what resembles flight. And when they choose, the horses pass us as if we are standing still. I whoop and holler, sounding like a complete lunatic. The boys follow suit. The herd disappears into the landscape, leaving nothing more than a brief vapor trail of dust.

If these animals can still roam free in the West, there's a betting man's chance that we may also outpace the reach of society between here and the Atlantic.

You had me at leeches!

10

"Every mother's son will rise and fall some day."
—Lynryd Skynryd

July 11   670 MILES
Near Hell's Canyon Campground, Montana

Considering the cargo, our eighty-mile-per-day pace is a speed metal band's tempo. Yesterday a real thunderstorm forced us into our first dead sprint. Sixty miles south of Helena, Montana, quarter-size raindrops kept me hammering the pedals even though I'd already put in a full day's work. Blowing by Hell's Canyon Campground I wanted to stop, desperately needed to stop, but knew that if I pulled off the road for even a two-minute pit stop to check for a pavilion or picnic shelter I could be putting us in the center of a storm that meant business.

For the better part of an hour we stayed in front of the worst of it. Each time I slowed my pace even by one mile per hour, the raindrops swelled in size and number.

Then, just as the skies opened, another campground came into view. Sweet weeping Jesus, for better or worse, this would be home. Wet and weary, but safe under a sizable pavilion, I planned to sleep like a caveman as soon as I could get the tent pitched.

Lightning blew away a chunk of mountainside across the river. Such a wild sight that I turned to Quinn for confirmation. He screamed in what I thought was fear until I realized what he was saying.

"Camera! Camera!"

Ansel Adams, eat your heart out. He was calling for his digital camera.

"Count the seconds. Tell me when you think the next one will hit," he howled over the din. "I'll try to get a picture of it."

It's twisted, the euphoria only a seven-year-old unleashed on summer safari can know. He was channeling some half-crazed war correspondent trying to document the carnage occurring around him. I didn't tell him that professional photographers with specialized equipment hunker down through storm after storm all season to catch the perfect strike. Which meant he'd probably frame a stellar shot on the first click.

We counted the beats between flashes and booms, but our attention was quickly diverted by the discovery of a dead pelican beside an equally dead fish. Good eyes Enzo. We were so stunned that, during a lull in the storm, we stepped out from under the overhang for a closer look. Quite a mystery here. We mulled it over from different angles. Quinn took a picture. The thunder returned with a vengeance, drowning out further communication.

It was 6 P.M.—time to call it a night. The boys played Crazy Eights inside the tent, using my lifeless hip as a table. I drifted off to their laughter.

I heard Lynyrd Skynyrd's onetime sound man before I saw him. Near midnight, a pickup truck dropped his wrecked body and worldly possessions next to my tent, then fishtailed out of the rain-soaked campground. Thick sheets of precipitation drove across the pavilion, but Rodeo's cigarette stayed lit. I offered to assemble his shelter, and he talked while I labored over a rancid military surplus tent. Not so much out of kindness, but because it might let me get back to sleep faster.

The arm sling and second-degree burns had been acquired in a recent motorcycle accident. He'd just been released from the hospital—sans transportation—and, as the bass player for a Skynyrd tribute band, needed to be at a gig in Bozeman by midday. (How one plays bass with burns and broken bones must be a tribute-band trade secret.)

I showed him my bike. He understood I wasn't his ride ticket. Still, being a Florida boy, I spoke his language, lyrics, and liner notes. "Every Mother's Son," "Gimme Back My Bullets." Rodeo began calling me Brother. By morning light he appeared even more damaged than I remembered, Keith Richards' harder-drinking cousin. As we pedaled away, Rodeo squinted at our rig and shook his head. "Our fans, with their braided rattails and Bic lighters, they think they're Freebird, man. But this . . ." He spread his battered arms as wide as he could. "You really are Freebird."

11

"In West Virginia if you run over an animal, you can legally take it home and cook it for dinner. A law passed in 1998 lets drivers keep their roadkill, as long as they report it within twelve hours."
—*Roadkill Trivia*

July 12   710 MILES
Wheat, Montana

We christen the highway between Helena and Big Sky, Montana, "Roadkill Boulevard." On a roadside breakfast break we notice what looks at first blush like a beaver about the size of a small suburb in Baltimore, freshly killed and fully intact. Quinn argues that it's actually a nutria.

Nutria are rodents of unusual size brought to the United States to combat the spread of cockroaches across the South. They did little to stop the roach, because really, nothing up to and including Tammy Faye Baker and nuclear war will stem the multi-appendage, armor-shelled march of La Cucaracha, but what the nutria established was a rather successful beachhead of its own. In Louisiana, their victory can be tracked by how much government funding has been thrown at the infestation. In a depraved moment of marketing madness the chamber of commerce or tourism bureau or some arm of civic-funded bureaucracy launched a statewide dining campaign and contest. The region's five-star chefs—respectable men and women in the big white hats—were brought together and challenged (while paid handsomely with public funds, I'm guessing) to create recipes showcasing nutria as a delectable entrée. And if you thought Rocky Mountain oysters or cow's tongues were hard sells, try cooking up three-foot rats for local food critics. That's right, epicure critics from newspapers, monthly periodicals, and TV outlets were invited to a big banquet featuring nutria in every way imaginable—over dirty rice, in soup, sliced across salad, stewed, broiled and poached. The marketing genius behind this gala must own his or her own pair of brass plated Rocky Mountain oysters. I imagine a massive Macy's Parade-sized blow-up of the nutria dangling from the chandeliers of the convention center ballroom for this fiasco.

What did Hunter S. Thompson once say? "When the going gets weird, the weird turn pro."

Politicians, local luminaries, celebrities and city officials all sat down to plates of rat while the cameras rolled. Footage, later aired on a PBS travel show segment, was priceless. Even seasoned black belts in the art of babble had trouble containing their revulsion as they nibbled nutria stroganoff and forked up lemon nutria in a light cream sauce.

Incidentally, sauces were heavily featured on the menus. The evening threatened to crack wide open when one well-known critic announced, upon her entrance, "I smell a rat."

I share all of this with my boys, who lose themselves in fits of laughter. To someone driving by we might resemble a demented pack of hillbillies reveling over our luck, as we prod, poke and giggle around a gigantic beaver.

"What are Rocky Mountain oysters?" Enzo asks. Fortunately, we're only yards from a pasture of cattle.

This creates another round of fall-down laughter and much finger-pointing at the bull's anatomy. And to think, some experts call experiential learning a flashy, failed experiment.

I talk up roadkill cookbooks and websites, but get no takers. Access to all-you-can-eat buffets and their mother, an exceptional Italian chef in her own right, play into this. I still think it would be a riot to share something exotic with the boys: frog legs, chicken feet, armadillo soup. It's a fight getting Quinn to eat his vegetables, so I know it's a lost cause. But they're all for watching me choke down anything we find along the way.

"You guys have heard about the time I pedaled up to a gang of Florida good old boys practicing the not-so-ancient sport of armadillo bowling?"

They had not. But anything involving animals playing sports gets their attention.

We park upwind of the massive nutria carcass, pass out water bottles of Gatorade as if they're longneck bottles of beer, and settle in for underpass storytime.

I braved the Florida border not so long ago—helping mom settle back in. Like Jack Nicholson, who thought we couldn't handle the truth, Mom couldn't handle Oregon's winters. She lasted a year and some change. Who can blame a woman who spent the better part of her working life fighting seniors for lane space on the A1A and the Tamiami Trail of the Sunshine State? Now that she'd officially become a senior it felt like an inalienable right (that of driving very slowly with the turn signal on) had been taken away. I think every time Mom stepped aboard Portland's clean, quiet mass-transit system, a little piece of her died inside.

On a sweltering ride (and trust that taking to the Florida asphalt after April 1, while not making you an outright fool, is being foolish enough to let yourself be enveloped inside a gigantic humidifier) I spied a group of three not-so-wise young men, all fans and followers of the mullet hairdo, all advertising their favorite beers and monster trucks above the bills of day-glo orange, John Deere green and duck-shit yellow baseball caps.

Before anyone phones the politically correct police, I did an involuntary residence, a stint if you will, in Florida. In technical jargon, this was also referred to as my childhood. Somewhere between the feathered-hair years and the parachute pants experiment, I even sported something dangerously close to a mullet, visualized myself behind the wheel of a Camaro and whored my favorite BBQ joint across the bill of my cap. This, of course, gives me politically correct immunity with no statue of limitations. I *was,* for a time, one of those boys.

Then someone shook me hard, changed the radio station and hoisted a copy of *Catcher in the Rye* into my mitts. If that doesn't cover me, too damn bad. Now I'm someone else's stereotype. Anyway, I have a pile of rocks here and I'm not afraid to throw them at your cliché. Doesn't everyone keep their favorite glass house repairman on speed dial?

That said, if anyone can find a twisted level of lively distraction on a Tuesday afternoon, my money will always be on those rough-and-ready boys of rural Florida. From out of the corner of my eye I'd caught what appeared to be lawn bowling under the carport.

With twenty miles of palmetto bushes already behind me, I thought the request of a cheap Lite beer would break up the ride nicely. I looped back, coasted down the crushed-shell drive, and leaned my rig against a poster of the Dixie Chicks. Someone had taken a pen and added devil horns and the words "Semper Fi" under their fiddles.

Nods, handshakes, a beer can salute from the gentleman holding the "bowling ball."

"Hey, y'all. So whatta we have going here?" (The proper use of "y'all" buys one an introduction. Like insects using antennae or spit trails to identify each other, it distinguishes you from the Canadian Snowbirds and all those Winnebago Warriors fleeing Michigan. After that it's up to your knowledge of NASCAR and pure deep-fried instinct if your plans include avoiding a solid beating).

Sonny introduced me to their pet armadillo—Dillo. There's a Zen-like purity in their choice of names for what I would learn amounted to a member of the family. The bowling alley was a muddy stretch about the distance of a horseshoe court with empty Miller bottles set up in a familiar triangle at one end.

If only ESPN would put me on staff. Hand to God, Dillo would tuck and ball up just before one of the three unwise men released. Sonny threw a decent spare. During that hallowed instant of silence after the bottles stopped spinning I was rooting for Dillo to unfurl himself and make a break for the underbrush. Instead, he righted himself and started back with that lopsided little gait, the one that armadillos still use to move about.

Evolution is a fickle master with a warped sense of humor. Incredibly, Dillo voluntarily brought his muddy shell back to the carport. In this pet they had a built-in ball return.

"It doesn't hurt the little guy?" I asked. And what sort of answer was I expecting? As if I were putting the question to a research team of biologists from the Columbus Zoo.

For the first time, the three not-so-wise men gave me a good looking over. While I had the "y'all" down, I *was* pedaling a bicycle. *It could be he's with those eco-folks over in Gainesville.*

Green Ballcap scooped up Dillo. That's when the already surreal went right over the redneck rainbow. Why hadn't I noticed the baby bottle filled with beer before? He popped it into Dillo's mouth-area thingy, and the animal when right to the teat. While these gents would be hard pressed to locate the Pavlovian Effect if it marched up and salivated on them, here they were putting it to practical use.

"We only roll 'im in the soft mud," Yellow Cap noted. To punctuate this he pointed at a nearby hose they used to water the area. "Dillo loves it. Damn near can't get him to quit. Smartest animal we ever had."

Everyone looked at the armadillo sucking from a baby bottle. Yep, Einstein on the half-shell.

Sonny chimed in with, "Smarter than all our dogs."

And that clinched it. Any vague plans I might have been cultivating regarding the liberation of Dillo were dashed at the thought of hounds being released on a sticky Florida afternoon. The three not-so-wise men still had their fur raised and their eco-radar up.

"Give Dillo a roll, why don't ya?" Sonny said, taking my beer bottle from me. This was not a question. It was the Southern-fried version of a scene from "The Sopranos." I was the deep-cover cop having to snort the dope, or pistol whip someone to prove loyalty.

And here I wanted to go to my grave without the stain of armadillo-bowling on my permanent record. When faced with a B-movie masquerading as your life, when staring down the barrel of the preposterous, as I see it you have two choices: fold, and roll the damn rodent . . . or escalate the craziness.

"Hell, boys, isn't there a rule 'bout keeping an armadillo off the alley for thirty minutes after he's drunk his lunch?" I laughed in the same way President Bush does when he wants people to think he's made a funny. Before my audience could turn on me I upped the ante.

"Got an even better idea! If you gentlemen will allow me, Dillo being so sharp and all, I bet he'd enjoy a bike ride. Yeah, let's put him up on the front panniers. Sonny, you can show him where the shifters are."

Their crooked smiles indicated that I was on the right track here. "Got a camera around?" I asked, taking back my beer.

So Dillo had his first photo shoot. Only once, when I was pedaling to the top of the driveway with the animal poking out of my oversized Arkel front bag, waving Sonny into position for an action shot, did I harbor thoughts of a proper prison break. But I reasoned, rightly or not, that if they'd trained one armadillo to bowl, who knew what the next critter recruit would be indentured into.

Besides, the three not-so-wise men really did seem attached to the little armored tank. I'm only guessing here, but I suspect being a bowling ball in the backwoods of Florida is better than being the soup du jour.

Enzo wants to hear the story again. Quinn wants to find an armadillo.

With each dead animal we roll onto, over or around, the morning quickly devolves into a game of green eggs and roadkill ham.

"Raccoon liver sprinkled over shredded wheat?" I ask.

"Lettuce, tomato, and titmouse sandwiches," Enzo counters. He's never even seen a titmouse.

"Bald eagle quesadillas, anyone?" Quinn's really warming up to this game.

Our two-wheeled train falls silent. "Bald eagle?" Enzo sounds crestfallen. "Eagles are protected 'cause of DTT." Close. This is what happens when you marry a biologist.

While the West's blue highways have turned up the occasional asphalt pastry, the next twenty-mile stretch is a stinking, steaming gauntlet of entrails and death. Dr. Seuss gives way to Stephen King, in a hurry.

An especially blown-out opossum, bulging eyeballs and dripping entrails, sobers the mood. It's time to distract with a music lesson— the lyrics to Oingo Boingo's "We Close Our Eyes" seems appropriate. I get them singing at top volume, if not on key, and hope the carnage eases up before my little men are scarred for life.

What baffles me is that the shoulder is wide, the traffic is light and the road is arrow-straight, all conditions that normally allow autos and animals to live in relative harmony.

"Where are all the cartoon birds with those long necks?" Enzo asks.

He's talking about buzzards, and it's a good question.

By my count we've seen dozens upon dozens of finches and starlets, all feet up or flattened on the pavement, their final flights taken, but what he's asking after are the vultures, those cosmetically challenged cleaning crews of the tarmac. In what is an anti-Hitchcockian twist, no birds are present, and this includes vultures. We scan the fence lines and look to the skies; nothing in flight. I start to suspect a modern equivalent of DDT or some other toxin is at play here. The death count ends abruptly when we cross the property line onto an organic wheat farm. This could be just a trick of geography, or something more significant.

At the counter of Wheat, Montana, a kitschy chain of sandwich shops prefabbed to look like grain silos, I ask the boys if they still have appetites. Ridiculous question; Quinn can read now, and the word *brownie* appears about a dozen times on the big board.

"You're talking about Roadkill Alley," the girl behind the counter says with too much perky enthusiasm. "No one knows what to make of it. But something's been going on the last few summers."

A farmer standing behind me pipes in.

"A bunch of scientists were out there earlier this year taking samples. It gets thick with dead critters by August."

He leans towards the counter, "I'll take a chicken sandwich and Coke to go." Then turns back to us. "You know it's bad when the coyotes won't even pick at 'em."

Thinking about the gigantic pit quarry or mining installation we could hear banging, motoring, and drilling through the night or the hint of sulfur on the air as we rolled past its front gate, I wonder if Erin Brockovich should think about setting a summer-home base of operations in this part of Montana. Or if I'm just throwing windmill punches needlessly at the biggest industrial landmark on the horizon. I can't help but eye the water glasses she slides across the counter.

"Filtered," she says, reading my mind.

For that I'm pleased, in an egocentric way, but soon my thoughts turn to that abundant line of roadkill, a battlefield really, many of whom may not have met their demise under a wheel or against a fender at high speed. I'm thinking of the birds and other creatures that do not have access to bottled imports. The phrase "We all live downstream" pops into my head. Knowledge can be power, but today the small amount I have on hand just makes me feel feeble— aware that something's wrong along a twenty-mile stretch of Montana . . . but unable to fix it. This is the beauty and the pain of passing through—it's hard to find a foothold, hard to be more than a tourist.

The sun comes out after lunch. My mood and the day warm up a little. Maybe I can outrun the unease of Roadkill Alley. At Interstate 90 we're faced with a decision. One road sweeps south for five miles, then north for another ten before mirroring the interstate for the last seven to that day's destination—Headwaters of the Missouri State Park. On the map, this road looks like the letter S, which someone tipped on its side. I silently curse the Interstate and its direct route. Normally, I love meandering along country roads, but even discounting our morning run through the valley of death, we're nursing a slow leak with no visible source (forcing me off the bike, into the trailer for the floor pump and over the back tire every fifteen minutes). And if that isn't enough, we're battling a whirling wind that keeps hitting us head-on, no matter which direction I'm pedaling. That's when I see a sign. Not from God, but the Montana Highway Division: FARMER'S ROAD.

I have to read it twice to make sure I haven't flipped around the letters to the more common signage, "frontage road." Nope. Quinn confirms the wording. The way it appears to parallel the interstate deep into the distance is mighty tempting; no matter what they're calling it, it looks like a frontage road to us. What's a few letters between friends? Cutting off much of our north-and-south ride would let me set camp early. It would give me time to find this leak before the evening mosquitoes send us into the tent around five in the afternoon.

Even though Quinn pretends he's outgrown the tune, he sings "Old MacDonald" along with the rest of us as we make our way down broken blacktop. Enzo likes it when we exaggerate the animal sounds. Quinn enjoys making every animal's verse end with farting noises.

When the road shifts from crumbling asphalt to gravel, I laugh it off. Once it becomes dirt and our pedal pace slows to a fast walk, I start looking for an escape clause. We've come too far to turn around, but the tractor ruts (for that's really all the road is at this point) keep teasing us. The path winds away from the Interstate for a mile then comes within a hundred feet of the fence line again.

If we really are on a road to nowhere, then finding our way back over that fence is going to be problematic. Imagine a little picket number, or better yet, one of those rustic barn wood deals that Hollywood cowboys are always jumping over. They vault it with style, in one fluid motion, thus demonstrating their virility.

This fence is nothing like that.

I throw a stick at its wiring to measure the voltage. So it's not charged even though it looks like it could be. Small consolation, since I will still have to scale five or six feet, then negotiate the barbed-wire hazard capping its top. Never mind what deal with the devil I'll be making to get two boys and a couple hundred pounds of gear onto the other side; there has to be a back door to this farmer's road somewhere?!

We keep our pace and our hopes up until the deeply edged John Deere tracks turn to baked earth cracking in all directions. The afternoon is undeniably hot now. Quail startle us when our commotion startles them. We flush a dozen of the funny-looking fowl out of the bushes. This is no stealth operation I'm running here. I keep pushing our considerable load along a path that has diminished to single-track.

The boys are having a blast, though, catching grasshoppers in their upturned helmets and spotting snakes sunning themselves on the edges of the trail. Each one slithers away before our arrival. I caution the boys not to chase after them since this is certainly rattlesnake country.

Their mood is infectious. A switch gets thrown inside my head. We're fine. The road is right over there, separated by razor wire, sure, but we're not lost, the animals appear alive and well around us, we can always turn back and, frankly, where else do we need to be at this instant?

"It's turning into a real adventure now, boys!" I announce with spirited exuberance, and I'm not just trying to pump myself up. A lazy summer afternoon in the Old West with my sons is about as good as it gets.

Quinn pummels me with grasshoppers. Enzo whacks the tall grass with a stick in hopes of terrorizing another batch of quail. I feel all the tension leaving my body through a series of deep sighs.

A holding pond surrounded by scrub pines and cattails marks the end of the road, literally. The path leads right into the water. I leave the bike back up by the fence. We play at the water's edge while I gather my thoughts. Turning back is always a stubborn man's last option—always. And I'm a stubborn man; ask anyone. There's something defeatist about such a choice, even when it's the right one.

Back at the bike, we survey the fence line. I spot the road we want. It crosses the interstate a quarter mile ahead of us. We're so damn close. This complicates things. Combine a man's no-turning-back gene with a glimpse of the finish line and technically, you've made the decision for him.

"What about this spot?"

Quinn finds a segment in the fence line that lacks barbed wire. It's still a five-foot hurdle, but I'm nothing if not an optimist.

Once I muscle the trailer, minus its wheels, over the fence, we're fully committed. The boys appreciate the way it bounces off the earth and the grunting sounds I have to make to accomplish this task.

After three portages, one section of the rig at a time, and all of our gear, I feel like I could use a proper lie-down. I settle for taking one knee while I contemplate which child to hoist over the wire fence first. Quinn's the obvious choice. He won't bolt for the interstate, but Enzo's lighter. I decide to picture this as a prison break in hopes that a spike in adrenaline will revive me a little.

Both boys perform flawlessly. Like refugees escaping a totalitarian regime, they scale the fence as though their lives depend on it. Enzo sings the theme to *Spiderman* under his breath. All I have to do is keep my hands on them for guidance. Just when I think we're home free, Quinn, standing across the wire from me, à la visitor's day at San Quentin, mouths a perfect O of surprise and points at something behind me.

Best-case scenario: angry rancher. Farther down my list: perhaps a very big rattlesnake, or—and only because it would be the boy's ultimate fantasy—Godzilla looming over the Montana skyline, getting ready to squash.

"I think that bull would like a word with you, Dad."

It's impressive how such a large animal can sneak up like that. I bet *he* doesn't flush quail from the bush. When I turn, the horned and hoofed beast is only a few feet from my face. In reality, it could be a male cow with horns, but I was always rather fuzzy on what categorizes bulls from steers, and even from cows, for that matter.

With a herd of cattle mulling around behind him, the bull resembles a union representative set to start negotiations, or the mascot of a football team (from Texas, perhaps) awaiting the coin toss.

It would be nice to lie about what happens next, have it sound like I handled myself in a way that would make the Marlboro man proud. Instead, I let go with a grade-school-girl yelp and pin myself against the fence. The bull, steer, cow or whatever it is, remains unimpressed, or perhaps he's deaf—it's pretty hard to tell with bovines. What my screaming does not accomplish is to move the animal.

"It's really turning into an adventure now, Dad," Enzo says.

"Olé," Quinn adds.

It's my turn to scale the fence as if I've been running the streets of Pamplona all week. I fully expect a horn to penetrate my back or stab into my bum. When this doesn't happen . . . and when I'm safe behind the fence, I discover my backbone. Still, the yell I let loose with is completely uncalled for. My schoolgirl has turned into a lion. In my defense, to celebrate getting through my first seven years on the planet, I was treated to a special birthday petting session at the Pittsburgh Zoo. A cow, bull, or steer backed onto my foot while I was distracted by a billy goat sporting a tantalizingly long gray beard. Classic pick-and-roll move by the billy goat. Like grifters, I'm told, those petting zoo animals work in teams.

The cow-on-foot experience included pain, a sense of betrayal by Mr. Billy Goat, whose coarse coat I only wanted to comb, and perhaps the genesis for a bit of buried fear regarding close-in work with cattle. Whatever the case, that stationary animal in Montana takes the brunt of my verbal catharsis. The boys crouch instinctively from the force of my outburst. There's this pregnant pause while my howl echoes through the valley. Then the grain-fed animal soils itself and a three-yard area behind it, before bolting in the direction of the herd.

A mini-stampede takes the group to the opposite side of the holding pond, where they await my next move. From that moment on, I am a comic genius in Quinn's eyes. Between fits of apoplectic laughter he cannot heap enough praise on me.

"You scared . . . the . . . the . . . the crap out of him, Dad."

Feeling more like a bully than a comic genius, I can't deny I'm secretly thrilled that my antics are the parental equivalent of home-made speed to my son. Enzo is pleased as well, but takes a more philosophical view of the proceedings.

"Everybody poops," he says through a shit-eating grin.

Slow-leaking rear wheel, slapstick humor, and the rest—we leave the poor cows in peace and limp our rig into camp . . . just behind the mosquitoes.

12

"If you want to see what children can do, you must
stop giving them things." —Norman Douglas

JULY 15   750 MILES
Big Sky, Montana

A cloudless sky, so wide and blue it makes me want to reach into
deep space just on the other side. This is what hangs over Big Sky
Resort's distinctive summit all summer. We ride a ski lift up, then

hike to snowline, where we take one long, respectful look at snow in July . . . before complete anarchy breaks out.

"Snowball fight!"

It's three in the afternoon, the sun is directly overhead and I'm truly thankful to be alive. Not in a spiritual sense, though there's always that, but as framed by the more tactile, flesh-and-bone definition. Snowballs come at me from all directions. Quinn's accuracy is better than his brother's, but Enzo's fearless storming-of-Bunker-Hill approach while he gathers handfuls of snow (and the occasional rock) on the run more than makes up for his buckshot technique. I go down in a blaze of snow and glory, crying "uncle" all the way.

Snowballs made of hard summer-pack graze my head today, and they even hurt a little, but I don't care because we dodged a real bullet back there on the highway.

It started with a call to Dax, Big Sky's publicity director and life-long ski bum.

"Not to harsh on your groove of cycling cross-country by bike, but there's a twenty-mile stretch through Gallatin Canyon that gets pretty gnarly."

"How gnarly?" I asked. I had him on the phone a few days earlier. Dax is helping line up our first pampered rest stop of the adventure.

"I wouldn't ride it," he offers. "And I'm up for almost anything."

By now I've heard a wide range of views on the condition and treachery of various byways and roads around the globe, but when a fellow athlete, one who obviously manages risk in his chosen sport and who actually lives in the area in question, raises a red flag, I have to give it serious consideration.

As much as this cross-country epic looks like child endangerment, I do put the boys' safety at the top of my list. In fact, right now the list has only three items on it:

1. Keep the boys alive and laughing.

2. Ride like it's the last day I'll own a pair of legs.

3. Call in that cell phone payment or haul around another useless piece of plastic. (Could use it to stir pasta round dinner time.)

Most people don't know the first thing about what makes a stellar cycling experience—it's because much of our lives are seen through the filter of the automobile. Cyclists angle for back roads with wide shoulders and visual beauty. Lower traffic flow, sure, but it's more about the type of traffic. RV and certain truck traffic is bad, and on any road we look for clean sight lines and several safe exit strategies. Switchbacks and long climbs are not inherently evil, despite what most drivers think, but shoulderless bridges and tunnels of any length are to be feared.

"You can't ride through Gallatin Canyon," someone else tells me. This time it's Roy, our campground host. I'm taking a wild guess that he hasn't been at the helm of anything smaller than his thousand-foot RV in years. Still, this is the second time Gallatin Canyon and imminent death have shared the same sentence. I perk up.

Roy's wife comes bouncing down the steps of their bus. B looks like a gracefully aging Ann-Margret and acts like your favorite aunt, the one who doesn't smell like cabbage and doesn't do crossword puzzles before noon. I know her name before Roy makes the introductions, not because the miles have unleashed some hidden psychic skills deep within me, no, it's airbrushed on the side of their RV along with a woodland scene of the happy couple with Rex, their German shepherd.

"Hi, B." I stick my mitt out, but she overrides it with a smothering hug. I smell Chanel No. 5 and Ocean Spray cranberry juice.

"Is B short for anything?" I ask.

"No, sweetie, think Cher and Madonna, but better, 'cause they need a whole name. All I need is one letter."

The line feels well used and for good reason. I want to hug her again just for being so comfortable in her own skin.

"Those are cute kids," she nods toward Enzo, who, brandishing a light saber, stands over a prairie dog hole ready to bop it, or any creature foolish enough to make an appearance, on its head. I suppose the definition of cute varies from state to state.

"You wouldn't want anything happening to them," Roy points out.

Which is not categorically true; I want all sorts of things happening to my children. I want them to smack line drives during clutch moments of baseball games, smell the sweet bite of creosote bushes in the Arizona desert after an August monsoon, eat a pile of messy short ribs dripping in Kansas City's best BBQ sauce, then sleep off their food comas under the whispery shade of a willow tree. I want them to stick up for themselves when it really matters, and someday slow dance with that girl, the one who makes them uncool and cotton-mouthed, at the junior high school mixer. I want them to find themselves at a loss for words from the beauty of the world, and make up fantastical names for constellations under the open sky this summer.

What I don't want is something horrible happening to them. That's what he really means. It's a small distinction, but, when magnified through the video black magic of Madison Ave. and filtered by the unfounded fears of parents fueled by the nightly news, it's what cheats all of us of so much. It keeps too many kids of this generation inside the trophy cases of climate controlled cars, fully insulated houses and carpeted tour buses. Parents think they're being responsible by eliminating every possible risk, but that's just a fairy tale someone keeps selling them.

In the end, no one's safe. But it is possible to protect a kid from his own childhood. Don't misunderstand: Car seats and childproof caps have saved countless lives, and I own all that gear and more; but keeping kids under behavioral arrest, constantly lathering them in antibacterial hand lotions, moving them from one organized activity to the next in the equivalent of armored vehicles only narrows their vision, making them observers of their own days.

The trick, in my view anyway, is to manage risk while leaving room for kids to explore the world while they're actually in it. Cutting through the guidance-counselor-speak, just let 'em fall down a few times, get dirt under their nails and end even one day wet, tired, and hungry. Go ahead and let them reach for things everyone's forgotten are important.

"That's the deadliest road in the United States. Least it was a few years ago when the *Today* show did a segment on it, honey."

Roy raises his eyebrow in agreement, which is so big and bushy it wouldn't surprise me if that unibrow could drive the RV all by itself.

"And I can tell you that they haven't changed anything about it, so people are still dying on it just as often."

"Drunk drivers?" I ask.

"Some, but it's a narrow slot canyon with a river on one side and RVs and trucks in both directions; you don't have to be drunk to over-drive it. Fifty crosses in one summer before they stopped posting 'em on account it was spooking the tourists too badly. I even heard that a family member died trying to visit one of the crash sites."

"You might skate through, but why risk it?" B says.

Good point. I want my kids to learn how to reach and, on occasion, fall so they get back up stronger. But you only fall at terminal velocity once. We're in the thick of our summer of freedom, not the end of a season of cheating death. Farmer's roads notwithstanding,

I've already come upon byways I didn't like, stopped on a dime, unfurled the map and found alternate routes.

"When you make that right turn for the mountain, it opens up big as all outdoors. You'd only need to catch a ride for about twelve miles," says B.

People will go out of their way trying to respect the sanctity of the cyclist's cross-country quest. It's the travel version of political correctness. The goal *must* be to pedal every mile, or why else do it?! They surmise (correctly, in my case) that anyone trying to muscle a bike coast to coast must be half-mad and therefore handled with caution. Clearly, a ride of this duration is a lifelong dream—complete with ritual, mythology and rules built up around it. Every mile is sacred. I've met plenty of riders that fit this description to a T. Hell, I've been that obsessed cyclist several times out the gate. But after a hundred thousand miles in unimaginable places and circumstances, from Alaska's permafrost highways to Peru's shining paths and Australia's baked Outback, the only thing I hold above all else is the experience—of being untethered from the day-to-day world for awhile.

"Moments over miles" is our mantra. (Though with a magazine deadline and my kids' summer vacation counting down, these miles do weigh on my mind more than usual, but still surprisingly little.) This is to say that B seems overly concerned that losing twelve miles of pedaling might send my world into a tailspin. It won't.

I have to promise B we'll find a ride when we get to the Gallatin Gateway truckstop, or she'll kidnap the boys and hide them from me somewhere in the black hole of their travel trailer. She's already fed them breakfast and lavished my privileged urchins with coloring books, let them unhook Rex from his chain to chase prairie dogs, and loaded them down with seeds to feed the overfed birds lounging along the fence behind their camp slot.

"You promise, now?! I got grandchildren, so I worry as if yours were my own."

This plea follows us out of the campground and echoes across the wheat fields when we turn the corner onto the much bally-hooed Highway 89.

The road appears innocent enough to me. More than fine, it's wide with a fairly clean shoulder; but B's sweet shrill keeps cutting through the tranquility. We wait in the shade and drink Gatorade. I even pull the bag with my Pop in it out for a look.

"What you think, Dad? Worst road in America?"

He reserves comment, but he drove big-city traffic his whole life. Three generations ponder the miles ahead. I decide to hitch a ride.

"Not allowed to carry unauthorized passengers," one trucker says, not unkindly.

We burn twenty minutes trying for safe passage.

"Can't wait for you to break it down into three pieces," a man with a half-ton truck and heaps of fishing poles points out. I'm starting to think we'll be having truck-stop food for lunch.

"There they are!"

The boys run right over to B. It could have been the bagels covered in cream cheese and jam extended to each of them from her multi-bracelet-covered arms, but I've seen some of their aunts and uncles try unsuccessfully to bribe smiles, greetings and hugs with all manner of treats. B's zest for life brings the boys sprinting in her direction. That and her wardrobe is the fashion equivalent of a lighthouse off the coast of Maine in a fierce Nor'easter, a Technicolor hummingbird. She sparkles and bedazzles, twinkles and shines in a flea-market-merchant-meets-Bette-Midler-on-a-USO-tour way.

"I told Roy, them boys are gonna get drowned out in a fog of diesel exhaust and tire changes."

Roy hops down from the cab of his behemoth bus.

"And I told her you've made it this far without our help, but we were planning an outing to Yellowstone anyway. So we pulled in the awnings, lifted the air jacks and poked our rig into the truckstop to see how you were making out."

A man in too much leather carrying four hundred ounces of coffee comes up from behind.

"You still need a ride?" It's the trucker with authorization issues. "'Cause I found a driver off duty who agreed to load you up."

That's when the cosmic gates of altruism open, flooding us with offers. It's as if we're in the roughneck version of the Broadway play *Annie,* it's tomorrow and the sun has, in fact, come out. Three more invitations arrive over the course of five minutes. It gives Roy a good laugh, not to mention a chance to toss B the old "I told you so." Before they can go at each other like polecats in a back-alley brawl, I split the difference with them, though I wouldn't mind seeing Ann-Margret throw down with Unibrow for a few rounds in a sanctioned fight.

"B, we'd be privileged to load our rig onto this aircraft-carrier-sized vessel and let you deliver us from the evils of Highway 89."

Her bracelets rattle and ring with all the hugs she's handing out.

The boys stare with incredulity at what has only recently been a double-wide looking quite permanent in a campground slot only this morning. It has transformed into a tight, rolling tour vehicle. To be fair, it's still the size of a city bus, but where the better part of a small building has hidden itself is a real mystery.

"Where'd it all go?" Enzo asks.

Roy claps his hands together the way my neighbor's grandfather used to do when someone asked about his model train city in the basement.

"Well, let me show you."

B puts her foot down, literally. She steps in front of her husband and stabs an authoritative press-on fingernail at his face, coming quite close to slicing away a bit of explosive hair growth that has taken root in Roy's ears.

"You are not gonna go pushing all your buttons this morning, honey. News flash: This contraption is only interesting to you and half a dozen of your RV Association buddies."

On this count B couldn't have been more wrong. Entire segments of the toy industry are devoted to creations that mutate, expand, come apart and reconnect in different places and ways. Wonder Twin powers . . . transform into the shape of . . . an RV. One word, B: Legos.

But it doesn't matter. She has only to glance at my sons' enthusiastic faces and resistance is futile. Forget Navy SEALS extracting you from a war zone, or Harvard debate champions talking you through a crisis. A couple of grade-school boys will win over the trust or wear down the resolve of anyone—from terrorists to teachers—using a potent mix of dimples and gap-toothed grins. Enzo could make it cross-country on his own using only his big blue eyes and the occasional well-placed tear.

We spend the next half hour in a button-pushing expansion and contraction of Roy's monster on wheels. Watching him work is similar to being at Frankenstein's birth.

It's everything that's wrong with modern America, and the industrialized world, for that matter: the use of vast amounts of petrochemical products, bigger is better, more is never enough. All this is summed up from tip to tail of this beast. It's the Donald Trump-ing of the world, and it will be the death of us.

Not to be a thorn looking for a side, but at the very core of my being I know we cannot go on this way.

Civilization as we are forging it is an absolute wreck in progress;

a beautiful pill-popping, super-sizing, classroom-crowding, over-consuming, narcissistic, lipo-sucking, text-messaging accident busy waving to the crowd just before impact. It's hard to admit the truth when I'm making the acquaintance of so many salt-of-the-earth people enamored by all the wrong things. Finding them in ZIP code after ZIP code across America . . . well, this just makes it that much more painful.

What's most alarming and depressing is that I'm with the band, and we're playing the ship of fools booze cruise. It's hit open water and I find myself in the conga line shout-singing the chorus to "Hot, Hot, Hot" when all I intended to do was convince a few people to come ashore with me.

But it's not something I'm going to take out on Roy before lunch on a Tuesday. Roy, who, between raping the land five miles per gallon at a time, only wants to help us, offering sanctuary and safe passage in the belly of his beast. This rig, which, if it existed in a vacuum rather than a world demanding endless amounts of energy, cheap labor, easy credit and expendable soldiers, would be off the charts in a James-Bond-for-the-AARP-set sort of way.

Hell, even in this world it's a gigantic transformer toy and, against all my instincts, I'm ten years old again, drooling over all these lights, whistles and bells. I ask them to drop us at the base of the mountain. Roy can't fathom why we'd accept a ride through the canyon and then not let him take us up the incline.

"That hill could kill an Olympic athlete." (Roy must be watching a different Olympics, but I can't help puff up at the comparison, anyway. For the record, it's a monster of a climb for anyone who hadn't already beaten Lolo Pass)

"It's gotta be thirty miles to the village if it's a block, and you're hauling serious ballast, son."

As if I hadn't noticed the burden behind my rear wheel until now. Thanks for pointing that out, Roy. After the load-out, we're only yards from another victim marker. This one's not a cross, more of a diorama. There's a framed photo of the deceased as a beaming fifth-grader, but other personal items arranged by family and friends don't give away how old he was on that fateful day; several pages from an X-Men comic laminated to the wooden box, several guitar picks and a yo-yo leave me baffled. The Frisbee makes me think college, and the empty bottle of Maker's Mark. But the liquor could have been tossed there by some thoughtless drunk—insult to injury.

"I made one of these at preschool," Enzo tells B. He snaps a picture of the diorama before getting back into his trailer. I know he's drawn to these roadside memorials by the colors and trinkets, but lately he's been taking on the empathetic gaze of a true photographer. Sometimes he bows his head after snapping his shots. Sometimes he sings snippets of Ray Charles songs, but always he wants to play with the trinkets and tokens of affection.

The boys promise Roy and B postcards. We watch the ruin of civilization lurch forward and barrel back onto the highway. They could be anyone's parents. They are someone's, and though they've caused so much damage looking for the good life, I feel a soft ring in my bones, as if I'm saying goodbye to my own family after the holidays.

13

Some folks drive the bears out of the wilderness

. . .

Me I just bear up to my bewildered best

. . .

—Lyle Lovett

JULY 16   790 MILES
Montana/Wyoming Border

By dipping into the chutes and swells of Montana's Gallatin River, I'm able to scratch off four lines of my life list: (1) Come down a river faster than I pedaled the road against it on the same day. (2) Share a risk-filled rafting trip with my sons and have them beg for more. (3) Witness moose and bighorn sheep running along the banks from the relative safety of our inflatables. (4) Try my hand at fly-fishing the eddies where *A River Runs Through It* was filmed.

Running Class III water with the boys, and a few precious hours of solo casting (the kids' camp at Big Sky Resort took the lads for an afternoon), is like turning back the clock two hundred years, to a time when the pioneer spirit ruled our collective unconscious—when a trek over the next rise held uncertainty and required no small measure of courage. Watching dancing flies over the dark pools and creases of light reflecting off a still-pristine river, I realize that I've slipped into the skin of my ancestors, or at least can feel the afterglow of their presence.

High time I get my crew back on camp fare. We've been lounging around the largest hot tub in the West, a forty by ten yard lap pool heated to steamy decadence in the shadow of Big Sky's signature peak.

Between hot tubbing, Cartoon Network on cable, plush beds, snowball fights, kids' camps, fly-fishing, and a spectacular morning of river rafting, we've practically forgotten what bike saddles feel like. It's been little more than a day since I labored us up this mountain but it feels like forever; a lifetime in the span of a few densely packed hours. I now know Dax, our guide for this pampered pit stop, and many of the resort staff, better than some of our neighbors back home.

During the unbridled joyride down that winding mountain road, leaning tight into the corners and opening it all the way out on the steep straightaways, we find it in ourselves to reach for the brakes halfway down. We're stopping just long enough to continue Quinn's traveling tradition of collecting cycle shop stickers. We put them on our helmets the way world travelers once put country stamps on luggage.

Grizzly Outfitters lavishes us with claw-shaped stick-ons, encouraging words and some sobering news. The wind is blowing fierce through the southern side of the canyon. And because the highway opens up, sure, the cars don't kill as often, but the headwinds may have you wishing you were dead.

I shrug it off with a laugh and set my sights for the north entrance of Yellowstone. I call this my British explorer pose. It's all false bravado and power of positive thinking. Crap, but what choice do I have? The boys think I'm made of Teflon, so I carry on as if I believe their press releases.

There's little in this world quite as satisfying as rocketing down a mountain that you've earned your way up through blood, sweat, — and gears. And we still have some mountain left to enjoy. The curtain falls when we turn the corner.

Montana's not giving us away without a fight. My determination earlier in the day was a fist, ready to hammer through whatever lined up to take a beating from me. Now, full sun on our faces, headwind in our wheels, a herd of thunderheads chasing our tail from the north, playing a tense game of cat-and-mouse much of the afternoon, I feel ganged up on.

Over the course of an hour, thunderheads will rear up so close that I swear I can smell water even against the strength of the headwind, then the build-up backs down, peeling away to the east or west, but never disappearing entirely.

I try to ignore it and time our rest stops so the boys can feed sugar packets to gentle corral horses nosing through fence lines. But like Rasputin, the headwind refuses to die. My fist? Now it's bruised and bloody, and my pauses keep growing as fatigue sets in. Counting breaks, I've covered a paltry dozen miles in three hours. No land speed records in jeopardy today.

When I start coming up with excuses for stops, such as a metal cutout of a cowboy in draw-your-pistols position that the boys should pose with, I suspect it's time to toss in the towel.

"Let me get a photo of you guys in a quick-draw shootout with him."

Instead, they drape their arms around the fierce little gunslinger. Ah . . . my pint-sized peacemakers. I click off a few frames, stalling.

If legs are the cycling equivalent of six-shooters, I'm not ready to lay down my guns yet. There's gotta be one more bullet left in the chamber. Everything above my neck tells me today is my The Alamo; play dead and hope the Mexican army passes me over. In other words, set up camp.

Everyone knows afternoon headwinds never blow themselves out before dusk; it's right there in the Constitution, or it should be. I keep going. This is the point in the ride when you get angry or get off; a strategy that moves us three miles down the road, three shabby, hard-fought, grudge-match miles before an enormous grizzly bear stops us in our tracks.

Carved from a massive slab of first-growth wood, the folk-art piece sits up on its hind legs. It sports an expression of satisfaction to rival Buddha. Obviously it hasn't been pedaling into a headwind all afternoon. The carving reminds me of an oversized prairie dog, the 1950s matinee-movie result of atomic bomb mutation that could eat a Buick. This traffic-stopping creation is part of a larger complex called The Cinnamon Lodge. I will come to the conclusion too late that this establishment has neither cinnamon rolls (my first desire) nor available lodging (a close second). But at the moment, hopes run high. We take each other's pictures by the big beast before we venture toward the lodge.

"Haven't opened the back cabins for the season yet," the front desk cowboy says.

"And all these up front are occupied tonight, but the restaurant will turn on its grill any minute now."

My shoulders sag.

"We make a mean chicken-fried steak, and there's a side room full of toys for the kids."

If he knew how famished I am he'd pass on the hard sell, but I appreciate his spirit. Properly seasoned, I'd eat tire scraps. I have to inquire as to cinnamon rolls.

"Funny, we get people asking for those all the time."

He hasn't made the connection yet, and I'm too tired to help close that circuit. Plus I'm busy drinking a full pitcher of water.

"Homemade cobbler is on the menu today, though." Sold! What he doesn't realize is on trips like this, I order my pies whole.

I set the kids loose in a room of toy chests and head back outside to lock up what I can of the rig. It's mostly symbolic, but it always makes me feel better. And hey, it might slow them down a little.

The act of Kryponiting my rear wheel to a pole behind the bear carving wears me out. Pitiful. And just this morning I was a fist.

U-locks are never long enough. It's usually a wrestling match with gravity and how much the bike will give. It's better than a mobile Bowflex machine. After the workout, I rest against my panniers until the harsh gravel crush of a pickup truck's wheels through the parking lot ignites my fight-or-flight response. I launch to my feet, still holding tight to the locked bike. A leather-faced rancher encrusted to the driver's seat seems amused.

"Son, why you locking that thing 'round here? This is Montana. We might shoot you, but we won't rob you."

Good to know where you stand. I appreciate that in a state.

It's 4 P.M. I've morphed into a Florida retiree from Boca del Vista. Tucking my napkin under my chin, I enjoy an early bird dinner alone in a hall the size of an airplane hangar. When I place a second order of the daily special, my waiter (the same cowboy clerk from the front desk) asks if anyone else will be joining me. I laugh the lunatic's laugh, which causes him to bring me extra white gravy.

Apparently, lunatics can never have enough gravy.

After ten thousand calories, I feel human again. The thought of getting back on the bike is too much to bear, but it must be done.

"You won't make it to Yellowstone proper before nightfall," the Cinnamon Lodge cowboy explains. "The north entrance might be fifteen miles up the road, but it's just a sign and a rock wall. A well-made rock wall, [he helped build it] but it's still just a wall. There's no organized campsites, ranger programs or anything like that for fifty miles yet."

I can't hide my frown.

"If it's just good quiet camping you want though, Ramshead Rest is a mile up on the left. It's sweet—a compost crapper and a running creek. Filter the water or bring some with, and you'll be snug as a bug."

First rule of Bike Club: befriend the locals. The locals know the lay of the land. That's what I'm talking about.

Second rule of Bike Club; tell everyone about Bike Club; that way they'll know where to send the rescue party.

You'd think I was powered by rocket fuel for the final mile to Ramshead Rest. When you know it's almost over for the day, your body turns on the afterburners. Ominous clouds don't faze me in the least. We'll have camp set up before any rogue storm can drench us. A hayride of tourists pulls alongside as we make the turn onto a dirt road. My mood is so buoyant now that we even stop to answer questions and let some of the kids check out our bikes and trailer.

But sometimes the ride isn't over once you leave the blacktop.

"It's farther up than I thought."

Quinn grunts in response. He's ready to be off the bike, too. Enzo's asleep. Depending on conditions, a mile of dirt road pencils out to three or four traveled over asphalt. Even more if, as is the case this evening, one is pedaling slightly uphill.

We pass a convention of horse trailers, hunters and sportsmen hunkered around their fire circles, reminiscent of the Old West tent communities that sprang up around gold claim operations.

It's another quarter mile to the trailhead. I spot the campground marker and heave a deep sigh of relief.

We appear to have the place to ourselves.

There's a wooden hitching post to tie off horses, which I use to lock up the bike. It puts me in an outlaw frame of mind. A trio of Young Guns hiding high up in the Montana hills: Jesse, Josey and Clem.

"No fire tonight, boys. The posse can't be but a few miles behind."

Quinn shakes his head, but I get a smile out of him.

By the time I finish setting camp, the veil of clouds we've been under since the Cinnamon Lodge lifts, revealing a potent summer evening. Radiant sun rays cut low across the horizon. Every ridgeline and rock is bathed in ethereal light normally reserved for museum-quality Renaissance paintings. "Miracle light," a docent once called it. If Jesus, John Lennon or both stepped through its illumination, I would not be fazed. We'd offer them a Clif bar and a stump around the fire ring. See if John could play us something if he brought his guitar. Put the Savior on tambourine. Keep that funky beat, the one from *Jesus Christ, Superstar.* Can I get a Strawberry Field from the Walrus?

We wake Enzo, break out the light sabers and commence to slicing, blocking and fencing to exhaustion around a muddy horse manure corral. Our creek rushes at just the right tempo for soaking off crusted battle debris. Late-day sun warms our naked skin. I watch thick clouds of harmless insects, whirling dervishes above high grass. Enzo searches for skipping stones and Quinn announces that he thinks he's found a beaver dam. When scheming an adventure, this is how I envisioned our best days coming to a close.

The water numbs my limbs, freezing out the last worries of the day.

"Dad, what's a grizzly bear relocation drop site?"

His question dislocates me completely. The same way waking up in a smoke-filled room might cause one to ask: "Is it just foggy in here, or is my bed actually on fire?"

I sit up Indian-style in the rushing water and follow his voice to the trailhead community board, a place where the Forest Service posts its rules, regulations, maps, and educational materials.

One of the most miraculous days in recent memory was the moment Quinn learned to read. It stands out, a snapshot that I can call up at any time, to remind me that I'm doing something right.

Driving around downtown Portland, in search of a post office, Quinn grew so bored with easy reader material in the back seat that he took to trolling billboards and storefront advertisements for stimuli.

"Dad, there's a "Bare If You Dare" film festival at Hard Times adult video store."

My God, the boy's reading at will.

"I think they misspelled the word 'bear.' "

And he's already an editor.

It was woefully inappropriate reading material, but I let it slide because, hell, the little man was reading! Not sounding out one-syllable words at a snail's pace, but finding the words spilled out of his mouth. The dam had burst. I swelled with pride but performed a billboard-spelling pop quiz just to be sure.

"And the one with the stage coach?"

" 'Free checking.' "

"What about that basketball player one?"

"'Trailblazers; Ready or Not, Here We Come.' Aren't you always calling them the 'Jail Blazers'?"

Houston, we do not have a linguistic problem; though it should have tipped me off about things to come. Once your progeny can read, they can read everything! *Everything!* Control slips away like water through a net. With this new independence comes both power and risk. No longer is he ignorant of certain aspects of the world, but short on context and perspective in many instances.

Enough about the potential developmental damage a warehouse of expanding knowledge can do to a nimble young mind; the truly alarming thing was now my son could hold me accountable. The carefree days of breezing by toy stores or come-ons for milkshakes in the newspaper were gone. My job just got harder.

And this evening at Ramshead Rest, I can't pretend we are camped in anything but a grizzly bear relocation drop site. The ignorance of a few moments ago had been catastrophically blissful.

Still naked, I join my seven-year-old in front of a poster trumpeting the bad news bears drop zone.

"Hmmm."

Quinn cocks his head, eyebrows slightly raised . . . waiting for his father to explain this one away. You just know what he's thinking:

"Go on, Pop, show everyone that black belt in babble."

I check the dates on the flyer. Of course it's a current posting.

"Hmmm."

"Here's the thing, Quinn. We're gonna see a bunch of bears now that we're rolling into Yellowstone. We won't bother them and they won't mess with us . . . and even if they do, that's why I bought the bear spray."

Unfortunately, we'd been treated to a litany of bear humor and pepper spray jokes while purchasing the canister at a fire, search and rescue open house near Helena. I suppose firemen in Montana don't have that many open mike opportunities. Still, working his shtick on the elementary-school crowd was uncalled for.

"You know what a grizzly bear calls food bags hung from trees?"

We did not.

"Backcountry piñatas."

Enzo laughed and clapped. He took this as encouragement, but then Enzo laughs and claps whenever someone mentions the word piñata. I have news for this paramedic: if he didn't produce a papier maché pig, a big stick and a rain shower of candy at the end of his bit, things could get ugly.

"What'd the grizzly bear say when hit with pepper spray?"

He pauses, as if he's giving us time to order our two drink minimum and tip the waitress.

"Pass the salt."

Nice. Scaring kids is a public service now? He hands me the spray; I'm tempted to test it on him. Still he's not done.

"What do bears call tents?"

"Take-out dinners."

I shouldn't have worried though. Quinn's camping credentials and having a biologist for a mother, one who enjoys reading "Far Side" cartoons at bedtime, surface.

He laughs, then offers some notes.

"Bears don't talk or celebrate holidays, many don't climb trees, and they'd need opposable thumbs for that piñata or drive-through food pickup."

The word piñata sends Enzo into another round of clapping.

Back at Ramshead Rest, Quinn's taking the drop zone realization in stride. Me, not so well.

I'm projecting a fatherly air of confidence, which might be help-ing. Inside, though, things aren't as tranquil. A bear has to be pret-ty rowdy before rangers bring out elephant guns and hit him with the trancs. These are the troublemakers. And if I'm an ursine badass waking up stiff and hung over from a shotgun Mickey, I want two things: food and retribution. A father-sons campout in my drop site covers both of those counts nicely.

And then there's the shadow of Timothy Treadwell, a troubled L.A. activist, eaten alongside his girlfriend by a grizzly after ten summers shooting home movies on Kodiak Island. This summer we've passed several movie marquees featuring a documentary about the whole disturbing episode.

On the upside, if I'm a bear released back into the wild, my first instinct is gonna be to bolt as far and fast as possible. Actually, maybe where we are is the most bear-free zone around. Either way, I'm too tired and it's too late to do much about it.

Except this: "We're putting our food in the bathroom; all of it. The Clif bars, the toothpaste, every bit of food or flavor-related product," I tell them. I start sorting out packets of grub from the panniers, but I think better of it, cancel the assignments, and haul all the bags into the small brick building.

"Poop food." Enzo is over the moon about this. "We're putting our food in with the poop."

Quinn smiles, even while trying to take the high road.

"Enzo, we're not putting it IN the poop, just near it."

Saying it out loud is just too much for him. Quinn joins his brother's chorus of laughter.

"Poop food," he yodels. Now I have a choir on my hands.

I secure the gear by wedging our bags into a corner ledge win-dow as far from the actual seat as possible. The door, one of those spring-weighted locks (perfect for bear-proofing a bathroom) catches my finger on the way out.

My howls mimic those of a man being attacked by a grizzly; so much for maintaining a low profile. The pain retreats after a quick soak in the creek.

"Look, Dad," Quinn whispers.

I'm afraid to lift my head, but it's not the big bad bear parade. A majestic herd of elk crowd the other side of the creek. Some are wider than an economy car I drove in college. We stay quiet and close together, and play a game Quinn calls "Count the Antlers." It makes all our trips to the zoo feel like dress rehearsals. Chemicals rush my blood stream. Regardless of how the summer ends, this moment alone makes it worth the ticket price.

The herd leaves when it's good and ready, wandering back up the ridge in the fading light.

The boys are asleep before I have the tent door zipped. My body wants to do the same. Instead, I take up a sentry position beside the window. Pepper spray in one fist, flashlight in the other. Maybe a half hour passes, long enough to let me relax. Then the rain arrives, followed shortly by ominous footfalls. Something large and marching on all fours comes crashing through the understory along the ridge. Crunch, crunch, crunch, crunch . . . pause; four distinct animal footsteps at a time.

Half a dozen yards later, it pulls up, waiting, probably catching a whiff of us. When it's perhaps ten yards away, I go proactive, hitting the light and releasing the safety on my spray.

"Who's out there!" I project this question with the force of an amateur thespian doing theater in the round.

This assumes that grizzly bears understand English now. Correspondence courses, perhaps? The flashlight proves problematic. I've accomplished spotlighting the inside of the tent and blinding myself. Another drawback: I don't have a free hand to unzip the tent door. But it's only a drawback if I actually want a confrontation with the beast. I put the light in my mouth and, with plenty of trepidation, yank at the zipper.

I can sense a large creature out there in the darkness. Is it human nature to want to establish the danger? It's a shock to my system then, when words with a slight Hispanic accent echo down, the voice of God from above.

"It's only me."

The ranger is on horseback, and he's probably just as surprised to reach the trailhead and find the bushes talking as I am to discover he's not a bone-munching grizz.

He hitches up the horse, then ambles, slow and laconic, toward the bathroom. He moves in a way only someone with a full day in the saddle would. I feel a kinship. I feel forced to explain, over the wind and rain, that those bags jammed in the window space of the outhouse aren't garbage, but our worldly possessions hidden from wayward bears.

He nods without breaking stride. Obviously neither weather nor the bizarre antics of summertime tourists near Yellowstone has any effect on this man.

Back on his horse, the ranger offers a valuable piece of information, information I could have used earlier, but you take what you can get. Speaking in the general direction of our tent, he says, "It's always good to secure your food, this being bear country, but so you know, we haven't relocated any animals this season."

I cap the spray, but hug it to my chest as I drift off to sleep; hug it in the very same way my sons clutch their teddy bears.

14

"Sex is good, but not as good as fresh sweet corn."
—Garrison Keillor

JULY 17   850 MILES
Yellowstone National Park, Wyoming

Some would call it ironic, or at least significant, that the very next morning we come face to face with our first grizzly.

I like the circumstances better this time around.

We're a mile beyond the official entrance to Yellowstone, coming from the north. A real Steve-McQueen-on-a-motorcycle morning, bracing winds at first light have given way to sun across an expansive valley. Instead of a tent zipper there are several hundred yards, a guardrail, a steep grade, and a raging river between us and a massive graham-cracker-colored beauty. It's no trick of light or rustling in the bushes, either. This encounter is close enough to appreciate the details of this animal. The boys point and jump up and down.

I'm doing the same, and shouting inane questions at them such as "Do you see it?" (as if a half-ton bear pawing across an open field isn't the Mutual of Omaha equivalent of the Ferris wheel at a state fair), "Do you think it's hungry?" (what else would it be doing clomping around by the river grabbing at things swimming by?), and this brain-trust classic, "How big you think it is?" (now my boys are a special blend of field biologists and midway carnies who can guess anyone's weight to within a few pounds at fifty paces).

Finally, I just shut up and let the bear answer our questions with its actions. A fly fisherman a hundred yards upriver doesn't seem concerned when the animal starts moving his way. A hulking downed tree trunk seems to catch its eye. The bear rolls the massive log as we might move a breakfast sausage across the plate to unearth some eggs buried below.

"Honey?" Quinn suggests.

"Ants," Enzo decides.

We can't bring ourselves to move on until the roadway crowds with tourists. Thick with RVs and loud with clicking cameras, these are cues to the traveling cyclist to thread through the traffic and leave them the moment. Pedaling away, I'm selfishly satisfied that we'd been first on the scene, another fringe benefit of this graceful form of travel.

"Look at that," Quinn yells. We're ten minutes beyond the bear.

I scan for elk, eagles, possibly bison, but it's a steady stream of color coming in from the feeder road to our right that has caught Quinn's attention. From this distance I'm reminded of a dragon float at a Chinese New Year's parade, with Technicolor parts of its tail lagging behind. The riders aren't carrying gear on these high-end bikes, but I can tell by body types, pedaling positions, eyewear and even facial expressions that this isn't a race.

Up ahead, the Cycle America van pulls over. When we pass the driver, a bronzed, smiling college coed, she flashes a wide-eyed look at our rig, followed by an enthusiastic thumbs-up.

Buoyed by this, I pick up my pace.

"They're coming, Dad."

Quinn must think I think it's a race. Do I?

Here's my dirty little secret. Any time two sets of wheels roll ahead of me, a spike of adrenaline floods my system and I have to resist this deep-rooted desire to stand on the pedals and go. It's childish, I know, ludicrous even considering the load I'm hauling this summer, but there it is.

Beside the caffeine issues, (never coffee, by the way—always tea, hot tea, iced tea Chai) questionable aptitude, career choices and verbal diarrhea, I'm also unnecessarily competitive . . . or maybe all men deep down are dogs on the run—chasing shiny bumpers from dawn to dusk until one day the nice farm lady has to go all Old Yeller and put us down proper with one behind the ear.

I'll say this much: runs in the family. Quinn turns nearly everything into a race, mostly with his brother because he likes those odds; grabbing the most brochures at travel centers, washing up under campground hand-pump wells, live grasshopper gathering, dead crayfish tossing, pulling hair out of his own scalp fastest and who has the stinkiest shoes (which I always win, though I didn't even know I was playing).

So when a breakaway of three or four Cycle America riders calls out, "On your left" and whirls by, I almost bite, and Quinn approves.

"What are you waiting for, Dad?"

I know enough about pacelines and the anatomy of a bike tour to let them go.

They're the tour's rabbits. You can tell by the clothing alone. It's the most coordinated we'll see all day.

Let's start with an ugly truth that few in the cycling world will admit in the privacy of their bathroom mirrors, let alone bring themselves to utter aloud at a club meeting or while wobbling about on bike shoes before a Wednesday evening canyon ride.

But I'll say it. I'll speak the truth and shame the devil. I'll hold it up there in the harsh morning light for a good looking over. No, I'm not referring to blood doping or sundry drug use on the Tour. And this is not a segue into the age-old debate over helmet use— because frankly, that one's been put to rest for me—if you don't think your head's worth forty dollars, then why should I?

No, what those rabbits up ahead have put my mind onto is, well, is this: Who in God's name dressed you people in those outfits? For the record, it really doesn't matter, does it? Because therein lies the ugliest of truths—fashion is to the bike rider as plans for world domination are to the bovine population. But while the lack of an opposable thumb is the culprit preventing cows from climbing the corporate ladder and kicking off their wildly popular "Got Beer?" ad campaign and hooking all of us up to milking machines some- where in the backwoods of Vermont, I can only surmise that my Brooks-seated brethren are suffering some sort of mass state of delu- sion, call it hysterical color-blindness. What else would have us thinking we look fresh in those cycling duds?

Reality check—it's a Halloween parade every time we suit up and roll out the driveway. We're dressing ourselves like disgruntled rodeo clowns after a messy battle with a tube of kid's toothpaste. Refugees from the carnival midway—"Step right up, see the color- blind athlete don improbable clothing combinations." It's like catching a glimpse of Elton John's top-secret walk-in closet of fashion faux pas.

To be fair, there are precious few jerseys on the market that aren't the aftermath of a tragic accident down at the Crayola factory. And while the old-school wool jerseys look sharp, only sheep and creepy guys driving Porsches from 1979 would be seen in that material. Still, just because you've matched the teal in your spandex pants with the teal in your top, that only means that now you look equally ridiculous from head to toe.

And while we're on the topic of coordinating the uniform, unless you're a member of the U.S. Postal racing team, do not wear the outfit. I can't tell if that was actually Lance training undercover in my town, or a wannabe from accounting on a lunch-hour spin. If you're gonna wear that get-up, then be able to go faster than the Metal Cowboy, or, at the very least, bring me my mail.

Oh, and the wraparound eyewear does not, I repeat, does not make you look like a young Arnold in *The Terminator* or Fishburne from *The Matrix*. Last time I put on those glasses my wife thought a German exchange student from 1987 had hijacked her husband.

Am I so dense that I don't understand the utilitarian aspects of cycling garb? Of course I realize that the Lycra must be tight for aerodynamic purposes, as well as to prevent leg cramping. I also comprehend that sporting bright colors is to help riders stick out at dusk, dawn and in rush-hour traffic, to cue the soccer mom passing back juice boxes in the minivan that we are indeed coasting by in the left turn lane. Yes, those neons just might stop the businessman about to run the light and into you while he's on his cell phone. This has not been lost on me. But I've been to the zoo; I've seen the peacocks. At a certain point it's just showing off. I must ask, does the world really need another wild cacophony of purple and pink acid-trip trailers on display across the backroads of America, when a solid yellow background with a few tasteful red stripes will do the job?

One more truth while I'm in a confessional mood. I really don't

care what we wear in the saddle. Fact is, we've already been con-
victed by much of society as freaks. We're pegged as odd simply
because we know in our hearts and legs that the bicycle sets the perfect tempo for staying connected, if even for a time, to the beat of
the natural world, the rhythm of the road. Actually, I'm not here to
convict, but to praise that abandoning of convention in the face of
earth tones and other drab fashion choices.

Our ability to feel no shame while exposing those ample gams to
the world is, or should be, a testament to the human spirit. That
some of us thrill at inserting a forty-inch waist into a pair of shorts
sized for the body of a petite Romanian gymnast is inspiring. A gymnast, I might point out, who must vault into thin air from the uneven
bar to stick the fit. And here's to you, Mr. or Mrs. "No, Jimmy Buffet
is not back in town again, but I will ride with my parrothead, shark's-
fin, or cheeseburger bike helmet covering anywhere I damn well
please."

When I clip in those tight shoes, the ones that should really only
be worn by jockeys, when I smooth the body-hugging jersey over
my shoulders and across my chest (damn I look marvelous), when
I flex the quads under the snug confines of my Day-Glo orange
bike shorts (behold the beauty of these oak trees, baby)—a trans-
formation occurs. I emerge from my sedentary cocoon, and on
those first pedal strokes I understand with morning-light clarity
that the clothes *do* make the man . . . feel as though he can go faster,
farther, forever in psychedelic style.

I've come to believe with all my heart that anything is possible
. . . anything but making *People* magazine's best-dressed list.

So go ahead, slip into something a little more ridiculous. And
when you think they're all pointing from the back seats and bal-
conies of America, you go right ahead and point back. Smile and
wave, even. Woodstock is just a memory, but we, my friends, we are

the glam fashion rock stars of the road, so let's start acting like it.

The boys cheer on my fashion rant. This side of adjusting my meds, they know it's the best course of action when I get going like this.

It's not until half of the Cycle America's pack overtakes us that I throw my lot in with a clump of riders and try to match their cadence. They seem impressed; these are experienced journeymen cyclists as opposed to outright endorphin addicts—people with careers and families as a centerpiece of their lives, not a supplement to their riding. In other words, people who watch the Tour de France but would never seriously contemplate entering it. These are my people.

Someone asks about our daily average. A couple in matching jerseys and matching bikes directly ahead of my front wheel makes a few halfhearted attempts to up the pace, but when I don't drop back they ease off the throttle. No harm, no foul.

About ten of us fall into a comfortable line. It would seem that I'm not the only one with leader-of-the-pack tendencies who lacks enough fast-twitch muscle fibers to back it up. My real Achilles' heel, though, is conversation. My big mouth is a recipe for disaster if I want to maintain their pace. Unfortunately, at that moment everyone wants to know about our adventure. I do my best, but it's killing me. Two, maybe three more questions and we're toast. I'll start to slip back until we become a spot, then we'll be lost completely to the heat mirage lines dancing above the pavement in their rearview helmet or handlebar mirrors.

Imagine a man overboard stroking hard after a life ring, forced to sing something powerful like Queen's "Bohemian Rhapsody" as the boat begins to dump him in its wake. Focus and air intake are my friends, and I'm giving away too much of both with each answer. Unless . . .

"Enzo, tell 'em about the bear."

And he's off.

If Quinn is my heart and head, then Enzo is my soul and mouth-piece. Quinn isn't being rude when, at times, he offers adults one-word answers. He's busy thinking things through in a complicated world; pondering.

My hope is that from all those deep thoughts will emerge some-thing lasting and useful for the future. And Enzo? He's a people person of the highest order. I predict he'll never lose a night's sleep, he'll perform keg stands in college, and he'll publicize his brother's brilliant business to a glorious success without needing to be asked. This is their relationship already. It might change, but I doubt it.

It's no mystery, then, that Enzo is my conversational designated hitter. Smack it to the fence line, little man, while I try to conserve some energy and recover our cadence.

Tucked in tight and growing stronger, I listen to Enzo, backed up by Quinn's clarifications and helpful additions, entertain a pace-line of cyclists all the way to West Yellowstone—the gaudy facade of a pioneer town seemingly manufactured for the sole purpose of soaking tourist dollars. Every pancake house, T-shirt shop and hotel has the words Nugget, Gold or Geyser in its name.

The Cycle America group scatters into eateries around the main drag. Bicycles are parked at almost every corner and neon jerseys festoon the sidewalk tables and patio seats everywhere I look. We find pizza and a place to rest at an outdoor cafe's picnic table. License plates from all fifty states line the fence. The boys make up matching games, burn their mouths on pizza, and find relief inside thick milkshakes.

A girl in a sundress, about Quinn's age, is fascinated by our

adventure and mode of transportation. She riddles the boys with questions—Bonnie and Clyde style. Her mother asks if she's bothering us, but I encourage the conversation.

"Did you eat a baked potato when you were in Idaho?"

The boys' faces register something close to panic, as if we've left the stove on back home. We stare at each other without comment for a long moment. Sundress holds up a French fry, possibly as a visual aid. I shake my head.

"My God, boys, I don't think we ate any potatoes while in the center of the known spud universe."

"I'm from Idaho," Sundress adds by way of explanation. "And you really missed something. You have to ask for a proper potato not the russets, because most of the ones they serve in restaurants aren't even grown from Idaho."

Which actually makes sense since farmers probably ship most of their stock around the globe.

"Are you going to try one on your way back?"

You have to love the limitless ambition of the typical eight-year-old. She assumes we're gonna tag the Atlantic seaboard, you're "it"—then double back for good measure. What's an extra four thousand miles among friends?

"Are we, Dad?" Enzo is also a little unclear on our route particulars. Sundress's parents can't hold back a laugh.

"I'm tired just thinking about you and your boys pedaling from here to the other side of the park," Sundress's dad says. "Give me your address. I want to ship you a sack of the best potatoes you'll ever taste. The ones served in high-end steakhouses mostly. Each bite's a masterpiece. "

I've never been offered a sack of spuds through the mail. Sea monkeys, fruitcakes, Uncle Milo's Red Ants, but never potatoes.

"You people really know your taters." This is all I can think to say.

"That's 'cause we grow them," Sundress explains.

Her dad nods. "Potato farming; the best way to bury a dollar each spring and dig up pennies in the fall. But we love the life."

He says it with feeling, not as if he's trying to convince himself it's true.

The boys would like nothing better than to go dig up some potatoes with Sundress and company, but they're headed west and we have thirty miles to cover due east to Madison campground. Yellowstone camping is only permitted in designated spots. From the window of a car it might not seem like much distance between these enclaves, but by bike it's a solid push. We pose with the potato farmers around our bike before rolling past a line of cars backed up at the park tollbooth entrance.

That we don't have reservations at any campgrounds should concern me, considering these slots go lightning-fast through Ticketmaster months ahead of time. But I have some insider information that allows me to smile and wave like a Disney character in the Electric Light Parade. We pass the minivan hordes of glass-enclosed nature lovers. Many will pull in before us only to be turned away. It's sad, but it's survival of the fittest tourist. National Park small print includes this little-known rule: *cyclists or backpackers arriving on their own power can't be turned away.*

Whichever subversive Rebel Alliance member slipped that piece of pedal-pushing pork through Congress, I salute you, and I wish you the best at that secret Gitmo prison cell you'll be shipped to once this enlightened regulation is unearthed and lobbied out of existence.

I came into possession of said information during a few seasons as a contract employee for the National Park Service in New Mexico. The fact that the federal government offered me employment more than once is further proof that the End of Days is upon us, but it opened my eyes to a number of rights and privileges available on public lands.

I never want to come off as one of those self-righteous cyclists: extolling the virtues of the wheel, the fact that I'm burning no dinosaur bones, smug and proud that I've eliminated gym fees and car payments in one pedal stroke, blissful that I'm on the actual adventure that car dealers hawk in flashy ads but never quite deliver. I am, of course, a self-righteous fill-in-the-blank of the highest order behind closed doors, but then who isn't?

It's not humility that keeps me in check on the open roads of America, though, so much as who with half a brain cell wants to infuriate people at the helm of big metal wrecking machines? With the casual yank of a steering wheel, we could be squished right beside all those squirrels that juked left when they should have darted right. No, drunk drivers, the elderly and log trucks are enough for any cyclist to deal with. I do not need to piss off every driver on the road with the Gospel of the Wheel according to Joe. Smile and wave, boys, smile and wave.

I even manage to keep the gloating hidden during a genuine rock-star moment. Coasting though golden eagle country on the downhill roll to Madison, I have an instant of self-doubt. What if I'm working from outdated information? What if the ranger I confirmed with at headquarters was misguided, or Congress recently closed the cyclist camping loophole? Damn the torpedoes, we're not turning back now.

We roll up to a campground host building. It's swarming with more people than a Bombay train station; testy, anxious people, due to a sign indicating exactly seven campsites on standby status if reservation holders don't claim them by 5 P.M. It's 4:57. This has camptown riot written all over it.

And there it is: an open window at the end of a nonexistent line on one side of the building. The only thing missing is a powerful chord from a church organ and a sunbeam from the heavens shining down on it. The sign reads BIKER/HIKER. I'm reminded of carpool lanes left fallow in many big cities across America. Five dollars and thirty-one cents later (what federal accounting office settled on that sum?), we are kicking back in a campsite far from the madding crowd of generators and RV awnings. We share the distance of a wooded football field with exactly three other hikers and bikers. There's a communal shed filled with lanterns, spare camping gear, canned food and lawn chairs. As the boys spill into other vacant sites with their games of hide-and-seek and kick-the-can, I stretch out on a plastic lounger and taste something tart. Is that guilt? My inner Jimmy Carter wants everyone to get along. If an old peanut-farming former president can build Americans affordable housing one hammer stroke at a time, can't I lobby the rangers to open up this biker camp area to a few disgruntled drivers?

My lawn chair gives me an unobstructed view of the host building. Some of the tourists are openly weeping, others plead in foreign languages with the man in the funny green hat and overly starched shirt. They are signing the universal symbol for "please save our Yellowstone experience with a spot of dirt and a grill-covered fire circle."

"Rules are rules." I overhear another ranger scold a carload from Iowa trying to set up shop in a hiker campsite without the appropriate paperwork or lack of car. I feel a bit like a feudal lord sitting on more land than I need. They cast scornful looks in the direction of my lawn chair.

Awkward.

Until Oscar and his teenage son, Peep, set me straight.

"You think it was the Tahoe truck or the trailer of JetSkis that tipped off the ranger?"

Their bold laughter chases after the Iowans and their sulky departure.

I learn that this pair hiked up from Midway Basin Geyser. It's their fourth stop on a summer walkabout: Olympia, Rainier, Glacier, and now Yellowstone.

"We drive between parks, leave the car outside, and hoof it around the backcountry. We've earned this area. I'm not about to share it with a bunch of exhaust-fuming day-trippers overstaying their park pass and lazy bastards trying to poach our sanctuary."

Oscar walks around my rig a few times.

"Christ almighty, you've earned it too."

We decide to cook dinner together.

"The thing is," Peep says (his name is John, but asks that we call him Peep), "Dad gets so worked up 'cause that was us last year. We drove the hell out of the parks, through them more like it, but mostly we forgot to stop."

"To smell the lupines," adds Oscar.

"And we forgot to make reservations in advance," Peep says. "That's how we learned about the hiker/biker rule the hard way. Tell you, though, walking the trails has made all the difference."

"Night and day," Oscar echoes.

Exclusion has an upside. Though I doubt the Park Service saw this as part of its vision statement, segregation has made a couple of hiking converts in this father and son. I relax on my lounger and really enjoy the acreage for the first time. Later, we boil, cook, and consume dinner with a ruthless focus only people pedaling and hoofing around day in and day out can truly know.

"You can learn a lot in a year," Oscar says over a cup of hot cocoa. "For instance, twelve months ago, all I could think about was what properties needed to be flipped right now and how my taking a month off with my son to tour national parks could threaten my standing as top realtor in Jefferson County."

"It was a little tense," Peep notes.

Oscar shakes his head.

"That's putting it diplomatically. I was a proper ass."

"There were fights," Peep offers.

"Then you stopped talking to me, altogether." Oscar's voice loses ten decibels. His face creases with pain. "I'd become that father— the one whose kid doesn't talk to him anymore."

I'm not certain, but I think we all become that father at some point.

Oscar looks from me to my own sons, who are happily playing Crazy Eights together in the tent. His expression gives me my answer.

"It was something I worked to prevent John's whole life."

He puts a hand on Peep's knee.

"It got me thinking about a lot of things. Believe it or not, I never wanted to care about floor plans more than family."

My turn to nod. I have no idea what I'll do when Quinn and

Enzo are teenagers. Will they even acknowledge how we once were?

"That's why I flipped my last house in December. It's why I admire the hell out of what you're doing with this ride and why Peep and me are business partners now."

I ask what line of work they're in.

"I'm marketing a wedge device that stops any piece of furniture from wobbling: tables, chairs, dressers. And it looks good in the process; invented it during the downtime while showing houses. Might be the most useful thing I've ever done."

"We landed our first restaurant chain," Peep says.

"On paper I was an American Dream,"Oscar notes. "That said, America's in a world of hurt. Chasing its tail. Chasing any tail." Words fail at this point. After a bit, he comes back to it.

"But it's still the best place to try and start again."

Ah, reinvention. We need some of that mothering like never before. Someone's gotta stop being impressed by all the wrong people, enamored by all the wrong things—reinvent ourselves into beings of substance, creating things that matter . . .

I grin. "What's the company called?"

Oscar and Peep share a look. With a proud little underhand wave, Oscar gives his son the go-ahead.

"Steady As She Goes," Peep says.

No one need point out that it's Peep who came up with it; a wedge that brought a family back together. The whole thing gives me hope for a minute.

I hang deep into the night with a father and son who appear to have walked out of the fast lane with plans to right the world one table leg at a time.

In the morning they're gone. My fists are back strong and surprisingly steady.

We gobble up a few Clif bars, bananas, and raisins, then break camp before it gets too hot. But that's where our fairy tale opening ends and a life-sapping incline begins three feet from the campsite.

It's a climb that won't cut me loose for fifty miles. There's something especially demoralizing about facing a fierce workout before your legs have even registered the ride. I've had bad patches before, MacDonald Pass for one, and my vertically endowed pal Lolo Pass back in Idaho, but this assault at the camping equivalent of my front door is both insulting (to what I thought was my vastly improving fitness level) and frightening (like a brick thrown through a bay window) because it overwhelms me with doubt while refusing me time to feel sorry for myself.

To make matters worse, I've hammered out of the campground exit and into traffic in the wrong gear. This is catastrophically successful at slowing my pace to a crawl. After much swearing and chain slippage, which threatens to derail me into a ditch, I locate a tolerable level of punishment, dial it in and go to work.

A sardonic little laugh escapes while recalling a one-minute conversation I'd managed with Beth earlier that morning. I placed it old-school style—from a campground pay phone (cell connections being more miss than hit in Yellowstone).

"Don't you worry, Honey, today I'm granite. Pedal on water if that's what it takes to convert the natives."

Somehow Beth knows if I've had my morning caffeine or not; I sound like a Quentin Tarantino movie. What she doesn't know: Today it's all-natural, high on life and fresh, bracing Wyoming air.

"So what I'm hearing is that you're feeling okay."

We share a familiar laugh. Trying to make a few words last from the one you love and have left behind—it could be the hardest part of a road trip like this. Fortunately, she's driving out to meet us next week at the Colorado border.

"Child's play, Babe, I predict we'll catch the 10 A.M. eruption of Old Faithful."

"Have fun storming the castle."

With that the line went dead. Beth would spend the day imagining us in a state of euphoric cycling bliss. At least the cycling part was accurate.

We climb a punishing staircase of switchbacks. The train I'm pulling behind me must have been loaded with black Acme anvils when I wasn't looking.

Quinn allowed me a free pass the first time I unleashed a string of colorful verbiage, but this go-round he's casting himself in the role of a network TV censor.

"Uh, Dad, Momma made Enzo stand in the corner a long time when he used that word."

I'm ashamed, truly I am. And I try to apologize as much as possible given the limited amount of oxygen I seem capable of processing.

He's polite, but holds firm on what he will let through.

"Liam says 'hell' and 'damn' are okay words to use because they read them in his Sunday school."

Liam may be in for some rough weather with his parents until he learns the definition of context. But I do appreciate the way Quinn is trying to make accommodations for my situation. Give him a corner office and a bleeper button and my boy could work for NBC.

Later, when a Buick almost swipes us on a razor-straight stretch of highway south of Old Faithful, he will permit me to take the language gloves off, but for now I'm on a short leash.

Facing still another set of "ups" after one pathetic excuse for a "down," something more in common with a kiddie slide than a legitimate slope, I'm tempted to bark out a few choice phrases.

Instead, I opt for shouting the choruses to songs that sound like swearing but aren't. The Red Hot Chili Peppers and The Ramones, stripped of any discernible melody. Quinn approves, or at least offers no protest.

As a bonus, my shout therapy puts me in a rebellious frame of mind; taking the fight to them. Lyrics devolve into yelps, howls and the occasional defiant whimper, but it keeps us moving.

We're in pursuit of big-game animal sightings and Old Faithful, but first we must complete the climb out of the park's east basin. It's slow going.

Halfway to the top we pause at a scenic overlook. A river rages far below. I taste blood in my mouth while a Japanese gentleman in plastic snowshoes and a colorful Cosby sweater snaps photos of a landscape leveled by the forest fires a decade ago. Without comment he clicks off a couple images of our bike before returning to the moonscape of fallen snags dotted with pockets of new growth.

He seems to be enjoying himself, which only drives home the reality that people around me are on holiday, while I am not, not today anyway. I accept this and prepare for more effort when we hear "it." There's only one thing less visually appetizing than a hulking Euro-trash tourist bathed in biting cologne behind the minute wheel of a powder-blue convertible Mazda Miata. It's this same tourist unfolding himself from said vehicle in a skintight, jet-black Speedo. Already nauseated from the climb, this forces me to take a knee.

Forget terrorism; airport screeners and border agents could go a long way in protecting our aesthetic health if they'd confiscate those tiny swimsuits on the spot. Any male with a European passport from say, Italy, Norway, definitely the Netherlands, and the former Soviet Union for that matter, should be asked to surrender their Lycra loincloth upon entry. We could issue a baggy pair of surf shorts in exchange, of course.

"And the two pairs in your carry-on also, sir. We'll need them all."

It would mirror those gun exchange programs Detroit and L.A. are always sponsoring, only instead of Glock 9mms, it's meat packaging material passing itself off as fashion.

But our Euro-trash tourist's troubles run much deeper. He's chosen a ruffly cream-colored Panama shirt to complement his bathing floss. The fabric is open to the waist so as not to hide a vast array of chunky gold neck chains. Expensive leather slip-on loafers, sans socks, complete the ensemble. He removes his cigarette to get a better view. When I'm certain our scenic overlook couldn't get uglier, he realigns the Speedo just as a club remix of Ricky Martin-style disco opera blaring from the Miata's back speakers begins to skip. With this, our Japanese photographer turns his camera point-blank on Mr. Miata and starts shooting with abandon.

Enzo emerges from his trailer. "What's that smell?"

Mr. Miata climbs onto the narrow ledge for a better look. If I squint hard enough, maybe he'll pass for an Acapulco cliff diver.

No one can squint that hard.

I share a moment with the Japanese photographer. We shake our heads and offer shoulder shrugs in the general direction of Mr. Miata. Between my Lycra, that Cosby sweater in July and Mr. Miata's entire get-up, this could be the worst-outfitted scenic overlook in the history of the world.

Quinn is standing by the ledge when our Euro-trash hops down, botching the dismount.

"That will kill you, Mister."

It's not clear if my son is referring to the smokes, ledge, cologne, or disco opera. Possibly all of the above.

Mr. Miata offers Quinn a nod and a cheesy wink, then, utilizing what I'm only guessing is his entire English vocabulary, dishes out,

"Okay, yes, thank you, please."

It takes ten more painful minutes for the sound of that skipping CD to evaporate up the hillside. Even allowing a few more ticks off the clock, I spend the next half hour tasting sweaty cologne and cigarette smoke left in his wake. But all is forgiven at the top of the hill. It's just after ten A.M., but I could eat my weight in Jimmy Dean sausages, hot cakes, bark chips . . . anything properly seasoned, steaming, and on hand. That's when we stumble upon a roadside banquet fit for kings.

Standing in contrast to the deep green carpet of pines that crowd the summit is one of those white party tents people rent for weddings and arts-in-the-parks events. A Cycle America Food Stop banner billowing proudly from its mainsail brings it home. Sweet mother of pearl, I'm not alone in my efforts this morning. We've caught up to them. A herd of bikes line the far end of the turnout. Riders click about in their shoes, chugging bottles of brightly colored liquid. Some slurp at oversized paper bowls teeming with salmon corn chowder. I spot tacos, a deli plate, three different fruit salads, pot stickers (are those really pot stickers?), pre-stirred yogurt—not the fruit-at-the-bottom kind—rings of string cheese, and a table devoted entirely to desserts.

If, at that moment, someone in a crisp suit and elongated game-show host microphone offered us a showcase prize package, taxes prepaid, I'd knock him down in a stampede to this rest-stop buffet. There's one minor hitch. Technically, or in any other way, we are not Cycle America participants.

Quinn sums things up, nicely. "Shazamm!"

I have to put the brakes on my pint-sized posse before they get delusions that this spread has their name on it. It's gonna break their hearts and my spirit.

"There they are!" trumpets a man of exceptional fitness valiantly holding back old age. His face is that of Mr. Rogers, if Fred had chosen a lifetime of triathloning over children's television. I feel a firm hand on my shoulder as he guides me into the feed line. I could weep with gratitude. Temples constructed in Cycle America's name will not do justice to this act of trail magic. Maybe a new holiday named after them.

"You guys were the hot topic around the campfire last night," Mr. Rogers notes. "No one could believe you're doing this except we've seen it for ourselves.

With that we're mobbed by back-slapping cyclists peppering us with queries about our travels, gear, route and ETA on the East Coast. More than one rider questions my sanity, but all of it is couched in good-natured ribbing and exasperated admiration.

These people know . . . these people are covering some of the same ground, minus 250 pounds of "back fat," as one of them calls all that weight behind my rear wheel.

"It takes a helluva lot just to push an empty frame over this hill," says a thirty-something wispy, reed-like lawyer. I can't look away from the tight muscles in his legs and several crisscrossing veins the size of thick grub worms. He's just being dramatic now, but I'll take every kindness and kudos I can get.

It feels nice to bring some excitement and joy into their lives on a Thursday morning. Though not as nice as it feels to take serving after serving of pot sticker and crumb cake off their hands.

"Can I circle the parking lot on your set up?" asks Mr. Rogers. "I just have to know for myself."

To keep it authentic, I insist on adding 110 pounds of kids. Muffins in hand, my boys begrudgingly oblige. He makes two brief circuits with the boys before executing a shaky dismount. Mumbling "Jesus," in a manner very unlike the Mr. Rogers of my childhood, he hands the bike back over. Here's a man not easily humbled. "Jesus," he repeats louder for anyone who missed it the first time. Laughter and nods follow him back into the fold. No one else wants a spin.

Quinn and Enzo are immediately swallowed up by a pack of MILTs—Mothers In Lycra that's Tight. When I glance from my third bowl of chowder, Enzo is on the lap of a pouty-lipped lady sporting a ponytail and a shocking-pink Race for the Cure jersey. Another MILT has assembled a Dagwood-size peanut butter, cream cheese, and M&M sandwich for my littlest hobbit. He demolishes it just as another appears on his plate.

Quinn's been anchored in the fruit salad section for twenty minutes. I can't remember my life before this chowder and those juicy chunks of cantaloupe. They're gonna have to tear the tent down around us before we leave this culinary Eden.

This is trail magic at its finest. In a nutshell, trail magic is any unexpected kindness extended by people who owe you nothing. It can be as small as a bottle of cold water, accurate directions or someone stopping roadside to see if you're okay. Or it can be acts as monumental as a bike shop owner replacing gear for free or at cost, throwing in extra tubes because it's the next best thing to being on the adventure himself, or a Cycle America food stop when you need it most.

Then there's the granddaddy of them all, an invitation indoors when the road has worn you thin and darkening skies are about to go biblical. These good Samaritans go by the name "trail angels." The concept is as old as time, but most recently popularized in the backpacker community.

It will take a lifetime to pay back the kindnesses shown me around the world: keys to a boat off the New Zealand coast, arc welding repairs to my bike behind an Argentinean bar, a weekend in John Huston's Mexican jungle villa not far from where *Night of the Iguana* was filmed. Rides, showers, muffins . . . the list goes on and on, and now salmon corn chowder and cantaloupe join its swelling ranks.

Sometimes, if there's no trail magic to be found, you have to help it into being. A fellow cyclist and talented commentator pal, Willie Weir, calls it "initiating kindness." People want to help; it's just sometimes they need a push. That's when a not-quite-empty water bottle will appear bone-dry and you'll ask a family reunion or company picnic full of partygoers if they know where the closest water fountain is?

Next thing it's spiking volleyballs with Uncle Dave and sharing a checkered blanket with Bill and his family from accounting. You haven't lived until you've crashed a Daughters of the American Revolution regatta and annual picnic.

And you haven't lived until salmon corn chowder fuels your downhill run to Old Faithful. It turns an angry sun into a warm glow. Nothing's a burden now. I announce my e-mail address and let the crowd know they're all welcome at my doorstep. We linger around the dessert table, but all good rest stops must come to an end.

"Boys, let's go watch the Earth blow off some steam."

We'll be lucky if we catch the two o'clock eruption, but what's my burning need for an agenda anyway. That thermal heat phenomenon has been going off *every eighty minutes or so* for millions of years. It's not running out of steam any time soon.

Enzo palms a few M&M's for the road. I pretend not to notice.

15

"It is an important and popular fact that things are not always what they seem. For instance, on the planet Earth, man had always assumed that he was more intelligent than dolphins because he had achieved so much—the wheel, New York, wars and so on—whilst all the dolphins had ever done was muck about in the water having a good time. But conversely, the dolphins had always believed that they were far more intelligent than man—for precisely the same reasons." —Douglas Adams, *The Hitchhiker's Guide to the Galaxy*

JULY 18   920 MILES
Yellowstone's Midway Geyser Basin

Bison don't give a damn—you can see it in their eyes. At two or three thousand pounds, why should they? We notice a behemoth a hundred yards off to our left as we pedal into full light across Yellowstone's Midway Geyser Basin. There's no one but us and the beast along this straight stretch of road.

It's taking a bath in the ash fields. This is a thing of roughneck beauty to behold. I've heard these ash baths are all the rage in Europe's finer day spas.

Here's a visibly top-heavy animal, all chest and head. It looks as if by hanging a dime-store keychain from one of its horns, the damn thing would tip forward. And we're watching it kick up clouds of dusty powder as it crashes, rolls, and returns gracefully—yes, I said gracefully—to its feet.

The ground shakes again, thunder on a cloudless day. House finches back home perform these very same dirt baths in our backyard sandbox. As when the neighbor's dog rustles around on the grass just after it's been cut, frantically try to scratch an itch, this bison's movements are mirroring it to a T.

Needless to say, the performance brings us to a halt. We keep a safe viewing distance, officially listed as no less than seventy-five yards. A public service poster over the outhouse sink clued us in. We'd been brushing our teeth before bed when some retro-looking government-issued artwork caught Enzo's eye. It featured a massive cartoon caricature of a bison flinging an exuberant man and his Yogi Bear-style picnic basket high into the air. He appeared to be having the time of his life. Imbued with the same vibe as those 1950s educational posters of smiling schoolchildren huddled under their desks sharing an apple as the H-bomb blows, this charging-bison warning poster had the opposite effect on my five-year-old.

"Can we ride the buffalo, Daddy?"

Based on visuals alone, I found Enzo's question quite reasonable. I shook my head. Quinn read the copy aloud.

"Warning: Bison are wild, dangerous animals weighing up to 5,000 pounds, capable of crushing visitors underfoot and goring them to death. Minimum safe viewing distance: 75 yards."

There will be no buffalo rides, little man.

"I'd put some blood dripping from the bison's horns," Quinn noted. A budding art critic, he used his toothbrush to point out where he'd place his improvements.

"I wonder what's in that picnic basket?" asked Enzo.

Directly across the road a half-ton Chevy with a small Third World country hitched to its bumper rolls into position. A pile of German tourists settle in for the ash field bison bath show. We marvel as card tables, lawn chairs, binoculars, and strudel—at least it looks like strudel—are ejected from the travel trailer and set up right on the road behind their vehicle. This is accomplished with NASCAR pit crew speed. Another roll of thunder and all eyes are back on the bison, except for Quinn's.

"What about this bison?" he inquires.

Distract and conquer. It's the oldest trick in the animal kingdom. How many times did it work for Bugs Bunny and the Road Runner? Based on its size, this must be the papa bison. He's closing distance to our right, perhaps to join his wife, son, or daughter in the bathtub. I register the chocolate-colored beast when it's no more than twenty-five yards from our stalled bike, not in a full charge yet but taking measured, deliberate steps in our direction. There's no time for bicycle safety considerations or preflight checklists.

"Hang on, boys!"

I jam bananas and Clif gel packets into my front bag, stand on the pedals and manage an awkward, crooked line uphill. Whether you're being pursued by bison, big dogs, or wild-eyed rednecks in monster trucks, there's always an incline. Always.

"Ahhh . . . I wanted to stay and see what happened." Quinn registers this complaint over the din of my exertions and the blood pounding in my ears.

From the top of the rise we turn in time to observe our bison charging across the road at the exact spot we'd been moments earlier.

"That's . . . why . . . we didn't stay."

But no one's listening to me. The show just got exciting.

Never breaking stride, the top-heavy beast scatters petrified Germans in its wake. We lose sight of the animal for just a moment as it goes behind the trailer, but real horror-movie screams, the thud of falling tables and paper napkins taking flight tell the rest of the story. Physically, anyway, everyone appears to be okay. Quinn's pleasure at this bit of slapstick is so excessive that he falls out of his bike seat. Call me twisted, but a deep sense of peace washes over me when it's clear we're no longer at the top of the food chain. I enjoy living in a world where bison still don't give a shit about us.

16

"A ship in a harbor is safe, but that is not what ships are built for."
—Anonymous

JULY 18   940 MILES
Fairy Falls, Yellowstone National Park, Wyoming

It's too late in the afternoon to start a six-mile out-and-back hike, but we take a page from the bison's playbook and set out for Fairy Falls anyway. Lodge poles reduced to cinders and rock still black a decade later indicate that this part of the park was not spared the most recent cycle of forest fires.

New growth is everywhere, but subtle; you have to really look for it. Bone-dry, the wood and rock crunch underfoot for two unbroken miles. Chipmunks hide where they can find shade. We soldier forward, pushed by the promise of a gothic-size waterfall at the turnaround point. It's hard to imagine amid the steaming pools of pungent sulfur and denuded ridges. Everything changes about the same time we hear falling water faint in the distance. New pines and understory along the path have returned to the size of Christmas trees; a bit of the holidays in July, boys.

On its own, Fairy Falls would silence even the most jaded urbanite. But knowing that its cave walls, wide pool and cascading waters offered refuge for countless animals during the big burn—predator and prey alike—makes it hallowed ground.

It also makes me wonder if I've had it backwards, if this ride is more refuge than risk for me. It had been business as usual back home for too long, blending in with the mess, living safe and uneasy while watching the world die from the comfort of the couch cushions.

To stop fighting because the causes feel lost—that's what I've gotten good at. And it's not enough even to turn up music that talks about a revolution while risking my son's world through so much hand-wringing and inertia. Go along, get along, count on the next invention, or leave it to a Senate floor full of grade-inflated Ivy League debris to think for generations to come. Sorry, boys, I could have done more but then I might have missed my favorite TV shows.

The bike's putting some of that fight back into my bloodstream, but I can't forget I'm leading more than an army of one these days. Look, kids, hailstones—let's rush out!

Still, it's been too long since corporate honchos held me in contempt for holding them up to the light, people followed me to something other than an author signing, and I championed an uncomfortable choice simply because it was right.

Taking on lost causes and relishing a good bar fight once crowded my dance card.

Wasn't I the wild-eyed idealist who saved a gopher tortoise habitat from becoming a science museum's overflow parking? (Insult to injury, the museum had the stones to try to use the very environmental education funds I'd secured in the tortoises' name, to do the paving job.) And wasn't I the guy who got death threats from a Canadian conglomerate just for asking—okay, just for staging a successful national media and political campaign (see old "20/20" tapes for my finest hour)—to relocate their irradiation plant away from an impoverished black community . . . say, to one of the far moons of Jupiter.

It's been too many years since I took a threatening corporate phone call from an ice-water-veined lobbyist.

This uncluttered time with my boys and the road reminds me of something wild-eyed Mr. Whittaker used to say to us eighth-graders at the end of every drama production. He'd pull us into a tight circle, have us bow our heads and announce in his best Hamlet: "Barn's burnt down, now I can see the moon."

A cryptic plea for simplification in all things and a revisiting of one's roots, paradoxically delivered by a oversized drama teacher in full beard, tights, face makeup and Henry VIII costume. Something in its sentiment has stayed with me to this day. The only question I haven't puzzled through is how to burn down the barn *and* raise a family.

We strip off the little we're wearing and wade in, under and around Fairy Falls. Part of me hopes we're mistaken for three blond bears by any puritanical tourists venturing onto the trail during the remains of the day. The rest of me, the parts I hope hang around for a while this time, doesn't care.

17

"You got to be careful if you don't know where you're going, because you might not get there." —Yogi Berra

JULY 19   1,070 MILES
Franklin, Idaho

Nearly 1,000 miles into the ride, I stop pretending and admit it's time to see a doctor. I haven't swallowed properly since Helena. Now, standing over my handlebars in downtown Franklin, the oldest town in Idaho, I sound like a pack-a-day smoker. Winds were so strong at the southern gate of Yellowstone that downed trees littered the roadway ahead of us for thirty miles. This forced us to turn west and ride a sheltered valley down the spine of Wyoming on the Idaho side. It works out to be one of the finest detours of the ride. Labeled a scenic byway, we rename it The Land of the Lost. I keep an eye out for Sleestacks and dinosaurs. Those tourists crowding Yellowstone are missing something spectacular just a thumb's width to the left of their AAA Trip-Tik maps.

It could be 1805, judging by the roaming wildlife, miles of unspoiled forest and lack of mechanical devices we encounter. Not a big leap of the imagination to picture an entire continent in the same vein, a tsunami of primordial forests, unspoiled grasslands and teeming rivers spilling over in all directions until it reached the coasts.

This daydream splits me in two. The half that loves milkshakes on demand, anything produced by HBO Pictures and March Madness betting pools mourns the end of the modern world. The other half, my inner Jeremiah Johnson, is doing backflips over the death of big box stores, Bluetooth technology (which reduces phone users to babbling fools wandering the streets talking to themselves like absolute loons, stop it, just stop it!) and people complaining about the service at Olive Garden.

I sing refrains from that Talking Heads gem, "Nothing But Flowers." Of course the shelter of that valley is temporary. The modern world still exists just around a bend. It hits us hard and without warning: a frontal assault of billboards and buildings that almost turns me back. But one advantage of the modern world, one I require like no one's business, is a qualified physician. I'm guessing Jeremiah Johnson never set a bear trap for a bottle of antibiotics.

I don't want the kids to start worrying, but I'm pretty confident I have the early stages of lockjaw. Chewing Tylenol helped me drift off to sleep the previous three nights running, only to find myself bolt upright with the worst case of dry-mouth on record.

"With a lung capacity of 99 percent and resting pulse of 48, you're the healthiest patient I've seen all year," says Dr. Bart Brower, an urgent care specialist out of Idaho Falls. "You're sucking dust and dry air and God knows what else in massive quantities for up to ten hours a day. What'd you expect?"

"More like fourteen hours a day, sir." I want him to have all the information.

He stares at the photo I've produced of the rig and the boys climbing up MacDonald Pass. I can tell he's studying it the way one would phenomena that are recognized but remain unexplained by science. He hands me back the picture.

"It'll stop by Kansas, when the humidity overwhelms you." He offers up a wicked little grin. "That's when you'll wish you were back on this side of the Front Range with your throat on fire."

I nod in the manner of a weary boxer taking corner advice between rounds with no intention of heeding it.

"Until then, gargle with liquid Benadryl, shoot as much saline wash up your snout as you can stand, breathe through your nose . . . and pray for rain." He hands me a card. "Here, I've seen so much of this in athletes during my time out West that I had remedy cards printed up."

It's comforting to know that reports of my impending death were greatly exaggerated by my hypochondria and simple road dust.

Still, gargling with children's Benadryl four times a day is no picnic. When I toss back the pink bottle of liquid under the shadow of a gnarled, barn wood gray building packed with hay, I'm struck by the significance of the words in front of me. In whitewashed letters covering thirty feet in all directions of this historic barn are the words:

While I can't vouch for Dr. Pierce's credentials, tonics, or much of anything beyond his progressive advertising savvy, my Dr. Bower's remedy seems to be beating back the worst of it. Word to the wise though: never ask your seven-year-old to administer a bedtime saline rinse by flashlight unless you enjoy saltwater shot up your nose at speeds brushing against the sound barrier. Though not medically possible, I swear some of it exited out my ear. We soldier on.

Beth meets us at the border. The reunion is Hollywood in its scale and intensity. Bike abandoned for a mad dash across an open field. Three sweaty, stinky boys accost a road-trip-weary wife and mother. Gatorade stands in for champagne. She's a vision. She's the cavalry. You'd think we'd just completed the first around-the-world voyage by raft the way we're carrying on.

It's to be the end of the road for our three-man brigade. Beth is slated to haul gear, and occasionally a child, over the worst ups and downs of Colorado. What's more, my trusty photographer, Brick Johnson, is en route to Gunnison, where we'll rendezvous like modern-day Pony Express riders. There, we'll add a trailer and child to Brick's burden (a spiffy, sleek sidecar that Beth has hauled by car—it reminds me of a Wallace and Gromit gadget), thus lightening my load by half, sweet weeping Jesus, *by half!*

The next twenty-five hundred miles are going to be a cakewalk to the coast. I'll have adult company, shared campground duties and half the weight. Did I mention half the weight? I haven't dared utter this last statement aloud since we left Oregon, for fear I'd jinx it. But now that Beth has arrived, the floodgates open.

The reunion isn't an hour old when I begin waxing nostalgic and poetic at length about the burdens and joys of pedaling 14 feet of boys, bikes and loaded bags. I feel like I should read my acceptance speech and take my Legends of the Road statue with me to all the post-ceremony parties.

"I'll require a monument built in our likeness, after I'm long gone, of course. And songs written about this summer. Hot damn, who's a badass, honey?"

Beth mentions how much she's missed my self-effacing modesty.

"But in this instance," she adds, "You really do have something to crow about." She gives me a playful pinch. "You know my study group has a pool going, divided by which state you'll quit at or keel over in. I keep telling 'em they don't know who they're dealing with. So you know . . . I took DC. We should clean up."

We share a long kiss, much to the horror of two little boys enjoying car air conditioning for the first time in weeks. Get a room.

I sit back while moving under something else's power for the first time in weeks. The afternoon sun feels comfortable on my skin.

"It's probably nothing, but Brick's been leaving garbled voice mails on the cell phone all day," Beth says, putting the car into third.

I nod. "He's probably just updating his location and ETA. I'll check my e-mail later." With that I don't give it another thought, and if this were a scientific thriller that, sports fans, was the moment when the virus escaped the lab.

A little background on the enlistment of my own photographer for this ride. Usually I fly solo, but let the record show that the Metal Cowboy has not gone diva on anyone. The purse strings at *Men's Journal* were planning to hook me up with a photographer one way or another, so I thought I'd beat them to the punch and search for potential ride partners with photography chops. I didn't want to end up eating the dust of any Armstrong wannabes decked out in Postal Service race team Lycra and a camera. Or worse, a postmodern shutterbug bent on making it all about self-expression in a repressed world; think Yoko Ono on two wheels. There was no way I was going to pedal around a cornfield naked with a guitar for the sake of art. Recruitment on my terms made sense to me at the time.

One of my loyal readers, a seasoned cyclist with world-class photojournalism skills and a decent sense of humor, just happened to be planning a sabbatical from his newspaper job. In the final planning stages of an around-the-world bike ride, he wanted to know what part of the U.S. leg I could join . . .

"How does all of it sound, Brick?" He was ecstatic. "And how would you like a high-paying photography assignment thrown in for good measure?!"

DATELINE: ROCKAWAY BEACH, OREGON, MAY 1, 2005

It's a get-to-know-Brick-Johnson weekend out on the Oregon coast; a shakedown cruise to see if four amigos would be compatible for the long pedal east. More than a few things that weekend should have set off alarm bells, but discounting the dwarf encounter is my fault. That's when I really dropped the ball.

This side of the big top, you just don't see that many dwarfs going by bicycle. Even under Barnum's Technicolor tent it's something of an anomaly. Oversized clowns on tiny trikes? Certainly. But dwarfs on bicycles? That territory is reserved for indentured black bears sporting crazy muzzled smiles as the bullwhip keeps them in line (their locked-down grins masking primal thoughts along the lines of, "Unclip this muzzle, you cowardly bastards, and I'll show you three rings of carnivore spectacle. Please direct your attention to the center ring where I'll be batting the limbs off some of your paying customers. Look, all I wanted was a thousand acres of Alaskan riverfront property and three squares of salmon a day . . . and this, this is what I get? And quit with the whip already, can't you see I'm pedaling?").

Quinn pauses, mid-stroke, during a pitched plastic light saber battle with Enzo on Rockaway's beachfront. This cease-fire lasts long enough to point and gesture wildly at a little big man on a child's bike. He turns out to be one stone-cold, street-smart dwarf; the slickest operator under four feet tall in all of Oregon, possibly the entire West Coast. Later in the weekend we'll witness him scamming motorists out of their gas money, but that's another story.

I turn in time to see a stubby pair of legs guiding the ape-hanger handlebars of an immaculate Orange Crate single-speed bicycle (circa 1967) away from Rockaway's neighborhoods. This determined dwarf coasts into the gravel lot of the corner pump-n-go grocery. He rolls up as if he owns the place. For all I know, he does. I manage to get Quinn to stop pointing after the dwarf brings his bike to a stop directly in front of us. What children don't appreciate about politically correct behavior could fill a flatbed truck.

Raising children is like living with a Fox News Network host who has forgotten to take the morning medication. It gives me hope. Not for Fox or the republic in general, but for lively, inappropriate outbursts by my boys. I'll actually mourn the day they stop blurting out damaging statements in public.

Once Quinn sees the sleek paint job and Georgia O'Keeffe style curves of that Schwinn up close, the dwarf's proportions become little more than an interesting afterthought. Something to bring up at Capri Sun cocktail hour on the playground, if conversations regarding Pokemon cards and wall-ball ever falter. Besides, this dwarf's bicycle really is the main attraction.

If some pimp daddy wanted to acquire the tightest kid's rig ever made, he would immediately bird-dog this ride from across the bike shop, strut right up to it and introduce himself in that sexy Barry White baritone.

Quinn circles the bike slowly, taking in every weld, braze-on and bend. Those pink single-speeds with pompom tassels and polka dot seats might be flashy eye candy for pimp daddy's girls to parade around behind him, but once the Orange Crate catches his attention, our hustler would be as good as in the saddle.

Back in the day, I'd seen my share of tricked-out Crates. Schwinns styled up by the fourth-grade crowd with aftermarket horns and all manner of baseball cards fanning their spokes; from no-name rookies to all-stars. Still, the dwarf's transportation choice puts them all to shame. It's about less being more.

He's shunned stickers and pompoms, ball cards, speedometers and horns shaped like hot dogs for a spotless spit shine and one stark, but effective, accessory—a set of real bones (deer, dog, human?) crisscrossed between the handlebars and secured with a length of clear monofilament line, ten-pound test from the looks of it. If the dwarf leaned his head forward between the bars, he would form a Jolly Roger with his face. He leans forward.

Quinn and Enzo pull back, drawing up their plastic light sabers in a defensive move. The dwarf eyeballs us, nods once, dismounts. It's a good thing, too, because his "Pirates of the Caribbean meets the Yellow Brick Road" pose was starting to creep me out. He addresses my boys directly.

"I knew the guy who was supposed to play Yoda."

Properly stunned by this information, my sons drop their guard. The dwarf sees his opening and shadowboxes a few karate-chop moves in their direction, to show them who's in charge. With that taken care of, the dwarf lights up a cigarette and offers Enzo the handlebar of his bike.

Enzo holds the Orange Crate upright with the proper reverence, like an undersized valet taking his job to heart and hoping for gum balls or cheddar goldfish in the way of tips. The dwarf crushes his cigarette butt under his boot after only a few puffs, borrows a light saber and goes into what I feel is an excessively flowery demonstration of swordplay; far too many flourishes with the wand and crane movements with his free hand. Clearly, I'm not the target demographic, because my boys love it.

That's when Brick emerges from the depths of the grocery stop and shows me how little he knows about kids. Until that moment I'd seen him as the only individual properly unbalanced enough in all the right places to agree—under no duress, drug consumption, or sleep deprivation, mind you—to share the duties of a coast-to-coast bicycle adventure with my pint-sized posse. But there is the possibility that he simply had no idea what he's agreed to. You see, at forty-one years old, Brick is a bachelor.

This weekend is parenting boot camp for the man. It's a given that the boys will break him like balsa wood under a well-made work boot at some point in the ride, and there's nothing I can do to stop it. How he responds when beaten down is what I'll be grading him on. The train wreck between adults and kids comes down to simple mathematics: a pair of finger-painting mercenaries under ten years of age, even ones reared with manners training and/or a healthy fear of parental reprisals, could weed out a thick nest of terrorists before breakfast—with little, if any, mess.

It's called psychological warfare. The weapons at their disposal are countless, but here's a best-of list for you: sleep deprivation, repetition, dimples, and tears are the big guns. Ruthless, a child at the top of his or her game can cut the unsuspecting adult's tolerance in half cleaner than a guillotine. Anyone without a flesh-and-blood link to a child, a direct DNA connection, is vulnerable, exposed; think Native Americans greeting thse pilgrims and their boatloads of smallpox.

"Oh, live a little, Chief, and accept the white man's tacky gift blankets. Stop listening to that paranoid medicine man. What harm could a few throw rugs do around here?"

Even as a parent, you aren't fully inoculated. It takes booster cups of caffeine, a backpack of action figures, crayons, and early reader books. You also must acquire a bump-and-roll approach to the day—hit an activity, say clay-making at the library, or T-ball at the park, then, at the height of their happiness, roll on to the next thing, no hesitation, no bargaining, no deal-making. Your instinct will be to squeeze every drop of time and pleasure out of each project, but this is a rookie mistake and the fast track to tantrums, tears, and, left unchecked, the destruction of public property.

Take Kenny Rogers' advice and know when to walk away and know when to run those stroller wheels the hell out of there. A network of parents with similar-aged play friends is paramount—so you can shuffle and trade one of your kids for one of theirs. This minimizes infighting. The best parents are like scouting coaches working the roster of an underperforming or injured farm league team. If your lineup remains the same for more than two or three days, trust me, the pitching will go south and you'll be left wondering if other parents threaten their children this much and deliver on the mother of all timeouts.

These are the ground rules. These are the standard procedures that Brick is not familiar with. It's not his fault. Nor is he versed in the proper care and feeding of kids. This means a steady stream of fruit, cheese, carrots sticks, goldfish, sliced apples and juice boxes (100 percent fruit juice, not concentrate, which is essentially sugar water) throughout the day. Think of yourself as the host of a housewarming party that won't wrap up for several decades.

And pace yourself; you'll be stocking the veggie plate for the foreseeable future. Less than twenty-four hours in the company of my little men and Brick has already excused himself for several solo jogs, a stroll down the beach, a look at the sunset and this leisurely aisle-walk through the grocery. It's looking a little shaky. Does he have what it takes to endure the human frailties and close company of four guys—two of whom have only recently seen their testicles drop?

He's had an opportunity to feel what it's like to cart a child and a bike trailer around when the kid is awake and full of questions about the world. He scored high, emerging relatively unscathed.

But it's the dwarf encounter that should have shaken this partnership plan to the core.

By the time Brick arrives, I've lent the little big man my spare saber and the trio is doing battle in the parking lot. A lit Kool sags from the dwarf's lips while he parries, jabs and regales the boys with stories of how Yoda was originally cast as a dwarf in robes and makeup, until that bastard Jim Henson and his job-stealing Muppets signed on.

"Muppets have been taking work away from us for decades now," the dwarf explains, repelling a two-sided attack from my boys.

"Imagine if *The Wizard of Oz* had been done with Muppets. It would have sucked the soul right out of that production. Urban legend has it Henson was poisoned by a dwarf's talent agent, but I know it was his kooky religion that killed him."

The boys slice the dwarf in half. He pretends to die in the sand and gravel, cigarette never leaving his lips.

Brick hands me a bottle of Snapple, my mid-day caffeinated medicine. "Looks like your boys have made a friend."

I nod. "For the record, I think they like to be called little people these days."

"What? Kids have a preference now?"

And that's when it dawns on me. Brick can't tell the difference between a chain-smoking dwarf and a seven-year-old. We're in trouble. I let it go for a while, just to see how long it will take him to make the connection. When the dwarf pedals away and Brick is still without a wiseass comment as to why a grade-schooler would be smoking in steel-toed work boots, I ask if he noticed anything odd about their playmate.

"He had an awesome bicycle."

So Brick sees the four-foot-and-under crowd as indistinguishable from each other. Maybe I've been a parent for too long, but it seems like a pretty easy catch. Still, desire wears blinders. I really want someone to carry half my load across America. So when Brick changed our game plan in the eleventh hour, I should have seen it for what it was.

"I've always wanted to roll across the Golden Gate Bridge, over the High Sierras, then through Death Valley," he said into a cell phone a week before we were scheduled to hold to the high country beginning at my doorstep. "This has always been my dream, Dude, always. I guess I should have been clearer on that point."

Here's what should have been clear to me: He was choosing the Mojave Desert over my children. He was choosing a suicide ride over temporary adoption. I tried to defuse things with humor. "And my dream is to crabwalk naked the length of Antarctica." When he didn't laugh, I knew I'd lost my sidekick, at least until Colorado.

"Come on, mate, this is crazy talk." When all else fails, start imitating Crocodile Dundee. He could get people to do anything. I drew on 100,000 miles of cycling experience to make an argument against Death Valley in July. "People die out there just standing in place," I said.

He threw the Badwater Race back at me . . . a bit of athletic insanity wherein folks run 135 miles from below sea level to the top of Mount Whitney through Death Valley in one day. I'd written about that race, about how hundreds start but only dozens complete it in a good year. How insurance companies wouldn't underwrite it in its early incarnations, and that competitors go through dozens of shoes, which literally melt off their feet in the desert heat. Brick thought that sounded like fun.

"I'll meet you at the Colorado border," he said. "Don't worry, I'll be fine.

18

"The man who goes alone can start today; but he who travels with another must wait till that other is ready."
—Henry David Thoreau

JULY 20   1,155 MILES
Logan, Utah

When Brick's e-mail arrives we're relaxing around a pool on the cusp of Utah. The boys know their time with Beth is limited, so they're clinging to her like remoras on a shark. The heat's oppressive already and we haven't dropped out of the high country. I love Utah—it's where their mother and I met. But I have every intention of climbing into cool pines as fast as my legs can pedal us over the Colorado border. Like I said, I love Utah . . . but it's time we started seeing other people.

The e-mail has one of those red exclamation marks in front of it. It's supposed to indicate the utmost importance, though usually it's code for spam. But Brick's note lives up to its exclamation-point status.

"Cowboy, I've been trying to raise you on your cell phone, but reception bites hard out here in the desert. Seems I took a little fall outside of Vegas, lost consciousness for a few moments. I'm told I hit an orange traffic cone. Scuffed myself, and the bike, up a bit. Where are you? Has Beth joined you with a car? I'm gonna try limping in to Green River, Utah. Can you guys meet me there? I have a new bike on order to Moab."

In Green River—hundreds of miles in the opposite direction of our planned Colorado rendezvous—we learn that Brick has a knack for the understatement. The entire right side of his body is an unbroken scab. His bike's front fork appears to have been spot-welded with Frankenstein craftsmanship by sixth-graders on peyote. Worse, the one-two punch of the High Sierras and the Mojave's life-sucking depths have ground Brick into something just this side of saltpeter. Physically, he resembles hammered shit; emotionally what Brick really needs is to be life-flighted to a quiet place, a spa in Arizona perhaps, where soothing professionals would wrap him in warmed rain forest leaves, submerge his battered frame up to its neck in the cool paste of Sedona clay, followed by a flash rinse of Evian water, before tucking him under silk sheets. There he could sleep off the next six months, until the nightmare faded and he's able to talk without something bordering on manic, false enthusiasm. He's trying to put the best face on things, and I appreciate that, but it sure looks a lot like painting lipstick on a pig.

"Dude, it was an out-of-body experience. I'm wasted. But a bit of Mexican food and a proper liedown by the RV park's pool should put me right."

If by putting himself right he meant passed out across a plastic lounge chair in 120-degree weather, in wind gusts whipping red dust so hard it raised welts on my skin, then Brick was going to be right as rain (of which there was none in Moab's forecast for some time to come).

I drag his lawn chair into the shade, with him still in it, while I decide what to do next. The following morning, loaded down with Green River melons (nectar of the gods grown in such an unlikely environment), we head for Moab. Brick's in no shape for riding, but he does anyway on that busted-up bike, no less. It's his quest to cover every mile around the world in the saddle. Every mile is sacred. The short haul into Moab seems to suck the last light out of his eyes.

His new rig won't arrive until the weekend, so he suggests we all hole up in town until then. There is no way in hell—with Moab in July being as close as you can come to it on Earth—we're staying in this inferno for more than a night. Beautiful as its stark landscape is, July is high season for Gila monsters in Moab, not humans.

Temps dip into double digits around 5 A.M. I sleep like an extra in *Road Warrior:* twitchy, sweating, and restless outside the tent in only my bathing suit. I break the news of our departure to Brick over breakfast. Whereas he hasn't wanted our company from San Francisco to here, he's talking up teamwork with a vengeance now.

"Come on, guys, it's a dry heat."

Before beating it out of that dusty inferno in search of Colorado's mountain towns, we leave Brick one of the trailers. Am I abandoning him at his darkest hour? Absolutely, but staying in this heat any longer amounts to child endangerment.

He insists on hauling only his essentials with him, opting to retrieve the bulk of his bags when we meet back up in Telluride, for when we form this all-star team for the first time since Rockaway Beach.

"It'll be a blast once I have the new bike and we're cruising Colorado?" Brick says, but it comes out sounding more like a question.

When we drive away Beth can only shake her head.

"You begged him not to ride through the desert in daylight . . . in July . . . alone. What'd he expect?" She shakes her head. "New age or old school, man is a dumb animal."

I'd argue with her but she's making too much sense—and she might have been speaking about me. I know what it means to do foolish things on a bicycle. I wrote the book. I have an idea of what Brick has been through having myself pedaled across the Australian

Outback for no more reason than it was there. Still, in the ugliest recesses of my heart, I also want to put some distance between us. His hollowed-out eyes and broken spirit were scaring the boys.

Besides, Jackson Browne is headlining a sold-out concert in Telluride's city park; the same park in which I've just wangled a campsite for the weekend.

"We only have a few days together," Beth points out. "I'm sure that makes me a bad person, but I want you guys all to myself."

Hopefully Brick will find some shade, a truckload of Bactine and his mojo on the climb out of Moab. This break will bring him back to life and find him ready to share half my load the rest of the way to the coast. It's my turn to make confident statements that I don't believe for a second. But those are problems for Future Joe to deal with. At this moment I have a long climb out of the desert to make myself.

I pick a spot thirty miles east and a thousand feet higher than the natural kiln that is Arches National Park in July and Utah in general. We unload my bike at the Colorado border. Beth takes the boys ahead, and for the first time on this journey I'm a solo cyclist tooling along and toiling through the far reaches of the West; John Ford country.

I replay all the spaghetti westerns of my childhood. My dad yelling stuff like, "The ambush is coming from behind those rocks, you half-wits!" at the TV screen. I wanted to tell him to calm down. Even at eight I knew it always ended badly for the Indians. Now that I'm cycling through that matinee-movie world, I eyeball a few clumps of rock ahead with mock suspicion, then actually do freak out for a minute, before reminding myself that all the Indians left standing today aren't out here but on the reservation getting their gold back one casino complex at a time.

Towering mountains in the distance, red rock arches in the foreground, and the rolling hill I'm on is heading in the same direction as the temperature, straight up. It's all meaningless threats, though, when you lose 250 pounds in one day. I'm light as a feather, skimming the blacktop the way you might clear the ice if you'd been born in a pair of skates. By 10 A.M. the heat has sweated away some of the advantage that losing my load gave me, but the views are Technicolor and the air so tight and clear that it would be criminal to complain.

I'm maneuvering my bike in the same manner that a Kentucky born good ol' boy drinks bourbon and handles automatic weapons—that is to say, loose, fast, and on the outside edge of control. Make no mistake; people could get hurt, things could get broken today, but I'm not changing a thing—not my riding style and certainly not my attitude.

I'm carrying nothing but water and a cell phone in my jersey. Purists could call this *cheating* during a loaded cross-country tour, but I don't see any of them on the road with me this morning. The handlebars shift expertly in gloved palms as I attack each hill with a devil-may-care approach; part work of art, part outright vandalism of gravity and good sense.

Around lunchtime I find the family stationed along the covered porch of a general store. I'm still in one piece, which I owe to dumb luck and low traffic patterns in rural Colorado. Whatever the reason, it has my confidence soaring. I savor this feeling because if there's one thing about the road, it can make you Popeye-strong and Hello-Kitty-weak all in the same day.

I step into a deja vu moment. I've been here before? Not likely, but something aligns in my brain that triggers emotional vertigo.

"It's from that scene in *Thelma and Louise*," Beth offers. "Right before they drive off the cliff."

"That's it!" I look around, nodding and grinning like a fool.

We drink cold grape Nehis with our legs dangling off the porch. The boys play countless rounds of fetch with a scrappy little stray barking and dashing about like a lunatic between tumbleweeds. Thank God it's not a greyhound or I might be tempted. Thelma and Louise . . . this sets me thinking about other lost causes and bold statements.

"I don't relish doing the rest of the ride without support, honey," I whisper into the back of Beth's shoulder length brown hair.

She drapes an arm over my shoulder.

"You don't know if you'll have to yet."

We stare out into the distance, at the deep gap where those badass girls drove over the edge. Could you end a movie better? I don't think so. I fear my Louise will be a no-show. Brick has displayed superhuman heroics just making it this far, but he can't catch up, I know it in my bones. Still, I'm a free man in America, and as we've proven in the past, perfectly capable of pushing things over the edge and taking a lot of innocent people down in the process. I'll be fine.

But I know Beth's only trying to help rally me, so I say, "Maybe you're right."

Back on the bike the badlands force me to forget everything philosophical, existential . . . everything but the operation of my limbs and the military coordination of tendons, joints and muscle over mind. Hours of head-down riding occur before hints of a breeze break through the tight canyon corridor. It narrows and shades out the worst of the summer sun. Water rolls and breaks in a rocky bed to my right. I'm cooler just knowing it's there.

I'm beginning to feel like my best on any given day could be good enough. This myth wears well on me all afternoon. It helps to imagine throngs of people lining the roadway as I hammer up the tight pass into Telluride. They'd all be whispering that the emper-

or's new clothes made of Lycra look mighty spiffy today, but I'd be too proud of my efforts to hear anything unflattering over the cheers and applause, delusion and daydreams. This is how every cyclist makes it cross-country.

Telluride, it turns out, could be another country. The slot canyon forms a gateway of sorts. A hidden high-altitude valley with nearly vertical mountains on all sides reminds me of the Alps, though I've only seen postcards of the Alps so I guess I'm reminded of postcards of the Alps.

I'm overtaken by emotion and have to pull to a stop. This is where Dad made his final stand. Since it was a heart attack in his sleep, stand probably isn't the right word. And while Telluride wasn't on our original route, it haunts me now that I'm here. It wasn't his chosen place, nothing meaningful . . . it wasn't where he returned year after year, just a gorgeous spot where Pop poked around town his final few days, remarried my mom in a chapel off Main Street, before he died surrounded by packed luggage in a rented timeshare.

I think about leaving his ashes on Lizard Head Pass, but I don't know if he ever made it up there, and I'm pretty sure he wouldn't feel at home for all time on a mountaintop. He was more a man of the people. Since Portland, I've been doling out a pinch here and a dash there, places I think he would have liked or would have asked me to send him postcards of; he never wanted snaps of Rushmore or the Eiffel Tower; he was forever asking about places off the beaten path. And he would have been drawn to them, if he'd gotten out more. Telluride was one of the first stops on what were to be my parents' traveling years.

I left a sprinkle of the old man at Old Faithful because he liked things that blew up. And some at the crossing where wild horses almost leveled us, since Dad would have appreciated that story like no one's business. Still more by the bison-charging incident, for the same reason.

Mostly though, I've been leaving a shake or two at quirky spots, like the Pin And Spin bowl and laundromat in Idaho and, other roadside attractions one could imagine fitting right into a Coen brothers film.

Inherited along with his ashes was my father's filing cabinet. It turned out to be something of a set of operating instructions.

This steel-and-chrome, four-tiered beast consisted almost exclusively of well-organized old insurance forms, check stubs, subscription renewals and a cryptically labeled, massive ring of keys to places that no longer mattered. After much digging, I excavated two files that brought him back to life for an afternoon.

The first file was labeled "Things that make me laugh; politically incorrect or otherwise."

Packed with cubicle-related cartoons, phallic humor, hate-your-boss jokes and all manner of altered interoffice memos by an extremely creative individual slow-roasting in the bowels of corporate America, this collection of rabble-rousing treasures I will cherish always.

The other file is tabbed: "2DOB4IDIE." Now this could be something, and while it appears he was channeling the liner notes of a Prince album when creating the file's title, it causes blood to start making strange noises in my ears. I pray for epiphany, grow hopeful for a few answers to the puzzle of Dad's life. I know I shouldn't, but I actually root for insight. It contains precisely one item: a refrigerator magnet for Sargent's Pizza Emporium. Apparently, the epiphanies never came, so Dad ordered pizza instead. Priceless.

I order myself to skip mountaintops over Telluride for my Dad's final send-off, opting to leave bits and pieces of him at every free-spirited entrepreneurial altar to lost causes and kingdoms of non-conformity we can find . . . and Sargent's Pizza Emporium, if we should stumble upon it.

19

"The difference between 'involvement' and 'commitment' is like an eggs-and-ham breakfast: the chicken was 'involved'— the pig was 'committed'." —Anonymous

JULY 26   1,475 MILES
Crested Butte, Colorado

"Is that U2 she's singing?"

The karaoke machine has been working overtime tonight in the Riviera Ballroom.

It's a pitched battle between a convention of harpists and members of the annual meeting of chemical engineers letting their poorly-styled-at-Supercuts hair down. Tone-deafness is winning.

Truth be told, U2 was a stab in the dark based solely on the way her hair and black jacket hark back to a young Bono.

"Wham," shouts a chemical engineer, louder than necessary. It's as though he's just solved a Rubik's cube, or has decided to imitate a slamming door. "Wham!" He shouts again. "Wake Me Up Before You Go Go!"

I'm pretty sure he spit in my ear that time. If I could feel the offended appendage properly through several rounds of Scotch and sodas, then I might be upset.

I'm mourning the fact that Brick has officially thrown in the towel. Or celebrating, depending on how I look at it. But if that's Wham she's singing, I'd better lay off the liquor. I despise Scotch, but the bartender tells me that amaretto sour is a girl's drink and pours me a Scotch and soda instead. He insists that I will thank him for this someday. I also hate soda water, but I'm waved off with an explanation that it was Hemingway's drink.

"You being an adventure writer on assignment and all, it's the right call."

I point out that things didn't end so well for Papa. That's when the karaoke machine cranks up, the bartender feigns hearing loss and a pack of engineers scoop me up under the mistaken impression that I'm one of their own, or possibly because I'm not. For the record, if you're a chemical engineer, letting your hair down amounts to unbuttoning the top button of your shirt, followed by a slight loosening of the tie.

Beth and the boys are upstairs in the palatial suite of our Crested Butte pampered rest stop. It's been several lifetimes since we pulled out of Telluride without Brick in tow, but only forty-eight hours off the clock.

While my family wandered around town and took in reading time at Telluride's phenomenal library (it's amazing what a Hollywood vacation-home tax base will buy), I burned a day driving Beth's car up and down the *Thelma and Louise* highway, hoping to help Brick over the mountain. But he's a ghost. No one manning the registers in tiny, two-aisle food stops has any information. Nor any of the post offices' counter help along the route. A pair of motorcyclists filling up at an ancient gas station (still operating on tumble-digit pumps) say they've been sightseeing all day.

"Shoot, we'd remember a six-foot-four-inch cyclist pulling a kid's trailer up that hill."

The area is a cell phone black hole. I blow ten bucks on a phone card that appears to have been issued by a dot.com company gone belly up years ago. I use it to pick poppy seeds out of my teeth as I grow hopeless in the lengthening shadows of the afternoon. I turn up the radio and strain my eyes down dirt roads that feed into the highway. By dinnertime I'm back in our Telluride city park campsite. We talk it over, load the entire family up once more and drive the highway halfway back. I could pretend it's out of respect for Brick, but by now I just want my trailer back.

Rain dumps on downtown Telluride. We'd spent the previous night camped above 11,000 feet on Lizard Head Pass. Whereas that storm was more bark then bite, something along the excitement lines of John Krakauer's *Into Thin Air*—without the death and drama—tonight truly feels like an End of Days storm. It finds me shoring up tent stakes in the dead of night, a caveman protecting his clan by diverting streams of water into lakes I've dammed in the corners of the tent, flinching at each flash of lightning, all while wheezing and coughing in an effort to swallow. You see, I'd allowed my liquid Benadryl reserves to run dry earlier in the afternoon.

At daybreak we take decisive action. We dry out over breakfast burritos in front of Baked in Telluride.

"I left word with the owners." Beth nods. "It's Brick's favorite eatery in town so when he comes through they'll pass on the message."

We've e-mailed, called, looked and sent up smoke signals, but now it's time to move on down the road. Sixty miles later, while poaching Wi-Fi outside a hotel parking lot in Montrose (I enjoy balancing the lap top on my front bag and typing), an e-mail arrives. No red exclamation point this time. I lean over the handlebars and read with growing bewilderment.

"Pulled trailer for five hours before dumping it at a general store in Bedrock. Don't know how you do it?! Averaged about three mph. That thing feels like dragging aardvark snot up a mountain. Will meet you in Telluride on Tuesday."

Along with most of the skin on the right side of his body, Brick seems to have lost all concept of time. Regrettably, he's also lost the trailer I need to safely complete the ride. Beth forces me to keep heading east with both boys, panniers, trailabike and a sidecar trailer, while she goes back. It'll be a four-hundred-mile circuit to retrieve the trailer from what she hopes is the *Thelma and Louise* store. On the return portion she'll hand over Brick's stuff somewhere in Telluride and close out our failed experiment in pedaling partnership.

I pull two boys, gear and myself over another mountain, trying to forget that one of Beth's goals in Colorado was to help me avoid multiple Continental Divide crossings with a full load. Instead, the other bike trailer and Brick's luggage are the only ones getting a free ride.

Around tea time that afternoon something shifts. We've been calling the road home for close to a month, and I feel us going native. It's the point in an epic at which everything becomes loose again. Your mind lets go of a former life and accepts the rhythm of the road as its future. We pee outdoors without shame, inspect ourselves for ticks around the campfire, eat from one pot, grin in the face of eighty-mile days, and stop cursing headwinds and soft shoulders. With or without a sidekick, support, weight sharing and all the rest, it just feels so right to be back on the road.

Once again, momentum is my friend.

I brake the bike briefly at a rodeo arena beyond Montrose to watch the rise and fall of eight-second dreams. Quinn and Enzo witness mutton-busting for the first time. I pledge, with the seriousness of a Supreme Court judge, to look for another rodeo along the route so they can mutton-bust to their hearts' content.

We peer over the sheer granite and sandstone gorges of the Black Canyon of the Gunnison, where Abraham Lincoln Fellows and William Torrence invented modern rafting by mistake, using rubber mattresses to explore its impervious depths. The river is all blind curves, hidden boulders and white spray splashing in every direction.

"Dad, did they really go into that water on mattress pads, not knowing what was on the other side?"

Quinn is fascinated in the way all of us get when passing a car accident.

"Sometimes the only option is to keep pushing forward," I say.

We eat yesterday's truck-stop popcorn on the precipice and re-imagine the mayhem of our fellow adventurers before camping in their footsteps.

I hope Beth is all right retrieving our trailer.

Just south of Gunnison, Colorado, I stumble onto a rare treat: the collision of federal highway dollars and summer construction schedules: brand new downhill blacktop, sealed and dry and wait-ing to be christened, safety cones still in place. Think pool balls rolling true over a newly felted table.

For days we've struggled with rough roads, dodging potholes, weaving between steaming chunks of roadkill, gigantic tire scraps, and broken pavement. At 40 mph, the posted speed limit before fines double, I pump my brakes exactly once. I could have stopped on a dime, but don't. Howling and punching the air with my fists, I recognize a moment of open-road clarity. I'm twelve years old again, praying then that I will have the balls to set aside even a sliv-er of my adulthood doing vulnerable things just like this. I tuck and go small and fast the rest of the way to the bottom.

The twenty-eight miles up to Crested Butte test my newfound faith. After shifting into the highest gear for a quick descent, I can't get it to go back onto the lower rings. No amount of coaxing, jam-ming or cursing works. What I'm riding now is essentially a fixed gear bike, and it's frozen in the worst possible place to take on an all-morning climb. A quick assessment of the situation reveals that it's the sidecar preventing me from moving the derailleur. A clamp has the cables in a stranglehold.

There's a pretty good wind at my back, I'm a robust, still rela-

tively young man, and I want to make it to our pampered rest stop before Beth, so I can ready the room and take care of her for the trouble I've put her through retrieving my junk.

The effort in one gear is manageable if I remain in motion even while I feed myself a steady diet of Clif gels. I can't afford to give up any momentum with fuel stops. I'm sweating like a plow horse. Quinn wonders aloud why he keeps feeling the occasional raindrop on a cloudless day. I shake out my head Labrador-style and feel rivulets of sweat run down my neck.

At the eighteen-mile mark the wind changes direction and the true torture begins. Each mile marker I eclipse is my own mini-Everest. Enzo has fallen asleep in the sidecar and Quinn is asking questions about the proper care and feeding of hermit crabs. But I have no extra air to answer. The crabs will have to fend for themselves.

That's when Quinn helps me realize that I will never be invited to join Mensa, but he might have shot.

"Dad, what if you lifted the chain into a lower gear by hand?"

And with that, the last three miles into Crested Butte take us about five minutes.

Another harpist finds her way to the karaoke stage. This one performs Alanis Morisette's "Jagged Little Pill." It's jagged indeed. The masochists in the room offer up a standing ovation. I'm thinking, *don't encourage her.*

No one hires harpists for their vocal abilities. In fact, music for the harp is specifically written as instrumental only. This leaves a lot of frustrated players either born without the ability to carry a tune or—and it's only a guess—suffering such ringing in their ears from all that close-in work against the strings that they can't hear what they sound like anymore. The rest of us can, though.

Listening to these women warble and shriek reminds me of a Star Trek episode that damn near tanked the franchise—it involved a half naked Spock strumming a futuristic harp and singing into the camera. Fortunately the writers explained it away with an evil twin scenario or some rare space sickness. Except for pointy ears, karaoke night in Crested Butte is just as odd and unbelievable.

"Alcohol and karaoke were invented at precisely the same time." Bill from ADM informs me. "You wouldn't have one without the other." It appears that business cards were invented at the same time as chemical engineers. Everything grinds to a halt until I accept each of my rotating tablemates' cards. This ritual goes on all evening. If I ever need someone to whip up a food additive while I'm passing through Oklahoma, I have the number.

Donald from New Mexico butchers a Bobby Darin medley. Rodney from California sets the Temptations back several decades, but at a certain point in the proceedings it all becomes endearing. Maybe it's when I'm recruited to sing back-up on a Huey Lewis number. In case you're wondering, we stopped the heart of rock-n-roll from ever beating again.

"You were aces up there," another ADM engineer says, spitting into my remaining dry ear. "Let's sign you up for a song."

It gets kinda hazy after that, but I do remember too much applause for my unfortunate interpretation of "Purple Rain."

It was touch-and-go for a minute when I refused to relinquish the microphone to a harpist who looked like David Letterman's mother. I wasn't leaving those hot lights until I'd performed all of John Belushi's *Animal House* speech:

"Over? Over? It's not over until we say it is. Was it over when the Germans bombed Pearl Harbor?" (Germans?! Forget it; he's rolling.) "Hell no!"

It was the right room for that material, and enough alcohol had flowed that my rally cry for committing to the rest of my bike ride was misinterpreted as a plea for . . . more karaoke, of course.

By the time I asked "Who's with me!" The answer was everyone. I even got a howling thumbs-up from the bartender. Engineers who'd never owned anything more daring than Volvo station wagons now owned that room—they stood on tables, beating their chests and screaming at the chandeliers. One had his shirt entirely unbuttoned. No one asked who Brick was, or why I was dedicating the whole speech to him. No one cared. They were having a karaoke conversion and I was leading the revival.

Before the Riviera Ballroom careened completely out of control, straight into *Lord of the Flies* territory, I handed off the mike for a soothing Karen Carpenter number. From where I teetered at the side of the stage, Letterman's Mom nailed it.

Those few hours in the company of stringed musicians and math whizzes helped me resolve to continue huffing, sweating, and bleeding, if necessary, to the nation's capital. Also, it reminded me I should stick with my girlie drinks, no matter what the bartender wants to pour.

20

"Remember—as far as anyone knows, we're a nice normal family."
—Homer Simpson

JULY 30   1,650 MILES
Colorado Springs, Co

The dividing line been Mountain West and the plains couldn't be more clear-cut. There's no transition. It's Rocky Mountain High one minute and amber waves of grain the next. Colorado Springs is the mountains' last gasp. We spent a few hours wandering around a geological wonder called the Garden of the Gods, but ask Enzo and all he recalls is the homemade fudge in the visitor center gift shop. It's amazing how many free fudge samples three boys can eat without fully realizing it. We kept circling like planes over LaGuardia. One minute the tray was full, the next we're slinking out the door before anyone's the wiser. I'd yell at the boys, but I ate more than anyone.

Brick proved that the desert in July is no place for a cyclist. As we make our way across an unbroken vista of prairie grass, I fear that the Midwest doesn't have its welcome mat out either.

Swallowing without the aid of Benadryl is possible again, so there's that. But the good doctor was right about the humidity. It feels like a bully holding you down for lunch money.

We don't get more than a few sweaty hours into the Front Range before making the acquaintance of our first tornado watch. It's sunny and still where we toil, but the horizon in several directions roils with an unnaturally green line of squalls. A farmer informs us about the weather watch. He has a radio strung up behind the seat of his tractor next to an orange Igloo cooler and the ugliest dog in three counties.

To take our mind off potential twisters we play roadside treasure hunt. Enzo invented the game, but Quinn gave it shape and texture by adding rules.

What can be spotted on the side of the road just off the shoulder is simply amazing—we've identified church pews, cookbooks, pillows, a tunable guitar, kegs of beer, bungee chords, beach toys. Much of it hasn't been thrown away deliberately but blows off passing cars by accident, making it high-quality stuff indeed.

That's part of the game. If you think it's been tossed out on purpose you have to be the first one to yell "trash." On the other hand, if you think some poor sods pulled into their driveway wondering where the hell their lucky sweater or pool floatie has gotten off to then you holler "treasure."

Most of the game consists of scanning the roadside ahead. If this were an NCAA sport it would be baseball or golf rather than, say, rugby or football. It operates at a meditative pace, which allows me to ride in peace while keeping my boys busy with something that actually holds a payoff at some point. The downside—my Zen is abruptly and loudly interrupted by outbursts and arguments as to who saw said trash or treasure first, and what category it falls under.

Often I'll slow, or brake completely, for longer visual inspections. Each player is allowed to switch an answer only once. That's the other rule: if you think it's a treasure you must defend its use and viability in its current state. Deciding who is right and who was quickest on the draw would undoubtedly make this a contact sport if we weren't on bicycles. Quinn's faster, but Enzo devises an ingenious defense to level the field. He simply deems everything a treasure, then uses his powers of imagination to justify the call.

The concept "one man's trash" comes up a lot.

Enzo is especially good at describing novel uses for discards; a flattened beach ball doubles as a hat, for instance. If no one's buying that, he switches over to a yarmulke.

I act as the commissioner of baseball when it comes to rulings on the field. My decisions are final, and the boys respect that to such a degree that they rarely let it get to the arbitration stage.

One benefit of roadside treasure hunt is that we end up finding things we need. From my years of touring I knew going in never to purchase bungee chords. The roads are littered with them—which begs the question: Is the bungee not up for the job of securing America's loads? Or is it America that has not learned how to properly use the bungee? Either way, the answer is always the same: free bungees.

We've discovered that shoulders in the summertime are awash in pool toys, floaties, rubber rafts, beach balls and such. So plentiful, in fact, that we've taken to rescuing them from ditches and fences, using them at the next hotel pool, then leaving them in the shallow end or distributing them to newfound friends by the three-foot depth markers.

Enzo relishes playing the part of Santa Claus in July.

"Who wants a beach ball?" he'll yell to a family of stunned tourists. Or he'll simply rain toys on appreciative preschool-aged twins in matching lifejackets—ho, ho, ho-ing his way around the cabana area.

With Quinn it's closer to a cast member on "The Sopranos."

"Here you go," he'll say, all casual and easy as he pushes a raft or floatie across the water on his way out. "You paddle away with that now."

At one point we'd scored so many neon floatie tubes and beach balls roadside that the trailer resembled the junk truck out of Sanford and Son: fat rainbow colored snakes poking in all directions.

Even Quinn noticed the wind drag.

"We gotta find a hotel with a pool, Dad."

When the threat of tornadoes and smothering heat gets to be too much along the Front Range, we pull into Tymes Square. It's nothing like New York's famed intersection, but this unremarkable box of rooms has something you wouldn't find in the Big Apple if you searched for a million years.

Their billboard proves that concise, teaser advertising still works: SEE OUR LION, STAY FOR OUR JACUZZI.

Beth is already parked in the lot when we pull in.

"There really is a lion," she confirms.

The boys turn to me. Eager and attentive, dancing and darting around my heels now like house finches at a feeder.

Their expressions say it all. "You can either dash our hopes, Daddy, or give us what appears to be a hotel out of the Chronicles of Narnia. It's your choice, but no one need remind you that there are still those teen years to survive with us."

I mop my sweaty, wind-blasted face with the back of a bike glove, stretching out the anticipation.

"Let's get a room."

Beth flashes a key card. "I already did."

So much for the illusion of power in this family.

Tymes Square lives up to its hype. No, it eats its hype for breakfast with feral, primal teeth.

Walk into the lobby and you've stumbled upon a taxidermist's life's work. Badgers frozen in furious mid-leaps by the fireplace, a massive moose staring down through a face of melancholy confusion—as if to say, "What the hell happened to regulated hunting seasons?"

The wolverine crouching by the candy machine with a dead pheasant in its mouth is a nice touch. It scares at least three children during our initial tour. Honest to God if this isn't Teddy Roosevelt's hunting lodge as imagined by a senior outing club of country craft scrapbookers. The wallpaper is all hearts and checkered picnic table covers. Sociologists might read some deeper significance into the juxtaposition of potpourri-filled baskets and Norman Rockwell paintings beside bobcats and weasels in teeth-gnashing poses, but Beth nails it on the head.

"Here's what happened. Married couple going on thirty years. He's a hunter, she shops exclusively from QVC. They retire to fulfill a shared dream of hotel ownership. Only they never discussed the actual contents of those dreams, or better yet they talked about them every day, talked up a blue streak, but never listened. When it came time for one of them to compromise, for one of them to give up their dream, for one of them to look away. . . ." Beth points at the bear's head wearing a blue bonnet, "No one blinked."

But it's the lion that seals things for us. Parked in a place of honor at the breezeway entrance, this regal animal comes complete with an outrageous creation myth. The front desk clerk has told it so often, and with such bravado, that he's convinced himself of its authenticity.

I like that in a storyteller.

"I'm not claiming it's the brother of Simba from *The Lion King*— I'm telling you it is." He comes out from behind the counter. We follow him into the breezeway as he spins a tale of two lions, Hollywood, and the unnatural instincts of one King of the Front Range.

"How'd he die?" Enzo asks, feeling around the fur for bullet holes. The boys appreciate stories where good conquers evil, but if you can't deliver that, you'd better make it end in a hail of bullets.

"Heart attack. He was nine years old."

The boys look crestfallen until the manager shows them a scar on its back leg. We give the hulking animal a good once-over as if we're considering a car purchase. I'll say this for Simba's brother, he has perfect teeth. Not that I want any future lion encounters at this range for comparison, but those are damn nice choppers.

That's when the manager's story jumps the shark. He couldn't let the beast stand in the lobby for all time with a shred of wild kingdom dignity.

"You're looking at one of the most gentle creatures that ever walked the Earth."

"Really?" I roll my eyes. Beth pokes me in the side.

"So docile that the owner's little girl rode this lion every day of her life."

I decide not to ask how long the little girl lived. According to my research most people only get to "ride" a lion once. It's why you see more of a market for pony rides at birthday parties.

"Can I ride him?" Enzo asks.

You set yourself up for that one, Mr. Night Manager.

First the bison; now my youngest son is disabused of any access to the back of a gigantic stuffed animal. Is there no justice in this world?

We ask the man if he'll snap a few photos of us with The Lion King's brother. It would make a shocking family Christmas card photo—if we were the sort of family that ever got our act together in time to do those things. We did it one year, but while you can tell yourself that mailing Christmas cards in July is an act of hipster irony, it isn't.

Beth takes the camera back. The boys execute a variety of poses starting with the lion, then vogue for the lens with dead wildlife throughout the hotel. And when I say the boys, I'm including me.

Each time we enter or exit the lobby, I can tell that it takes every fiber in Enzo's body not to grab that flowing mane and ride Simba's sibling bareback into glory. Instead, he pets the beast tentatively while singing the chorus to "Hakuna Matata."

Roadside respites don't get much better than this. The hot tub is hot, the pool is cool and complimentary breakfast offers the promise of waffles you get to make yourself. By dinnertime, though, the skies outside look threatening enough that I ask Quinn to read aloud from the tornado evacuation procedure mounted to the back of the door.

"We're supposed to head for the basement," he surmises.

"I wonder what animals are stored down there?" asks Beth.

We could always follow Plan B, which involves all of us hiding inside a bathtub the size of a dorm-room refrigerator.

The lure of the lion made me break one of our cardinal lodging rules of this road trip. And that is, if it doesn't offer animated entertainment on the boob tube, keep going. Beth works the remote like a soda jerk, but it's all inappropriate live action: *Scarface,* "Six Feet Under," and some soft-porn silliness on USA network. The adults in the room so desperately need a break that we settle for ESPN's professional eating finals.

This will prove to be the granddaddy of all bad ideas, sure to bite us in the ass in no time. It's TV as bizarre spectacle, a parody that isn't in on its own joke. Brazenly revolting, yet hard to look away from—the boys cheer on a slight Asian woman with the ability to open her throat at will and consume more food than a herd of marauding rhinos. We will learn she is the heavy favorite, possessing so much game she regularly embarrasses guys five or six times her size.

And with stage names like Cookie and The Shovel, these are gentlemen who don't embarrass easily.

"She's the tour's leading money winner, Dick."

Beth looks at me. We're thinking the same thing. *There's a tour?*

We reap the rewards of parenting-by-television over dinner at Denny's. Table manners, never easily achieved in our home to begin with, go out the window starting with the first course. It will be years before the boys discover that Denny's is not fine dining, but that's no reason to waste food and act like jackasses. I hear myself channeling everyone's father on a family vacation, but it must be done.

Then Jell-O arrives and it's all over but the slurping. I figure if you can't beat your children in public anymore, join them in a Jell-O eating contest. Beth thinks I'm an embarrassment, but that's because her side dish is salad and it's hard to be a competitive eater of lettuce now, isn't it?

We aren't asked to leave at any point, but I think that has more to do with Denny's generous policies on inappropriate behavior. Twenty-four-hour establishments tend to let a lot of things slide.

We linger around the Tymes Square lobby after breakfast. Today we'll break the barrier between Colorado and Kansas, a line Beth can't cross. She has nothing against the state, but her final grad school field study starts shortly, and we've already paid the tuition. This side of clicking together a pair of ruby slippers, my wife has a long drive ahead of her. The boys spend time with top-flight taxidermy and their only mother, but a late start comes at a cost. And I'll be asked to foot that bill. It's so hot that by 10 A.M. the pavement burns uncovered flesh—my uncovered flesh—when I step out before I've put on my bike shoes. Simba's brother reserves judgment, but fellow hotel guests give me sideways glances and double-takes when they realize I'm about to ride a loaded bike contraption into this steam bath.

21

"Ah, I wanna ride the pony."   —Sid, *Toy Story*

JULY 31   1,710 MILES
Burlington, Colorado

"No, no, you go on up ahead, find the fat shade of some big tree in this town right here." I thumb the map on top of my handlebar bag. It's hard to read with all the sweat dripping onto the plastic. "Some place called Burlington." Eyeballing the thin red line under plastic once more, I determine it can't be more than fifteen miles.

Enzo has been successfully transferred from the bike trailer to car seat without waking him from an afternoon nap.

Despite the heat and wind we're having a pretty good time. The bike brings out the best in Quinn. He especially enjoys those moments when it's just father and son. He loves his younger brother, needs him like oxygen, but he would sell Enzo for scrap if it got him some more time with his old man. This is understood. This is how it works in our family.

I appreciate his naked desire, these unabashed flaws. I hope for them, in fact; makes him more human in my eyes. It's those perfect little soldiers and Junior Achievement yes-men you have to keep an eye on. When they snap, it's all over but the memorial services and gun control reforms.

Blame it on this being Beth's last day and the luxury of our Colorado escort, but I toss my extra gear, even my cell phone, onto the back seat. I linger inside the rolled-down window, letting the air conditioning flash-freeze a jacket of sweat that covers the top half of my body. Paradise isn't seventy-two virgins in the afterlife, no sir; it's working freon in August along a rural country road.

As soon as Beth's car crests the hill ahead of us, Quinn wants to pull over for a look around the grounds of the Cavalry Cemetery. He's turning into quite the photo hound. Headstones are on his list of subjects, and this batch looks promising.

I don't want to get off the bike when we've just gotten back on, so I pedal us off road, onto sacred ground, and weave our rig expertly between neat rows of family farming history. Quinn documents their existence from the saddle. I'll soon discover that every town from the Front Range to the Mid-Atlantic comes equipped with a water tower, grain elevator, cattle auction (which in better times doubled as a rodeo arena), and a cemetery.

Something about this dead man's detour feels wrong, but I can't put my finger on it until we hear a flag whipping against a pole in the steady breeze. What's odd is we're a half mile from any buildings.

I nearly give myself whiplash trying to trace the source of the sound, which is growing louder by the second.

"Uh, Dad?"

It's Quinn's trailabike tire, deflated, dislodged and flapping hard against the pavement with each rotation. Goat heads! Nasty little buggers, ninjas of the thorn world. Goat heads will insinuate themselves into the ridges and linings of tires, then go to work like time-released cyanide. You never pick up just one goat head. How could I have forgotten? These agricultural welcome mats spike unsuspecting bike tires all the way across the Midwest. We may have ridden away with hundreds of them after meandering around that graveyard.

I grab for my bike pump and the bottom drops out of our afternoon. Vehicle support has made me soft. Damn it. I've failed to heed the central tenet of that benign paramilitary organization also known as the Boy Scouts.

"We're not prepared for this," I whisper into the wind. For the first time since Portland I've handicapped myself something awful, and for no good reason.

I instruct Quinn to run his gloved hands along every exposed surface area of our tires. It won't save us, but it might prevent a few flats. A long empty road and we've sent our cell phone and support team on ahead. I try telepathy. You'd think after a dozen years of marriage we'd have opened up some unspoken connection, a frequency that only two perfectly aligned spirits can access. Later I learn that Beth was buying ice cream cones and *Us Weekly* at that moment. No shiver down her spine or slight cocking of one ear, à la Lassie when Timmy's fallen down another well. We're on our own.

Quinn smiles up at me, a vote of confidence in his Dad. He'll learn soon enough that most fathers are just cardboard cutouts of their favorite superheroes, but for now I can move mountains. That one grin kick-starts me into action.

"First order of business, son, let's sweep all the tires for goat heads one more time. They didn't poke you through your bike gloves, did they?"

I inspect the little doughnut wheel on his trailabike. Some duct tape should keep it from flapping around; otherwise duct tape is useless in bicycle flat repairs. My own old man would be proud. It'll slow my rolling speed slightly, but we weren't breaking any land speed records to begin with. A few minutes later, we're back on the road. Take that, you Boy Scouts.

Ten miles later my rear wheel goes soft and squirrelly. The insidious thing about goat heads is how they'll pierce another tube just when you think you're in the clear. I have spares, patches and tire irons under my seat. Everything but an air delivery device. My kingdom for a bike pump!

We manage to wobble and spin another two miles before the rest of the tires start popping like party balloons. Five flat tires in ten miles. It's a personal best.

Quinn spots a hawk guarding a fence post just feet from our hobbled rig. We're only a few miles short of town. It's what you make of these things. We decide to make it a father-son foot parade in funny-colored clothing. As we walk, I wonder how much to berate myself. That's when Quinn slips his hand into mine, recounting some of his favorite moments of the summer so far. Somewhere between the snowball fight at 12,000 feet, a rocky mountain oyster taste-testing dinner, and the Aspen-to-Crested-Butte horseback ride, I forget all about the burden of a fully loaded bike train balanced in my other hand. You take your After School Special moments where and when they arrive. Only a fool would question the cost.

Our chariot shows up half an hour later, bearing bike pumps, cantaloupe, and ice cream. I'm disappointed when Quinn lets go of my hand for some cookies and cream Beth holds out. But ice cream's a siren song that's hard to resist.

We make our way by car through Burlington. I hold my face right up against the air conditioner and rejoice. There's not a chance that a town this size has its own bike shop, but I go through the motions—we desperately need to outfit the rig with Kevlar tires (the same stuff in bulletproof vests) and fill all of them with Slime for good measure. A drive-by tour at ten miles per hour proves me right, but we spot something even better in the process.

Under the shadow of the town water tower we find Kit Carson's County Carousel. I cannot overstate the beauty of this hundred-year-old gem featuring hand-painted animals—real horse hair for their tails—an operating organ at its center, and a perky tour guide selling rides for a quarter.

It's as out of place in this dusty high plains setting as, say, a day spa in Darfur or a tanning booth on Mars. How? Why? There can't be more than a few hundred Burlingtonians on the tax rolls. It's as if we've stepped into the pages of Ray Bradbury's ode to small-town America: *Dandelion Wine.*

Towering cottonwood trees and a gigantic all-wood play structure wait across the street in an adjacent city park, but at twenty-five cents a ride we're planning on testing a few different carousel saddles before the swingsets draw us away.

In 1928, the city of Denver decided the future would have no need for quaint carousels, what with flying cars just around the corner, so they worked out a deal with Burlington to unload the thing for a whopping twelve hundred dollars. This included packing, shipping, and reassembly.

It wasn't a few years later that Denver had seller's remorse. The city offered to buy it back, and offered and offered, but Burlington has turned them down for seventy-eight years. Today, just one of those horses is worth tens of thousands of dollars. More than money though, it's the town's history, and that's not for sale.

Someone did try to steal it, once. In 1981, a crew of hapless thieves, arguably teenagers chugging their first beers, made off with a handful of horses, hacksawed right from the carousel and driven into the night. A tri-state manhunt ensued (hell hath no fury like pitchfork-wielding farmers). All the animals were retrieved within six months of the incident, most within ten miles of Burlington. For the record, none were recovered in Denver.

These horses hold an honored place on the carousel. Plaques that commemorate the robbery and return dates as well as their recovery locations have been fixed above each animal. Quinn saddles up on a mustang found in a grain silo on my birthday.

I choose a camel so I can rest my back against one of its two humps, but there will be no relaxing on the Kit Carson Carousel. Along with one of the best backstories in the annals of amusement

ride history, this is one of the fastest merry-go-rounds in the world—and while it doesn't go spinning off its axis like Hitchcock's did at the end of *Strangers On a Train*—it goes fast enough to have you holding brass and leaning hard. Don't be surprised if you contemplate what you had for lunch and wonder whether you're going to be seeing it again so soon.

After a lakeside campfire dinner, it's time to show Beth what a clever man she's married. It's called "A Friend of George." This trick—a bit of tire-patching sleight of hand—has saved many a cyclist left holding flaccid tubes and deflated hopes by the side of the road.

"Give me all your loose bills, Beth."

She never likes the sound of that, but it gets Enzo's and Quinn's attention. I go to work impressing my audience. We need to cover all that goat head damage, but there aren't nearly enough patches to make it possible. George Washington's stoic face on the dollar bill is going to pull an assist. Where nothing—not tape, moleskin, newspaper, bubblegum—has the combined strength, flex, shape and thinness to fit and hold between a tube and tire, U.S. currency with a dab of patch glue gets the job done. Any denomination works: George, Jackson, Lincoln. I just rarely have more than George on hand.

I put on a professional bike clinic for the fireflies well into the evening. When it's all over, we have five working wheels again. No cash on hand, but working wheels.

It takes plenty of pumping up slow leaks to limp into Hayes, Kansas, but when the shop owner asks me how I'd like to pay for freshly Slimed tubes and new, nearly impervious Kevlar tires, I grin like a fool and instruct him to take it out of the old tires.

"We don't do trades."

I tell him to just look inside the tires.

"So, that urban legend really works?!"

So well that I believe I have change coming. He pulls thirty bucks from the trailer wheels and another fifty from my front tire.

"Could we get a photo of you guys for the newsletter?"

Leaving Beth at the border is one of the hardest moments of the summer. Being our second goodbye in so many weeks makes it something close to Chinese water torture, but adding to the pain, we know this is it until September.

It would be one thing if I'd wed a Hilton-by-the-poolside sort of spouse, but Beth lives for the road as much as the rest of us. Under any circumstances, I'd take her over all those big kids they used to pick first for the kickball team.

"It's your adventure again, boys." She tears up a little. "I want to hear every detail when you get home." Notice she says when, not if. That's why we love her.

22

"The safest road to Hell is the gradual one—the gentle slope, soft underfoot, without sudden turnings, without milestones, without signposts." —C. S. Lewis

August 1   1,912 MILES
Somewhere in Kansas

Our outrageous pace is the logical consequence of itching to get on with it, or beyond it. "It" being Kansas. More specifically, the gentleman's headwinds of Kansas, named for the way they blow hot, from a slightly southern direction, in no particular hurry; languid, even. These dilettantes overstay their welcome against my scalded skin. The extra hours of road work they cause find me pondering the state's enigmatic slogan, "Kansas: As Big As You Think."

What the hell? That's gotta be a "Jeopardy!" answer in search of a plausible question. Did someone run a contest and only adolescent boys raised on a steady diet of "Beavis and Butthead" episodes enter?

I'm forced to read these six words on sign after sign, billboard and travel brochure. I try engaging the retiree volunteer at the travel center in a debate about his slogan, but all I get is a vacant smile as he backs away. You know he's hoping that the day brings a few less-crazy tourists through his door.

I pedal along, feeling mocked and baited. And the kicker? It replaced the perfectly serviceable if not pedestrian slogan "Kansas: Simply Wonderful." Was there a lawsuit in which tourists proved beyond a reasonable doubt that the state was in fact more complicated than Nebraska and less wonderful than, say, Iowa?

In defense of Kansas's Mensa-level branding think tank, a host of other states have spent millions of tax dollars on equally bizarre, cryptic and inane official shout-outs. I mull them over mile after mile.

Connecticut: Full of Surprises. (Are we talking the cash and prizes variety, or snipers and ice storms? You gotta be more specific.)

Wisconsin: Stay Just A Little Longer. (Could a state sound any more desperate? It's like a blind date going nowhere or a drive-by at a distant relative's place—"No, stay, I'll put in some pot pies and break out Super Yahtzee.")

Texas: It's Like A Whole Other Country. (Setting aside grammatical issues, I was treated to a full-cavity strip-search in Texas once; not only did it feel like another or "whole other country," I can tell you where: a prison in Turkey.)

Delaware: It's Good Being First. (Now that's just childish bragging, coupled with some resting on one's laurels—it's been several hundred years since you've been first at anything, guys.)

Wyoming: Like No Place on Earth. (Except maybe Montana, oh, and a bit like Idaho, and we do have more than a little in common with Colorado and Nebraska . . .)

Nevada: Wide Open. (Didn't *anyone* on the branding committee see the double meaning in a state with legalized prostitution? Anyone? Bueller? Anyone?)

Tennessee: Sounds Good To Me. (Was this the slogan, or was it what the secretary wrote down from exuberant responses to a killer slogan we'll never know about? My guess: the committee is too embarrassed to fess up now that all those keychains have been printed.)

Alaska: Beyond Your Dreams, Within Your Reach. (Excellent, except it's the farthest state to reach from anywhere in the USA. Though it is within a stone's throw, if you reside in Russia or the Western Yukon.)

New Jersey: The Perfect Getaway. (Car. That last word must have fallen off during the printing process.)

Nebraska: Possibilities Endless. (Vacation plans, finite.)

Ohio: So Much To Discover. (Two words: Election Fraud. Could you do something about discovering that?)

All I can say is our tourism boards must have excellent lobbyists, and is that pork I smell burning through the halls of Congress?

"Dad, are we ever gonna stop for lunch?"

I pull the bike over at the next town and search for some pork BBQ. That and shade. All is forgiven when I realize where we are . . . Cawker City, Kansas, Home of the World's Largest Ball of Twine. As Big As You Think—now it's starting to make sense.

"After lunch, boys, we're gonna bag us the biggest ball of string on the planet."

They offer up enthusiasm, but no sense of confusion. The bizarre has become commonplace. My sons are no longer tourists, but full-fledged travelers.

Enzo pipes up from his covered caboose.

"We should probably start looking for the biggest cat in the world . . . and bring it here."

23

"I can resist everything except temptation." —Oscar Wilde

August 2   2,020 MILES
East Kansas

Under the right circumstances, slurred speech can be kinda cute, but this ain't happy hour, and I'm no one's Marilyn Monroe. I'm just a big white guy trying to fend off heat stroke in central Kansas. Tell you this much, there's an art to staying alive in temperatures above 100 degrees.

If that's true then the boys are DaVincis, both lathered in number 50 sunscreen, wearing solar protecting hats and pressing their water bottle mister fans into full service. I've ordered Quinn not to pedal, and Enzo's solar guard is fully extended. My children have the relaxed looks of folks vacationing in the Caribbean, while I'm suffering the effects of being their rickshaw driver through a Midwest heat wave. I find religion when the bank's electric billboard reads 113 degrees.

I've stopped several times before noon at gas stations and corner stores, drenching myself with water hoses. The effect is something along the lines of electroshock therapy; my body rattles in grand mal fashion. Minutes later I'm dry and baking again. At any corner store you might find me holding cans of sodas to my forehead as impromptu ice packs. Word to the wise: I put them back in the cooler unopened, so think twice before drinking your next unwashed can of pop if you live in the heartland.

Here are the ground rules: you must ride at sunrise and finish your last pedal stroke by 10 or 11 A.M. at the latest. You must dunk your clothing in water and hope the gods of evapo-transpiration are with you. When the clock strikes noon, all bets are off; your legs turn into pumpkin mush and even leather-faced fairy godmothers that spend winters frying their gams in Florida fold up shop. You're on your own . . . and may The Force be with you.

We've been out of the harsh climbs and deep woods of the Mountain West for close to a week now. The distances you can see across on the plains dwarf anyone's best efforts to gauge mileage. These sight lines make twenty miles feel closer to a hundred. It's the watched-pot theory: if you can see the horizon it never gets any closer.

I love the extremes of any journey; count them as good times, not something to simply be endured, but these good times are killing me.

Forgive me, Father, it's been thirty miles since I laid face-down in a pitiful little trickle of water and confessed my heat-fueled ambitions to the world. It gave me nothing more than a psychological boost, and I only managed to find it based on the knowledge that cottonwoods grow along water sources. I'm guessing thirsty cottonwood trees can hold out a lot longer than my body.

That's when I set off in a dead sprint for the next town. (I know calling it a sprint with two boys and a couple hundred pounds of gear is like calling Exxon a nonprofit organization. Okay, so I crack 15 mph and hold it there for several minutes at a time.) My CamelBak becomes a solar shower that I uncork and spray myself with on the fly. When a town water tower comes into view I find myself stupid with happiness, leading the boys in a spiritual or two as we roll up Main Street.

We circle the perimeter a second time, then a third. It's a scene out of all those apocalyptic movies, like *The Hot Zone* or *Outbreak:* sunbaked streets; bleached, muffled, lifeless, nothing stirring. No sounds either, no birds, even a generator or music from a shade-tree garage. Making our way down a side street, I fully expect to see spacemen in hazmat suits step out of shuttered storefronts.

"Car," Quinn calls over my shoulder. I chase after it as though we're a pack of junkyard dogs.

The Reliant K-car's owner has already beat a hasty path to the door of the farmhouse when we wheel up. But we know there's life in there, and that's good enough for us. The car windows sport homemade GO TITANS posters and shaving cream or soap-etched slogans extolling the team on to victory. Every inch of available window space has been used. Blind-spot city. From a traffic-safety point of view, I see now that there can be too much team spirit.

I ring the bell for an uncomfortably long time. After I give up, Mena Suvari's look-alike from the film *American Beauty* opens the door with a flourish. It doesn't hurt that she's wearing a blue and white cheerleading uniform with GO TITANS plastered across the chest. All that's missing from this movie set are rose petals fluttering down onto everything and the piano-theme undercurrent to help move the scene along.

At that moment I become the Kevin Spacey character. It's gotta be close to a full minute before I say anything, and it comes out all cotton-mouthed and stammering when I do. Somehow I convey the message that I need to submerge myself fully in a water source, pronto. And the boys could go for some spritz-mister refills. I know I have more requests, but I drift off task a little and into a cheer-filled daydream.

"Would it be okay to use that hose on the side of the house, and maybe that big bucket?" Quinn asks. He must assume that the heat's finally gotten to his old man.

She does us one better by pointing out a horse trough brimming with water of questionable origin, color, and quality. I flop fully clothed over the edge without a second thought, coming up for air just in time to catch her turning on a sprinkler for the boys. She rustles Enzo's hair before she disappears back into the house. It must not be heatstroke if I can still appreciate the female form to this extent.

My ability to smell improves in direct proportion to a drop in my body temperature. It alerts me that, holy mother of pearl, I do believe I'm currently bathing in horse swill. Our cheerleader returns. She's holding a tray of iced teas, causing me to forget that more than likely that's horse shit in my hair.

She poses a few questions about our adventure in a throaty little singsong voice. As much as I'm embarrassed by who I am at that moment, I'm now completely under her spell. I form some words, but have no idea what I'm saying. There's something about Midwest girls in uniform.

It's Quinn who finally breaks the trance. "Shouldn't there be some sort of sporting event going on for you to wear that costume?" He swirls around his tea a few times, all cool and casual. I know exactly what he'll look like at a cocktail party fifteen years from now.

Our cheerleader completely ignores my seven-year-old, opting instead to lean over the trough, hand me a glass of frosty tea and, in a flirtatious little whisper, answer the question as if I'm the one who's asked it. She offers up two words and a smile seldom seen outside of a Whitesnake video.

"Band camp."

And that'll do it for us, boys. I'm feeling much better all of a sudden. I down my tea in two gulps, saddle up and leave temptation—pouty, double-jointed, tanned temptation—back on the farm.

A quarter-mile beyond the town line, just as I ease up and find a pace I can live with, we solve the mystery of where everyone else is.

We hear laughter, splashing and country music.

"Can we stop for a quick dip?" Enzo asks.

They've built their recreation center under the shade of a cottonwood grove.

"Sure, but I'll need to shower. No one's letting me in smelling like this."

The pool teems with what I assume is the town's entire population . . . minus one peppy little vixen with a healthy amount of teen spirit.

24

"It doesn't matter who my father was;
it matters who I remember he was."
—Anne Sexton

August 3   2,152 MILES
North of Topeka, Kansas

I would have made a horrible hippie. As evidence I point to the fact that my first hallucinogenic experience arrives at forty years old and in, of all places, a Kansas cornfield. There's even parental supervision. That's right, I achieve an altered state in the company of my dead father—a guy who missed the 1960s because he was too busy working or watching golf to see if the revolution was actually being televised, let alone participate in it.

No amount of squinting into the darkness remedies these weird weather conditions. I bolt up from the picnic table I've collapsed across above Owens Lake.

"Something's definitely eating away at the stars."

If only this were the opening to a children's book I've been reading to the boys in the tent. Instead, it's a question I'm posing to my overheated, taxed, and tired brain.

The absence of any twinkle-twinkles across nearly half the horizon would be disturbing enough to a lucid individual. After a rude ride covering 116 miles over a day without end, banging down one beat-to-hell road after another on our way to this waterfront campground, past the point of exhaustion and to a place where drinking brackish liquid from a fungus-coated outhouse sink seemed like a reasonable choice, this weather phenomenon feels downright menacing.

If I'm still conscious—and that's up for serious debate—not hypnotized by miles of reflective white lines or just flat-out losing my mind, then something funky is definitely going down on the horizon.

There . . . did you see that? More stars chewed up by the darkness. All told, I've spent several years of my life voluntarily sleeping under the open skies, so I think I know the difference between cloud cover and . . . and . . . whatever the hell this is.

I squint some more, then glance to the tent where the boys are sleeping sound as cavemen. Back to the horizon; I shiver though it's gotta be eighty degrees at midnight. Time to mull over whether the aliens' mothership blotting out the stars will be populated with cute and cuddly E.T. types or those barcode baddies with detailed plans for probing my openings and poking around my soft spots. Other signs of the apocalypse: A breeze off the lake, pitiful and paltry as it was earlier, has come to a complete standstill now.

We're all familiar with the expression "still of the night." For me it evokes a sense of safety, a blanket of darkness and tranquility that pauses time and trouble for a few lush hours. But this particular silence is so still, so complete that even the insects have lawyered up and the familiar crush of own my foot steps has gone missing. I'm many things, but Ninja is not one of them. Why can't I hear my feet?

I stomp soundlessly through a waist-high field of grass en route to the washhouse. It's as though cotton has been jammed in my ears or wrapped around the world. The washhouse sits at the campground's high point, lacks a roof and sports only three of the customary four walls found in traditional architecture—a handball court with a large sunroof, really, with toilets, showers and an abundance of bugs attracted by the promise of water—though currently subdued and silenced from the heat, the freakish atmospheric conditions or both.

The building's design does give me a clear view of the tent. So that's something. And though I don't have to go, I check below the lid for wasps and spiders, then park myself under the half light of a halogen lamp . . . a bit of sanctuary to gather myself.

We must all have a bit of moth DNA in us, attracted to light when we feel threatened. Why else have I come up here? It's a familiar position, so I stay put on my porcelain throne and try for that peaceful place between exhausted consciousness and dream. I lean back. The blackness above is complete now. Maybe the roof was lost to a tornado? We are in Kansas, after all. Come to think of it, is a bizarre lack of stars some sort of tornado warning I missed in the safety brochure?

I drift now . . . eyes closed, feeling as dislodged and isolated as I have in years. I listen for any signs of life. Nothing. No cavalry coming for this road warrior, thank you. Aliens, tornadoes or just the weight of the ride I've signed up for . . . I'm gonna have to save myself.

My thoughts ricochet around, landing on the kicker line in *Cool Hand Luke*. Paul Newman, looking loose and youthful, cornered by the warden and his shotgun. Paul smiles into the muzzle. The warden, with a southern drawl and a politician's look about him, speaks his famous catch phrase: "What we have here, men, is a failure to communicate."

Sometimes I wonder what it would be like to look out of Newman's eyes for just a few moments. Rock solid, is my guess. I drift off on that image for a few moments.

"Never made it to Kansas until now."

The fact that someone has gained silent entry into this open-sky washhouse and now sits two toilets to my left, addressing me directly, should be cause for some alarm. Too many miles, too few stars and utter exhaustion allow me to take it in stride.

Besides, what child can't recognize his father's voice.

When I hazard a peek, it's my old man all right, perched on the edge of the john, just the other side of the lamplight. He's dressed from head to toe in Pittsburgh Steelers fan garb: black and gold jersey with Franco Harris's number across the front, scarf wrapped around his neck and '74 conference championship cap riding proud atop his head. He's my age, maybe a little younger, but since he was a smoker most of my childhood, it's hard to tell.

"I appreciate you putting me in our hometown colors, over those pinstriped monkey suits I worked in every day."

He spins the mustard-colored Terrible Towel with real gusto. I've missed his smile.

"Least I could do, Dad."

Our eyes lock. It's too much. I make my way over for a hug, but he waves me back.

"No touching. . . . I think it'll end the moment."

I step away. He gives me a little shoulder shrug.

"Hell's bells, Pop. Either I'm in a heartland Twilight Zone episode or there was some mescal in that fungus-covered outhouse faucet."

He removes the cap. There's that full head of hair he was quietly proud of all those years. "Call it a happy confluence of chemistry, weather conditions and heat stroke, son. Maybe I'm here, maybe I'm your vision, maybe I'm Memorex. It is what it is." He spins the towel again. I can almost smell early September afternoons in Three Rivers Stadium, roasted peanuts, and gridiron glory.

"Before this fades, though, I wanted to thank you for bringing me along."

And that's when I can no longer contain my longing. It's almost a certainty that I'm putting the words I want to hear into the mouth of this halogen-lit hologram of my dead dad, but it's damned effective nonetheless. We really should have done something like this ride adventure together when we had the chance. I don't blame him—here's a guy who, at three or four, was chained to a tree in the front yard so his immigrant parents could go off to work. Freed from that rope only to go to school, where they strapped his left arm behind his back so he would write like everyone else. The man was freaking Houdini to get as far as he did.

He clears his throat, takes a long pull from a stadium cup of beer and nods toward the tent.

"It's a helluva summer you're going after with those two."

We look over at the blue nylon dome. I sit back, trying to embrace, if not my Dad, then this altered state of consciousness. I've even remembered to put that patch of eczema behind Pop's right ear. It's all in the details. I blink hard and squint again just to see if I can clear the decks. Even that time I came down with viral pinkeye, all I experienced was sticky lids and some blurring of distant objects. This is full-on Hall of Presidents hologram hallucinations at work.

Figment or not, it kills me that we can't throw our arms around each other. Come to think of it, though, we were always kinda stiff huggers in life. I settle for some more conversation.

"It's good where you are, Dad?" As if he's just away at a timeshare in Costa Rica and not riding shotgun as a Ziploc of bone chips in my back bag.

He sets his beer down by the bowl. A few water beetles scatter.

"I'm just happy we're not in some manicured cornfield talking about building a ballpark. Costner always poured it on too thick for me. Hanks can get away with it, but Costner isn't fooling anyone."

"He was dead brilliant as the fugitive with a heart in *A Perfect World*."

"Don't remember that one. But I didn't get out to the pictures as much as I should have."

I shake my head; if only we'd done this sort of thing more when Dad was alive. It's the same story dating back to Cain, I suppose. What's hoped for and what's received.

Dad reads my mind.

"I do remember putting our canoe in the Hillsborough River some afternoons. Steering and drinking in back, while you got in some upper-body work with your paddle and kept an eye out for gators."

As I recall it was hot, hard work, and Dad usually had one of those thousand-yarders going behind his eyes, but we were doing something as a team. I burned it into my memory and marked it as the beginning of our world adventures together. We never made it beyond the banks, but I'm not complaining.

"Your Mom came along that one time, remember?" He shakes his head before taking a long pull off his cup.

"We scared her speechless with all those gator sightings. Not an easy state to achieve for her."

Dad swings his Terrible Towel again. I can smell his aftershave.

We nod, grin and stare into the darkness. I get my chattiness from her.

"Is this the part where I can ask you about the secrets of the universe?"

Dad laughs like he means it. "What? Like have I walked with God and what's Elvis up to? That sort of stuff?" Pop shakes his head. "Sure, I could tell you I've chatted with The Almighty. How's this for poetic justice: He's the spitting image of acclaimed atheist Karl Marx. Or let you think Elvis comes by every evening with his PB&B sandwiches singing us all Memphis lullabies. How about some hot tips about the future . . . one word, son: biofuels."

He's more relaxed than I ever recall, except maybe while watching golf and eating party pretzels on Saturday afternoons.

"Truth is, I got nothing for you." He's standing now, with his arms extended, palms upturned, a banker turning me down for a loan.

I shrug. It was worth a shot.

"Besides, I don't need to tell you that the answers to any questions that matter are sleeping down there in that tent. Hell, I came by out of envy more than anything else."

It's full night now. Still no stars or breeze, but I've forgotten everything but the contours of my father's face in that moment.

"The boys ask about you sometimes," I manage. "Quinn has that bear you gave him. Brought it along this trip, named him Stanley, after your father."

He nods. I think I see him wince a little.

"Wait, here's something for you." He smiles like he's been keeping the best secret. Like once he reveals this, it'll always be Saturday for us.

"You ready? Our Steelers? They're gonna take it all this year."

It's my turn to choke back laughter.

"Coming from you, Dad, this isn't Oracle of Delphi stuff. You ever bet against the black and gold in your lifetime? Super Bowl? They must not have Sportscenter where you're at these days. The Bus needs to take his knees into retirement, and our quarterback's riding high and heading for a sophomore slump. Sorry, Pop, the Steelers will be lucky to make the playoffs."

He shrugs, the same slow-rolling motion I recognize as my own. Seeing this brings me closer to the memory of my old man than any predictions, afterlife descriptions, or eczema patches. I'm nearly overcome by emotional vertigo. Quiet tears run the length of my face. Still, I can't let the Steelers statement go unchecked.

"*To* the Super Bowl, or win it?"

He affects the voice and inflections of sportscasters Howard Cosell and Chris Berman. "They . . . will . . . go . . . all . . . the . . . way."

We both break up over that one. I lean back, closing my eyes for a second.

"Funny, that's about the only plan I have in the works, too, Dad. We . . . could . . . go . . . all . . . the . . . way . . . to . . . DC! After that it's up for grabs, including where to leave what's left of you, and what to do with the rest of my time."

His words are soft and comforting. "You'll work it out as you go. I never worried about you."

I smile. "Funny, 'cause I worried about you all the time, Pop, even now. Not whether you suffered in the end—style points for that massive heart attack in your sleep on Thanksgiving morning, by the way—but mostly regarding your open-faced suffering all those years. I'd give anything to know we were worth it."

"Irish-Catholic. Suffering's in the DNA, though you seem to have inoculated yourself somehow. Maybe it skips a generation, or all those endorphins, eh? Better self-medication than stout and lager, trust me. And cheaper." He finishes his beer. "But forget all that now. I'm in the wind. It's still your run though, so do this if you can . . . stick the landing."

I let go of a long sigh and with it much of the day's searing heat, withering pain and maybe even a bit of the anguish over losing my dad right when I'd started to see him through a parent's eyes.

"Stick the landing for you. . . . got it."

Maybe Dad's a Russian gymnastics coach in the afterlife. But the sentiment works. The sentiment hits me where I've been hiding for too long. Inside a head full of half-baked dreams, paperback revelations and plans on paper. Whole empires have come and gone between my ears, glorious vistas and alternate endings.

"Sweet weepin' Jesus, son, not for me . . ." He spins the towel one more time, stopping as it settles in the direction of the tent.

In the incoherent words of baseball great Yogi Berra, the simple people's poet laureate, "You can't think and hit at the same time." Damn straight, Yogi. I need to get on with it. Batter up.

Dad hums a familiar tune. Something that has me filling in the empty spaces with Celtic drums and pennywhistles . . . it's from an Irish Rovers album he wore out on weekends while reading the Sunday paper. I'd spin in place by the credenza stereo, my dad glancing up from time to time. Dervish myself into a dizzying frenzy until I'd finally drop to the living room rug at his feet; tweaked, giddy, safe.

When I come around the stars are back in their heavens and my neck feels like it's been resting against cement blocks for several hours, probably because it's been resting against cement blocks for several hours. Oh, and our favorite Steelers fan has left the building, such as it is.

So what have we learned here? Drink only from reliable water sources and keep the daily mileage under one hundred on over one hundred degree days. But I am tempted to put a few bucks on Pittsburgh for the win. Talk about hometown spirit. My Pop had it to burn.

Coming back through the field I hear my own footsteps loud and clear. I snuggle the boys close. Despite the sticky, sleep-apart climate conditions, I don't let go. Instead, I fall into the deepest slumber of the summer; dreamless and unburdened.

25

"Whenever you find yourself on the side of the majority,
it is time to pause and reflect." —Mark Twain

August 4   2,190 MILES
Kansas City, Missouri

"Are they chasing us, Dad?"

Quinn keeps looking over his shoulder as a growing crowd of children, all black, some shoeless, stop whatever they're doing on the stoops and curbs of a North Kansas City public housing cluster to follow this crazy contraption through their 'hood.

Some of them suck on lollipops as they trot along; others carry sticks and well-worn bats.

"It's a parade," I tell him, hoping I'm right. We'd turned on 72nd Avenue as planned. Everything matched up on the map, except now we're looking at a cul-de-sac up against an overpass. This is not a through street. I ride the length of the neighborhood only to realize I will have to retrace my steps to get out.

It turns out there are two 72nd Avenues, but only one appears on the map—the one on the other side of the interstate. We're following the invisible one. It's how we divide things in our country. It's how we keep score.

The kids howl and holler as we pass; joyful yelps, which cause me to grin and slow down. They're all smiling teeth and pumping fists—pep rally-style. Some of them want a ride. Some just want us to circle back so they can run the length of the neighborhood again. Only the drug dealer sitting on the hood of his Town Car at two in the afternoon reveals nothing. His expressionless face holds even when he nods, offering safe passage through his kingdom while expending the least amount of energy necessary.

Big women, comfortable with their weight, wave from threadbare lawn chairs. They lean way back, drink from jars, and fan themselves slowly with strips of torn cardboard.

I pull over for a second, trying to get my bearings. Each street of the housing project looks similar to the last. Before my foot hits the ground we're mobbed. The boys shake hands, nod, and chat. Kids want to know where Oregon is.

"Right above California," Quinn hollers.

The ones who know where California is whistle and moan. We hear "No you didn't" and "That ain't right" from a few of the older kids in the crowd.

"Quinn, go into my back bag and get out all those extra bike shop stickers we've been collecting."

Now it does feel like a parade—Mardi Gras, to be specific.

Instead of beads, though, we're passing out stickers of grizzly bears on bikes in Montana, spiders wearing helmets from Moab and Rainbow Riders from River City Bicycles back home.

Stickers and kids make for a common denominator the world over. I see some applying them to Razor scooters and plastic balls before we've even finished distribution. Enzo gets into the spirit of things by handing out extra floaties and beach balls from the back of the trailer. This sea of limbs and laughter parts abruptly and quiets immediately when a motorized wheelchair powers over broken pavement. We watch a shriveled-up balloon of a man hit a top speed of 3 mph before bringing his rig in for a landing nose-to-nose with ours.

Everyone waits. He fingers a nappy gray beard with one hand and rubs furiously at the leg of his jeans with the other. Any more friction and his pants are gonna burst into flames.

"What do you know about that," he says, then waits a few beats for everyone's attention.

"I'd give anything to get rid of these wheels . . . and it looks like you'd do anything to hold onto yours."

A flash of fear runs down my back. Is this some sort of signal for the crowd to push us down and take our possessions? I have no reason for such thoughts outside of my own prejudices. Feelings I'm loathe to admit even exist, but there they are, revealed on my face as we try to pedal through the 'hood.

Maybe he recognizes something in my conflicted expression, maybe he appreciates that no one's free of their fears as long as two 72nd Avenues exist, or maybe he's just deciding whether to scratch his other leg into flames. Whatever his reasons, the old guy doesn't dangle us out there for too long.

His grin is broken and genuine. When he flashes it, I find my footing again.

"You wanna race?" he says, winding up the electric battery in a ridiculous imitation of NASCAR.

We're given directions to what everyone in the vicinity agrees is Kansas's best pirate BBQ, not the ones named in all the brochures and best-of lists. This one comes out of a pit barrel on wheels and moves from place to place, but everyone knows where. The lawn-chair ladies insist we buy a whole chicken, shred it, light and dark meat together, then mop up each bite with a piece of roll smothered in baked beans.

"It soothes what ails you."

This causes arguments to break out over side dishes, eating techniques and ordering combinations. Even the drug dealer comes away from the Town Car to add his two cents. I don't know what it means to be a member of the black community. I'm certainly not another white-boy poser chasing after a ghetto fantasy, but I do know what it feels like to be human.

I'm not knocking my roots too hard, but if I ever experience a reception of such spectacle and warmth in the suburbs, I'll eat my brake pads . . . because I sure as hell won't be tearing into BBQ this tender.

"Boys, you heard the ladies—mop your beans with those buttery rolls."

26

"All my life, I always wanted to be somebody. Now I see
that I should have been more specific." —Jane Wagner

August 6   2,190 MILES
Kansas City, Missouri

We'd made it halfway across the country only to have my childhood sweetheart hide herself behind a half-mad, insanely jealous
husband, who also happens to be the finest French chef in the
Midwest if not the entire country. Good God, the appetizers are
enough to make a grown man weep. I excused myself to the bathroom between courses so my children don't have to ask why their
Daddy's crying.

And I forgive my old friend for escaping into the kitchen and making sure we are only seen together in public places or with our kids. After too much drinking on Saturday night, the Frenchman offers up a glimpse of his rage. It's this misplaced, pin-wheeling anger that allows me to cash in my disappointment for empathy, if not understanding.

Over a three day rest-stop in K.C., I spend a few minutes with her here and there, catching snapshots and sound bites from the life of my childhood friend and teenage heartbreak. It was distance, not lack of desire, that ended things twenty years earlier. At least that's how I remember it. While the Frenchman's jealousy is two decades too late, it does offer us closure. Of course I would like more time to see if she's really happy, but that's not my job, if it ever was. Instead, our rest stop offers up something more lasting and valuable; unfettered time with her folks, my undocumented godparents, and with her two girls her folks babysit regularly. They're spunky little ladies who just happen to be the same age as my sons.

"Tell me again why my mom would think to buy my dad boxing lessons?" I ask Ben.

We're laughing so hard out by the pool that I choke a little on one of three famous heartland BBQ samples. We've been conducting taste-testing around the chaise lounge. For the record, while it's all slow-roasted ambrosia, none of it holds a candle to that no-name pirate restaurant rolling from corner to corner around the 'hood.

Not only are Ben and Cathy as close as family from the summer I spent in their home years before, these people are also the most direct living connections to my father's early adulthood. Back when my father was thin and frisky.

"Your dad comes into work one day with boxing gloves." Ben rolls his eyes at this point, indicating the improbability of my dad as a promising welterweight. "He's looking rough and worn out, but it was a stressful time so it could have been the job. When I ask about the gloves he's hiding under his desk, he tells me Claire's signed him up for boxing lessons."

"'She doesn't know how much they beat us up around here all day.' your dad says. 'Now she's spending my money to have me beat up for real in the evenings.'"

Ben, Cathy, Joe and Claire could have been the cast members in a Woody Allen film. Comfortable inhabiting the urbane world of the late 1960s, the foursome had been thick as thieves for a time and stayed close through phone calls and vacation visits after that. It's how I met their daughters. It's why my boys are playing with their granddaughters in the pool at my feet, and it's how my dad keeps coming back to life this summer.

He and Ben worked together for the American Red Cross; Dad writing ad copy and Ben pumping blood as a doctor. Family legend has it that my pop coined the bumper sticker campaign, BE A LIFESAVER: GIVE BLOOD. Mom also swears the Pet Rock idea was swiped from him . . . which is why these family legends need outside corroboration.

"Hell yes, he did. That man could have done just about anything." Ben removes the pipe that hangs perennially from the corner of his mouth. "I'm not just saying that, either. He was a helluva guy."

Cathy looks over at the bike, then back to my boys.

"I know what he'd think of this insanity," she teases. "But I have no idea how you're doing it."

That makes two of us. But I need whatever this is as much as oxygen, as much as they needed my parents' friendship when they were young and improving. "Just between you and me, when I heard what you were doing, I expected your boys to look like Civil War veterans by this point in the ride. But they're fine. I'm surprised, frankly." She laughs at her earlier concerns. "You're giving them the time of their lives."

Among other things, I think to myself. She's not the first person to hold this view. It's one of the hardest things to convey about our ride: helping people wrap themselves around the idea that we have to help a generation explore the world in something other than a hermetically sealed SUV. Kids are capable of much more than absorbing TV waves and being spoon-fed one activity after the next. When did second-graders need cell phones, BlackBerries, and a lifestyle aimed to grow ulcers the size of cooking onions? When did we stop trusting their imaginations to fill in the unscheduled hours of the day? It's not easy or even acceptable in some quarters to stage a breakaway. I'd mention our summer plans to some parents and you'd think I was selling my boys into slavery.

"Those poor bastards, all summer on the back of a bike." Unspoken was that I was putting myself first and my kids on a chainring leash for the duration.

"What about their routine?"

"What about their friends?"

The boys and their newfound Kansas City girlfriends didn't seem to be suffering.

By the end of the visit, Enzo and Sarah have agreed to live in Hawaii together when they grow up. I consider telling Enzo why long-distance relationships never work out, but I realize that none of these kids would be here if ours had.

Before we roll out early Sunday morning, I take a few of Dad's ashes into the garden where Ben often labors over the greenery of his retirement.

"Thought I'd leave a little of you with some old friends. Reminisce if you want."

Dad's not talking this morning. Just as well, I'm worthless before 10 A.M., unless I'm in the saddle.

And with half the country to go I'd better get in it.

Part 3

Missouri
to
Washington, DC

"A man encountered a tiger. He fled. Coming to a cliff, he caught hold of a wild vine and swung himself over the edge. The tiger sniffed at him from above. Terrified, the man looked down to where, far below, another tiger had come, waiting to eat him. Two mice began to gnaw away at the vine. The man saw a luscious strawberry near him. Grasping the vine with one hand, he plucked the strawberry with the other. How sweet it tasted!"

—Chinese parable

27

"If everything seems under control, you're just not going fast enough."   —Mario Andretti

August 7   2,230 MILES
Lees Summit, Missouri

People go soft all the time, but roads stay hard and unyielding year in and year out, unless it happens to be a stretch of shoulder in Jackson County, Missouri. Highway workers have all sorts of euphemisms when a municipality can't afford to seal its shoulders: putty, pudding, soup, gum, lava, cream of wheat. It all boils down, or up, to the same thing—a pliable paste that parboils in the summer sun until it's ready to swallow up debris; everything from AA batteries to armadillo shells to screwdrivers and fender strips. Each evening the uncovered blacktop cools, capturing its treasures much the way a spider lands insects in its web. Once ensnared, nothing gets free. The angles and patterns these pieces and spare parts create are works of art, really, unless you have to navigate around them on five yards of bike at close to 20 mph.

We'd already battled a plague of grasshoppers over sealed asphalt all morning. At first I do my best to dodge the little critters, but that's when they numbered in the single digits. It began as most games did that summer, with a Stars Wars theme.

"Pretend we're steering the Millennium Falcon through an asteroid belt. The grasshoppers can be the asteroids," Quinn says.

I wonder how the grasshoppers feel about this?

The boys make the appropriate starship propulsion sounds and crashing noises as I veer and juke the rig between critters. The occasional crunch under our wheels is greeted with jeers and howls. Enzo keeps score.

Quinn and Enzo aren't afraid of hopping insects, which is a good thing because by lunchtime thousands of them cover everything. The asteroid game has morphed into something closer to demolition derby as we mow through miles of undulating arthropods.

It's unsafe to wipe away the build-up of grasshoppers covering me and continue steering. I keep my cadence steady and let them land where they will. Quinn takes great pleasure in calling out how many he counts sitting atop my helmet and crawling across my back and bottom. Occasionally I have to spit one away from my mouth.

That's when we hit the soup shoulder and things get interesting. I'm dodging all sorts of obstacles melted into the roadway: old magazines, tire chunks. It feels a lot like pedaling over a hot trampoline littered with toys. When I reach back into my jersey pockets for a water bottle, I come out with a handful of insects clinging to the plastic container.

"These are my pets," Enzo announces from the trailer. God knows how many have infiltrated the interior, but when I catch a glimpse through my helmet mirror the sloped surface of the carrier cover appears to be a perfect landing strip for these bugs. It's saturated with grasshoppers.

When we reach the top of a rise I wonder if our first legitimate descent of the day will shake loose the insects. Many blow off, but others are there to take their place. It's not unlike a six-legged version of those battle scenes in *Braveheart*.

"Send in the Irish—they're cheaper than arrows."

The madness of dodging debris, shaking bugs off my glasses so I can see, and blocking out most of the boys' chattering and cheers make for a rather invigorating race to the bottom. Video-gamers, eat your hearts out. This is where it's at.

"Uh-oh . . ."

Though I'm still boggled by the physics behind it, I manage to dodge my front wheel around a five-foot length of car fender melted into the soup shoulder. It takes dead aim on my rear wheel, though, in retaliation, I suppose.

Bam!

Phosphorus-green Slime pukes and splatters from the severed wheel with the speed of an airbag deploying. The boys cheer as if a touchdown has been scored. I death-grip the drops of my handlebars, careful not to slam the brakes for fear I'll execute a dismount that even the Russian judges would be impressed by. It's similar to wrestling a steer into a rodeo chute, but somehow I bring all fourteen feet of rig to a safe spot at the nadir of the hill.

"Yes!" Quinn fist-pumps the air.

He's covered in green Slime, as is the trailabike and much of the trailer. A CSI detective could recreate the angle and speed based on how the various Slime trails have splattered across my children and gear. Stunned grasshoppers now painted neon green launch themselves into the tall grass. I'm no biologist, but that's not gonna help them come mating season.

In the future, when Quinn retells this incident, he will refer to it as the day the ocean came to Kansas (we're actually in Missouri, but I never interrupt a storyteller hitting his stride). "I looked up just as a big green wave of Slime washed over me and my bike and Enzo's trailer." He always waits for shock to settle on the faces of some of the more cautious adults listening to his tale. I will be held in low regard by these people for my risk-taking skills, but it's worth it to hear Quinn's closing line.

"It was the best day of my life."

When I'm confident that no one's been injured, I get off the bike, cue the laughter and dig out the digital camera.

"Totally wicked, Dad." Quinn is beside himself. "Can we do that again?"

I make a cursory inspection of the tire. It's been sliced to the bone, a clean guillotine cut that severed the tube and tire in half.

"Not unless you have fifty bucks and a bike shop handy. That was Kevlar."

Back in a Colorado hotel room we'd clicked to a rerun of *Ghostbusters*. The boys watched every frame. All I have to do is start the chorus and it's a *Ghostbusters* singalong the rest of the afternoon.

"I've been slimed!" Quinn says in his best Bill Murray voice. Spinning around, he falls into the grass as part of a dramatic death scene. Get that boy to a children's theater audition.

Enzo is about to taste a dollop of green goo congealing on the trailer. I don't blame him. It has the viscosity of pudding, but more than likely it's packed with poisons.

"Don't!"

"You can fix the tire, right Dad?" Enzo remains my biggest booster. But it would be easier to spot weld my frame back together using
the reflective properties of my eyeglasses and the power of the sun.

Since I bartered away our spare tire back in Kansas we don't have
many options. Kevlar might lull the rider into a sense of flat-tire
invincibility, but then laboratory stress tests never faced the soup
shoulders of Missouri seeded with Detroit's finest in steel bumpers.

The "Friend of George" trick isn't gonna work this time. We
need a friend of Michelin: a ride to the closest bike shop. On the
plus side, the Ginsu fender was so preoccupied with slicing our rear
tire in half that the rest of our wheels snuck by unscathed.

As we're about to move the caravan east on foot—destination, a
gas station at the top of the rise—a late-model truck pulls over.

"You're the guys, right?" the driver says. He's a well-dressed, boisterous man in his late fifties holding an expensive digital camera. I
notice an NPR member sticker in his rear window. You'd think after
traveling a hundred thousand miles by bike, over four continents,
I'd have more sense than to blurt out "Yes" to a loaded question
such as "You're the guys?"

For all I know he means we're the guys who hit his dog, robbed
the liquor store, defiled his religion . . . the list goes on and on, with
plenty of it ending badly.

"I read about you in Sunday's paper."

He's referring to the half-page article in the Kansas City *Star*
regarding our adventures. My childhood sweetheart sent us off with
a parting gift. Generous to a fault, she placed a few calls, then spotted a reporter in her restaurant and orchestrated an interview that
led to the handsome spread in the Sunday edition. People have been
honking, waving and buying us Gatorade and chocolate milk ever
since. "King for a day," I keep telling the boys. Quinn likes the king
part, but he's not impressed that it comes with an expiration date.

The driver sets down his camera to shake our Slime-covered hands. It shouldn't be any trouble catching a ride now.

"Family's not gonna believe I ran into you guys without some documentation. Would you mind getting closer together for a quick photo?"

I point to the tire dangling from its rim, and my neon-green kids.

"Be happy to, but we're in a bit of a situation here." I lift the seat so the rear wheel is even more on display. "After your photo shoot, what we could really use is a ride to the nearest bike shop."

He never loses his grin or boisterous delivery, even when he's rejecting us.

"No can do, guys. Lees Summit's where you'll find your shop, but it's in the opposite direction I'm going. I actually just swung back when I spotted you three celebrities. I crossed two lanes of traffic and an emergency-use-only median." He makes this sound like an accomplishment.

He nods vigorously before raising the camera to his face and directing us to bunch for better composition. A shining example of self-absorption married to merry callousness. What I should do is tell this guy where to put his camera. Being a fallen-away Catholic with Buddhist tendencies, though, even in the most offensive situations I'll feel a certain amount of guilt followed by an overwhelming sense of peace. The guilt must be residual—a pool of bad feelings placed there by countless "You suck and you know it" Sunday sermons of my childhood—like leftovers still hanging in the back of the fridge for no good reason. The sense of peace comes when I conclude that whipping a clueless member of the Missouri amateur paparazzi with a deflated bike tube will only bring me fleeting pleasure and set the wrong example for my boys. We smile for the camera (mine is more forced and tight than the boys') before pushing our rig uphill, as our ride drives off without us.

"You're the guys, aren't you?!"

We're not falling for that one again. It's a father of five, the sort of guy who plays weekends and Wednesday evenings in a slow pitch softball league, but wears the polyester blue athletic shorts the rest of the week.

"Which guys?" I say.

He steps out of the super-cab, long-bed, heavy-duty-something all-terrain truck. Boys' faces poke out from behind him, much the way cartoon chipmunks pop their heads out from behind a tree when the hint of mischief or food fills the air.

"That dad, from the *Star*, the one pedaling his boys by bike?" He looks hopeful. It's a big truck. I wouldn't even have to disconnect the trailer to fit it into the bed. But I don't want to get my hopes up.

"That's us," I say, bracing for another letdown.

"Man alive. That's taking it to the limit, padre." He high-fives me as if we're teammates. "I read the whole thing out loud at breakfast. Course you've made my life a living hell now. The boys want to go on something like this, but I told 'em it's not in my blood. It's not in many people's." His boys come out from behind him now, making their way less and less tentatively around the bikes and boys.

"Maybe we could do some sort of adventure more my speed— bass fishing our way across America. I could start that tour if they don't have one."

He's patted my back at least ten times already.

"You guys are really something."

My boys are brandishing light sabers now. His brood comes back with cap guns. The merriment begins. There's not a grasshopper in the tri-county area that should feel safe at that moment.

Before I can even get halfway through my pitch, he's loading the bike into the back of his truck. When I try to put us in the back with the cargo, he's having none of it.

"We've got room enough for all of you up here."

One look inside the super cab proves that softball Dad is not into hyperbole. There's enough room behind the front seats to host an awards ceremony or deliver a SWAT team to the scene of the hostage crisis. Inexplicably, there are even seven seat belts. I notice a Polaroid paper-clipped to the visor. There's a whole world in that overexposed image—his wife hanging lightly on his thick forearm, boys actually smiling rather than just showing teeth and fear for their father. He's holding a trophy. I was only off by a little. It's fast-pitch.

As we chat, I establish we're from two different worlds, but this guy has a sincerity to him, a way of interacting with his sons that makes us equals, brothers. I probably vote the same ticket as our NPR photographer, but look who offered us the ride. These are the little things that keep my view of the world pleasantly off-kilter.

When he deposits us at the front door of the bike shop, a fat chunk of me wants to take his sons along on the ride of their lives. The other chunk wants to tell their dad to keep driving until we get to their ranch-style subdivision home. We could turn on the sprinkler, pass out the squirt guns, crack open a couple longnecks and let NASCAR dreams race around us for the remainder of a summer afternoon. Forget for a while that resources are finite, the suburbs are a whopper of a mistake and working too hard to pay for all of it is the biggest confidence game this country is pulling on itself.

Instead, we gather everyone in the truck bed and click off a snapshot. This time I encourage him to take a few more shots. It's a photo I refer to now as a tale of two families, separated by things that matter, but in a perfect world wouldn't. Whenever we click through the photos from our trip, the boys stop me on that one.

"When can we have them over for a play date?" Enzo always asks.

I think about what my people call the "flyover states," the red states, Guns, God and Country folks. How it's easier to lump everyone into one box of values and write 'em off.

"I don't know when, Enzo." Wishing I did.

He looks at me as though I've missed an easy one; a slow pitch I should have been able to put out of the park.

"When it happens it'll be a good time, though," I add. "A damn good time."

28

"Forget your perfect offering.
There is a crack in everything.
That's how the light gets in."
—Leonard Cohen

August 7   2,270 MILES
Sedalia, Missouri

It's a day without end. The ones that start off too strong are omens. When we cover fifty easy miles before lunch, I tend to take on the personality of a boxer taunting his opponent for more, when what I should be is humble, listening for the bell and posting a respectable win on the judges' scorecards.

Now I've jinxed it and we're dodging steaming raccoon carcasses and possum parts with uncomfortable regularity again. Highway 50 is supposed to be the scenic way across Missouri, but it has yet to reveal its pastoral beauty. Maybe she's one of those pretty-on-the-inside states.

"I think I saw a nest of birds living inside the head of that one," Quinn notes as we blow by an especially ripe raccoon kill.

Those weren't birds eating away at the animal, but I let his version of events stand.

The sun is straight overhead. A steady incline, almost imperceptible, grows from an annoyance into agony. Then a wind whips up for good measure, battering us in bursts that are impossible to predict, some from several directions at once.

It's a sad state of affairs when a forty-year-old athlete in the best shape of his life reaches out to the valiant but window-dressing labors of his seven-year-old for some sort of redemption.

I'm not proud of everything that happened this summer, but only a full confession will do. I turn to Quinn and I plead.

"I need you, son. I need you like I've never needed you before."

While this may or may not have been the truth, in the moment it feels like it. A side note about Quinn's trailabike—it is of the highest quality, a Burley with six gears and an aerodynamic design, including a special spring-lock rack connection. This is key because it forms a solid extension of my bicycle rather than some loosey-goosey attachment along the lines of towing a friend's broken-down car back from the beach with a length of rope and some slipknots. It's so secure that I rarely have to look back to see if everything is working properly.

It has its limitations, though. You could put the strongest grade-school rider on it, a future Tour de France contender in that saddle, and unless the road is razor-straight and pancake-flat it doesn't pencil out. From an engineering standpoint, any tilt, any grade in the road makes it a net loss. Downhills are glorious, but then we aren't going downhill at the moment.

When Quinn doesn't answer my pleas with the proper amount of enthusiasm, that's when my parental training kicks in. Always make eye contact. It's the only way to be sure they've heard you. What I see next will haunt my nightmares; what I see next crushes my spirit. *Quinn has his feet up on the center bar.* His riding style reminds me of an English gentleman from one of those Merchant-Ivory films. He's having the time of his life. Waving when someone in a passing car toots, soaking up the countryside and throwing his head back so that the breeze can better reach the depths of his neck. Oh, for the love of God!

"Quinn, how long has it been since you pedaled?"

He cocks his head to the side. It's not without a certain amount of tenderness, but he's studying me. In the same way one might a pitiful creature that needs to be put out of its misery. Much the way Lenny eyed George when he had to tell him to pet the rabbits for the last time. It's the look a girlfriend holds when she means *It's not me, it's you*. It's the look doctors learn to hide when they know it's gonna hurt you a lot more than anyone else in the room. It's pity. But I never expected to see it from my son, at least not for another ten years or so. He breaks it to me.

"Dad, I haven't pedaled in two days."

And with that I go back to work; whimpering occasionally, but making little circles with my pedals and dodging roadkill.

It's good to know one's place in the big scheme of things.

"God, what's that smell?" Quinn says, coughing up a storm. It has to be something exceptional, because both boys have learned to ID the foul aroma of most approaching carcasses, and play through by breathing mouth-only until the olfactory dangers have passed.

There's only one dead animal that hooks into the corners of your mouth and makes you taste its essence on your spit with each swallow.

"Skunk!" Enzo announces at a volume and urgency reserved for Navy gunners as the first planes flew low over Pearl Harbor.

A driver has landed a direct hit on the poor creature, and from the smell of things, landed it recently. I pedal harder, but as we close in on ground zero my eyes water and nerves are alerted that tell me never to eat again.

From a car, the experience of a skunk imploded roadside is similar to opening a rotten Tupperware container of something residing far too long behind the ketchup. Sure, it slaps you in the face for an instant before you close the lid, toss it to the curb and put a new Tupperware container on the shopping list. From a bike, with the wind blowing in the right direction (it always is), you're *inside* that Tupperware container. Not only that, you're also encased in the sweltering confines of the trash can, with no escape because pickup isn't scheduled for days.

"Make it stop, Dad," Quinn says. Enzo just moans.

Even after we've cleared the blast zone, the odor hangs on. I get an idea from a film about the bubonic plague I watched back in high school. Digging inside my handlebar bag, I come out with what I hope is the antidote, or the citrus equivalent of a Band-Aid, anyway.

"Quinn, take this section of orange slice and rub it all over your nose and the space above your lip." I demonstrate on myself.

Enzo has some orange slices in the carrier from our last rest stop. We never drop below 15 mph during this rolling bit of triage. It takes a few seconds to see if it's successful, but that's because we've been holding our collective breath.

"Better," Quinn says.

My high school years weren't a total waste after all. There's still pulp in my goatee when the first legitimate downhill since Kansas City sneaks up on us. That *Ghostbuster* descent the other day was a screamer, but oh so short-lived. This one is robust and long and exists on account of a slow rise we've been laboring along since lunch. One of those slight inclines that feels like the promise of Social Security. It could pay off in the future, but no one should count on it. Thankfully, it's payday.

"Drop your orange peels and grab onto your grip-shifters, Quinn."

I always savor the shift, similar in emotional texture to that moment when the coaster finishes its last upward click, right before giving over to gravity. My legs tingle. Adrenaline is dispensed in the right amounts to keep me in control while right on the edge of it.

And what the hell do we have here? Another Chevy truck, this one the size of a small country, its wheel wells extended on either side in out-of-scale proportions—the automobile equivalent of lamb-chop sideburns. This gas-guzzling boat slows down to fill the entire shoulder lane a quarter mile ahead. I bring my rig up to full ramming speed anyway, on the chance that they're just dumping something out the window and moving on. When I peer up from my tight tuck the black truck is still there, only now a lady has exited the cab and is holding court in the only conceivable space I would have used to shoot the gap between the truck and highway traffic.

That folks, is how you ruin a cyclist's fuzzy rush. I burn off half a brake pad on each side pumping to a stop. There's at least another glorious mile, maybe two, of downhill between that truck and the bottom. My expression is one of scorn. I can order up an icy glare when properly motivated.

Dressed in Bermuda shorts and an oversized navy blue shirt featuring the stars and stripes emblazoned across the chest, a middle-aged PTA mom bum-rushes the bike, arms waving and all smiles. I try to soften my expression, but my face is having none of it.

"You're the guys?!"

I'm beginning to doubt the maxim that there's no such thing as bad publicity.

"My husband read about you boys in the paper. When we spotted your get-up on the other side of the hill, he said we should leave you to it."

I can only see the back of a man's receding hairline in the driver's seat. But from here it looks like the head of a wise man.

"But I told him I was having none of that and made him pull over."

A wise, brow-beaten man.

"I'm Emma, by the way." She reminds me of a hummingbird. "I have one question for you."

Only one?

"David—that's my husband—worked as a conductor on the train line for years. Just like his father before him . . ."

I settle in. Maybe the question will come in the form of a parable.

"Every Sunday for longer than I can remember we've been putting what's called a farmer's dinner on the table. It consists of more courses than you can count with your fingers; a right proper meal for a dad pedaling his sons across America. My question is this: How would you like to come back to our house in Sedalia for dinner, have a swim at the club, a sleepover, and we could do your laundry if you have anything that needs . . . freshening."

Clearly she's entered what I think of as my "ripe zone." Most people call it their personal space, but on me its radius and reach are too wide to claim as my own. It's clean-living sweat and grime; nonetheless it's still the aroma of the road: campfires, sunscreen, and wet Lycra coexisting with a few hefty burps from a pizza stop made less than an hour earlier.

Emma's smile is contagious and her offer outrageously kind. Considering that I've been cross-checking her with something between a glare and a wiseass grin since she broke our momentum, I'm blindsided by this act of unprovoked kindness and grace. I discover at that moment it's physically impossible to subtly shift a garish expression into beaming gratitude. Instead, I look down, stew in my shame juices for a long moment before collecting myself for what I have to say next.

"Emma, that is the *only* acceptable question to ask a fully loaded cyclist barreling downhill at thirty miles per hour on his first descent in days." I'm grinning from ear to ear now, convinced that she doesn't understand a word I just said. I try again.

"We'd love to take you up on your hospitality, wouldn't we, boys?!"

Enzo has opened his trailer cover. He holds up several floaties. "We'll bring our own pool toys."

Still racked with guilt over my initial approach, I want to cook up a way to feel better about eating their food and overrunning their home. When Emma suggests we load our bike into the over-sized truck bed, I suggest an alternative.

"Sedalia can't be more than fifteen or twenty miles up the road, right?"

Emma nods.

"It's too early in the day for us to call it quits (an outright lie), and I'll need to work up a farmboy appetite for that spread you have cooking back home."

She's giddy at our acceptance.

"Give me some directions and phone numbers and I'll call you when we hit the city limits."

We watch their taillights crest the horizon before resuming our downhill run. Little do I know that the shoulder will turn into a broken maze of danger, and our glorious descent is an anomaly. There will be bruising up-and-down rollers the rest of the way to Sedalia, none of which go down long enough to do a cyclist a bit of good or work up a solid head of steam for the hill waiting on the upside.

I think of it as my penance. Several times I curse my choice, but most memorably when I leave my sunglasses on the side of the road and have to circle back a half-mile to retrieve them. We take so many "short breaks" for Daddy to "grab a breather" that the boys actually get antsy for the bike. Though it doesn't seem possible, there are only so many ways to entertain oneself with grasshoppers, corn stalks, and light sabers.

During the worst of my efforts, Beth calls in a panic. She has to be at her brother's wedding in Canada, and she found all our passports but her own. I am somehow at fault for this. I ask her to call back after I can get to the top of the hill. She says she'll hold through my heavy breathing.

"Did you check in the box under the bed?"

Each time she calls back she is more irate. Now I feel weak and powerless in two time zones at once. When the cell phone rings again, I brush a grasshopper off it and hand it to Quinn. Maybe he can calm her down.

"She says she found it and that she loves us."

I wonder if this sort of thing happened to Lewis and Clark.

Our final reward exceeds expectations. There are drawbacks to traveling by bike during full summer, but there's also a timeless beauty found under the glow of sixteen hours of daylight. When we arrive at Emma's just after 4 P.M., it's as if another day begins within the first one. David is a calm, sage-like figure, not brow-beaten in the least, a rock of a man who has raised four children, succeeded in business and marriage and treats my boys like royalty from a far-off land.

He delivers a signature piece of advice over dessert in chairs out back. Staring me dead in the eyes as the sun dips low on the horizon, David allows a long sigh to escape into the evening breeze. I wait for the wisdom to set me free.

"Be kind to your knees, son. You'll miss those bad boys when they're gone."

I laugh until the fear of throwing up multiple courses of farmhouse supper slows my convulsions. David and my dad, almost the same age to the day, would have gotten on like gangbusters. I can see them, swapping stories and dispensing advice over beers down at Sargent's Pizza Emporium.

For this reason alone, I'm loath to turn in for the night and away from David's company. Emma, it turns out, is the unofficial mayor of Sedalia. If today someone were to hand me a heartland headline reporting that she had taken over the governor's mansion in a land-slide, it would not surprise me in the least.

It was the largest pool in the Northern hemisphere; Emma treat-ed the boys to a science adventure involving barn swallows getting ready for first flight from under the patio eaves; and if anyone asks, a farmhouse supper includes eighteen courses, not counting the vanilla ice cream over cantaloupe.

29

"Perhaps this is our strange and haunting paradox
here in America—that we are fixed and certain
only when we are in movement."
—Thomas Wolfe, *You Can't Go Home Again*

August 8   2,280 MILES
East Sedalia, Missouri

"You know the Katy trail is right around the corner."

Emma mentions this casually over a breakfast that's only a few
courses smaller than the farmhouse Sunday supper.

How could I have forgotten? Catching this legendary rail trail across the state of Missouri has been the plan all along. In my defense, I'm easily distracted by shiny objects and all-you-can-eat buffets. At eighty fully loaded miles per day I can't expect to remember everything, though this is a biggie. It simply slipped my heat-addled mind; that and the fact that although officials have plans to connect Kansas City with St. Louis via the Katy someday soon, this rail line converted into a 225-mile crushed-limestone bike path misses its mark on either end by fifty miles. Godspeed, you idealistic bureaucrats, Godspeed. But until then it's Highway 50 or nothing to get you out of the big city.

Once a corridor for coal and freight cars, completed or not the Katy is still a rare find. The name comes from the Missouri-Kansas-Texas Railroad—MKT, or Katy for short. That's how our August begins: on the outskirts of Sedalia, Missouri, a news crew interviewing us, cameras clicking courtesy of their unofficial mayor, then the distinct sound of Kevlar tires rolling onto crushed limestone.

Not fifty yards down the Katy trail everything changes. It's our first chance in 2,500 miles to forget about what could run us over. You don't always recognize tension until it goes away. My helmet mirror becomes decoration. While the limestone slows our progress down by at least a couple miles per hour, it's worth it to roll along under the shade of tall cliffs, virtual tunnels formed by thick vegetation and real tunnels cavernous enough to hold massive train engines and loaded freight cars at one time.

In addition to the nearly flat terrain and shade, there's wildlife, good fishing along the Missouri River, stunning bluffs and caves with Indian artifacts.

On our first afternoon, we park the rig beside a wooden bridge for no other reason than we can, and because the river below is just too inviting. The deer count is up to three before I get my helmet off. Enzo has already found a tree to shimmy. The cicadas hum and buzz in surround-sound as I pass out poles and bait.

"Dad, when we cycle across Canada, I want my own bike," Enzo announces from the high branches.

The addiction will not be skipping a generation. I take pride in this knowledge; a silent, swollen pride that only a parent feels when the space between generations is still close enough to touch.

Where the treeless landscape of Kansas forced me to take to the road at first light, under the hardwood canopy of the Katy we start our days as late as 10 A.M. I read from *Huck Finn* aloud by moonlight or flashlight in the tent and teach the boys how to shoot pool at local bar-and-grills that dot these converted depot towns.

An entire industry has built up around the bike. Little clusters of shops, homes and eateries that would have fallen into disrepair when that lonesome train whistle sounded for the last time have experienced the Second Coming. They've found religion, all right. It's called the Church of Latter-Day Cyclists. B&Bs with bike racks, bathrooms, shade and shuttle service at every depot station, maps to each business in town and discounts for anyone arriving on two wheels. Unlike four-letter-word greetings from road-rage-infused drivers who bellow at cyclists to get back on the sidewalks (where there aren't any) or simply those who run us off the road—into a hospital if we're lucky, the grave if we're not—everyone along the Katy has a smile and a wave for the cyclist, time to stop, chat, offer directions, even supply tips for the best experience up the trail. I know some of this is commerce at work, not altruism, but far too much felt easy and sincere to be an act. If it is, then Hollywood's missing a pool of untapped talent along the Missouri River.

To be sure, there are plenty of patches where the trail remains in direct sun, the humidity recalls somewhere in Indonesia during monsoon season, and I haven't lost an ounce of rolling weight gear since the Montana purge, but I couldn't care less. We've found the heart of the ride. We're untouchable and we know it.

"Dad, was it Lewis or Clark who discovered America?" Quinn asks.

We're standing beside yet another plaque commemorating the spot where Lewis took a leak and Clark maxed out his credit card. No disrespect to these audacious explorers, but enough already. We've been living in the shadow of their statues and roadside attractions since the Oregon Coast.

"A man named Columbus owns that title, son. It only feels like Lewis and Clark did. Maybe they had a better P.R. firm."

My boys will either make future social studies teachers furious, or keep them in stitches. Either way they can already find more places on a map than a shocking number of American adults. This does not make me puff with pride over my boys as much as it dampens my hopes for the future of the republic.

Everyone calls us crazy to pedal at the height of summer, but I just laugh louder and order more drinks—just a wee thimble of Scotch, (as a begrudging tribute to my karaoke bartender in Crested

Butte) with a Gatorade chaser—during the worst of the afternoon heat. We camp beside cornfields and nap in the mouths of cool limestone caves after searching the dirt for arrowheads and other evidence of the past.

If you know that Jefferson City is the capital of Missouri, you fall into one of two categories: sixth-grade honor student prepping for a geography bee, or resident of Jefferson City. As an unscientific experiment, and a cheap way to entertain myself and the boys when it's too hot to ride, we start asking people in towns leading up to J.C., "What is the capital of Missouri?"

Survey says:

St. Louis—6

Kansas City—4

"No, you're wrong. It's definitely St. Louis"—1

"Can I change my answer to Columbia?"—1

Jefferson City—1 (disregarded when we learn he grew up there).

"Who gives a damn? They're all bums living off the government teat and telling us what we ought to do with our corn subsidies. If you find the capital, give 'em this piece of rotten corn and tell 'em where I'd like them to . . ."—1

Something everyone along the trail does know about Jefferson City is that there's a long, dangerous bridge linking the Katy trail on the north side of the Missouri to the hotels and amenities south of the river. I reason that if they don't know their own capital, I'm certainly not banking on any of their travel advice. This will prove costly.

As a rule, museums close on Mondays. I discover Tuesday is when most of the Katy takes the day off. From mile one out of the campground until well into the afternoon, I can't find food at any price. Cyclists, not unlike armies, travel on their stomachs. Each depot town, separated by about fifteen miles, holds the promise of nourishment. And each dashes my gastronomic hopes.

Water is available at each stop, but unless I get something solid and boasting three or four thousand calories, my flame will go dark soon. I've eaten all the Clif bars, and those restaurant packets of jelly and sugar are almost useless, offering up the staying power of a cheap sparkler at an Independence Day parade. Whenever some relative handed me one of those sparklers I lost all hope that we would be blowing up something big later.

We wander through another two-street town off the trail. It's vacant but for a postal worker in her shotgun shack and two matching beagles, who lumber up to the boys and make nice in all the right ways. While I attempt to summon energy from winter stores of fat that no longer exist—who would believe that I'd ever miss my love handles?—the boys beg me to take two droopy-eyed beagles the rest of the way to Washington, DC. I find the shade of an ancient oak and slide down against its trunk.

"Forget for a moment that these slack-jawed mutts have an owner; together their weight has gotta be in the vicinity of fifty, no, sixty extra pounds on board."

Now my arguments aren't even following conventional parental lines of reasoning, or the show-stopping almighty closer line delivered by every exasperated parent at some point: "Because I said so!" But my rambling argument makes perfect sense to me in the moment.

"Forget about the dogs. Forget 'em because unless we forage for some grub, I won't even be able to lug you guys much farther."

Enzo chuckles.

"That's nice. Laugh at another man's suffering, why don't you?! That's cold, son."

I'm getting punchy. It won't be long before the boys start looking like Loony Toons cartoon drumsticks and chicken wings.

"No, Dad, I just like it when you say the word 'grub.' "

"Vaseline," Quinn contributes. "Now that's a good word to say out loud."

Enzo nods in agreement. Each of them sits Indian-style around me, identical beagles in their laps calling for belly rubs at the same time. If the moment gets any weirder we'll have to sign on as extras in the cast of *Alice in Wonderland*.

"What about sarsaparilla?"

Quinn is just getting started.

"Ichabod Crane." Enzo comes back with.

"Iceberg Augie," Quinn says.

It's a riveting verbal ping-pong match they've put into play, but it's getting us no closer to food.

"Watermelon," Enzo tosses into the ring. It breaks the rhythm they have going.

"Watermelon?" Quinn challenges.

Enzo won't admit defeat. He points into the woods.

"No, there's watermelon over there," he clarifies.

And just when I thought our Mad Hatter's tea party couldn't take it to the next level.

Sitting off to the side of the trail, nearly hidden by flowering plants, is a child's bookcase loaded down with watermelon, not one of which weighs less than thirty pounds. The bookcase reminds me of that game, Don't Break the Ice, or the other one, Jenga. I'm afraid the entire structure will collapse into rubble if I pick the wrong melon from the shelf.

"Ronnie's watermelon-sweetness-tester machine would be handy right now," Quinn says.

It's August, I'm peckish and the watermelons all look like winners to me. Let's give Ronnie his props, but I'm willing to take my chances. I hand Enzo two dollars to put in the honor-system coffee can and reach for my McGuyver.

The McGuyver is only the coolest tool known to man. It's what every kid thought he was sending away for in the mail when he joined a private detective, star fighter, adventure hero, secret agent decoder club. Instead, after six to ten weeks of painful anticipation, what arrived was utter crap; a dime-store pen knife or flimsy magnifying glass with less torching power than a pair of reading glasses. The ring always turned your fingers green, and that "secret" code? Nothing more than switching numbers for letters and writing words backwards. It wasn't so much that all your allowance money was sitting inside a Great Neck, New York, P. O. Box, but that your trust in mail-order products had been shattered. Thirty years after I lost my faith in comic book come-ons, the McGuyver arrived by mail. It makes up for everything . . . almost. I'm always going to be bitter about those sea monkeys.

The McGuyver is a Swiss Army Knife on steroids. If all your

favorite tools were gathered together into some sort of indestructible Gordian knot through alchemy, then miniaturized without losing strength, you would still have a pale imitation of the device I now hold in my hand. With three dozen tools for working on every part of a bike, car, anything mechanical, really; or alternatively for escaping from a terror cell in Pakistan, this is the Cadillac of travel tools. The magnifying glass is powerful enough to actually start a fire, there's a fish hook and line feature, fillet knife, and a screwdriver small enough to fix wire rim glasses. Once you've accomplished every *Mission: Impossible* activity you can find in a day, there's a bottle opener for celebrating. Unlike Rogaine, elevator shoes or beard dyes, my McGuyver makes me something more, not just giving me the appearance of. And it makes easy work of our forty-pound watermelon. We munch on half-moons of sweet ambrosia until our distended stomachs can hold no more. It's far from a steak dinner, but it'll have to do. I'll surf a sugar river of pulpy red juices into Jefferson City or die trying. Okay, that's a little melodramatic. Maybe I'd better pack the rest of the melon along in case of emergency.

"You've got a passenger, Enzo." I strap the remaining twenty-five pounds of melon into the trailer seat, using the five-point harness as if it were a toddler. It fits nice and snug by standing it on end. Our lunch looks like a forest-green barrel with the lid off. Enzo puts his arm around it, patting it a few times. "There, there," he says. I gotta find these kids some real playmates.

We reach the bridge into Jefferson City on fumes. I can't seem to bring the bike above 5 mph on the long ascent to the center spans. A noisy chopper pulls alongside us. I see Quinn flinch at an oversized rider's unnecessary revving. I look over in time to see that he wants to say something. Burning energy I don't have, I lean in. He stops revving.

"Bet you wish you had a motor right about now." His laugh is that of a hyena.

There are so many things I want to say in the moment, and I'm just the guy to say them. I don't get stage fright or come up with killer comebacks after the fact, an hour later on the drive home. Just before my mouth starts to misbehave and dig my own parental grave, I spy Quinn bird-dogging the proceedings with the intensity of a Wimbledon line judge.

Alone, I would have said something along the lines of "Your @#$% future heart attack will be sponsored by Harley-Davidson," or "Does your Momma make you wear all that @#$% leather in August?"

Instead, I offer him a placid smile. "This is just my speed."

Properly confused, he roars off with little satisfaction for his hard-hearted efforts. A perfect example of how having kids can make you a better person.

"Jesus, what an idiot," Quinn mumbles under his breath.

And that would be an example of how children learn a lot from the way adults (me) usually talk to themselves (me) and others in rush-hour traffic. Speaking of Jesus, and cursing in general, I've tried to get my kids to go easy on taking the Lord's name in vain, not because we're big churchgoers, but out of respect for those who are, or those who take semantics way too seriously, anyway.

We're not outright heathens, more the St. Francis school of divinity; our worship tends to be the hands-on variety: pulling ivy on Sunday mornings at Tryon Creek Park to protect the old growth, and putting hammers to nails or straw bales to chicken wire for Habitat for Humanity. Still, try as I might, kids say the darnedest things, little bite-size packets of truthful, inappropriate things.

A couple of Quinn's friends had a classic philosophical discussion going on a recent play date.

"What's God look like?" one of them asks.

They think for a moment.

"Like a smiling face painted on a cloud," Ezra offers. Standard preschool depictions underpin this answer.

"Like a hippie with no pants," Sam declares.

Whoa, Nelly. I have to leave the jungle gym, I'm laughing so hard.

Nothing, though, will ever top the time we learned What Jesus Would Pedal. My sons were a little younger, small enough to have them together in one bike trailer.

We were out for a quick rickshaw—Pat, myself, and the boys lounging comfortably in the carrier. Be it known that parenthood reduces the most carefree cyclist to a glorified pedaling taxi service, but I'm not complaining, banking instead that I'll live longer or, at the very least, expire with rather exquisite calf muscles.

Pat's sense of humor is as dry as a five-dollar martini, which is why I like to ride with the man. That and Pat's not psycho about racing me everywhere just because my byline appears in some national sports and travel adventure magazines now and again.

I notch up the pace, pushing for home because I've just remembered about a proximity birthday party. Everyone knows what I mean when I say "proximity," right? Those are people, often salt-of-the-earth folks, with whom you have nothing in common save for similar addresses. By virtue of location, and one innocent wave on move-in day, a semi-uncomfortable relationship has been allowed to fester.

Kitty and Stan haul us inside like they're hosting a game show. Pat tries to excuse himself, pleading no gift, no invite, *no mas,* but for my part his presence will turn out to be that of a lighthouse during the perfect theological storm.

You see, Kitty and Stan are WWJDs in a category so far beyond inappropriate I'm at a loss as to where to store it. WWJD is a genre of pop-culture T-shirt-inspired religious therapy that poses the question, What Would Jesus Do? Taken at face value, this works for say, ethical dilemmas on the scale of "Would Jesus bomb North Korea back to the Stone Age?" "Would Jesus sleep with his boss's wife during the Christmas Party?" "Would Jesus rig an election?"

But, as with Tabasco sauce and karaoke nights, a little is almost too much. Jesus as your personal referee, fair enough, but I think it's safe to say that when you're asking your personal savior to be your personal shopper and reveal what shoes go with that blouse, you've ridden this one right off the rails.

What caught my eye were the two massive matching birthday cakes, one ebony and the other of the ivory variety. After the candles were blown out and my boys had a piece of each cake in front of them, I waded in . . .

"Two cakes! Never pegged you guys as such sweet-tooth folk."

"We're not," Kitty announced. "But we couldn't decide on a flavor, so we asked ourselves, 'What cake would Jesus eat?' "

As Pat began to shake his head, I caught my friend's eye and gave him a pleading look that said, "Throw me a bone here, Pat. I've gotta live and ride on this street, so hold it together. It only takes one disenchanted neighbor to back over me with an SUV. Come on, Pat, they own dogs. Big dogs. Don't do it, my friend! Wait, wait. Ask yourself Pat, What Would Jesus Do?

"We were reading scripture—"

"King Solomon?" I venture.

Stan looks impressed, "How'd you know?"

"Lucky guess." Mensa club, this is not.

We're surrounded by party guests sporting bracelets and necklaces showcasing the letters WWJD. Why hadn't I noticed this before? Kitty slides another space shuttle-sized piece of chocolate onto my oldest son's plate. Quinn's expression is that of a lottery winner.

"Still," she muses, "I believe in my heart of hearts that Jesus would have preferred the lemon cake."

I'm about to say something regarding angel food, and Pat confides in me later that he had a comment about spice cake at the ready. But the unfettered truth flows easily and unencumbered from the mouths of babes. Quinn beats us to the punch.

Through chipmunk cheeks of chocolate icing he declares in a voice to reach the rafters, "Mmm hmm, that Jesus doesn't know what he's missing!"

The room falls silent. Now that's comedy, son. Wrong room, but that's finely spun gold, little man. Forget that absolutely no one but Uncle Pat and Daddy want to bust their guts with laughter. Forget also that for the next year Stan and Kitty will most likely release the hounds at the sound of my passing freewheel. Still, that's some solid, A-list material.

We don't hang around long.

Miles later, the boys are sleeping it off in the bike carrier, chocolate-covered smiles revealing a moment of childhood sloth and privilege. Out of the blue Pat leans in conspiratorial-like with,

"Joe, something's been bothering me for the longest time . . ."

I brace for a discussion about proper seat height, achy gonads or hand numbness on long rides. Such queries come with the territory, but I didn't expect this from Pat. As much I like him, I have a rule not to ride with people who use me too often as an advice column on wheels.

"What bike you think Jesus would ride?" Pat's as droll as they come.

For the record, Stan believes the King of Kings would pedal a thirteen-seat tandem, with Judas slacking in the rear.

Yep, I asked him, and rather than siccing the hellhounds on me, Stan delivered. It turns out Stan believes Jesus likes a good joke as much as the next guy. Kitty, we're still not sure about.

After our motorcycle encounter, it takes the better part of an hour to work through the valleys and summits of Jefferson City. At some point, like the sirens of Greek mythology the red and green colors of a 7-Eleven sign come into focus.

I pull over as if we've arrived at the gates of the Taj Mahal. In a way, we have.

"Anything you want, boys."

"Anything?" Quinn is incredulous, sensing some sort of trap.

"Anything!" I repeat.

He hops down and we stumble back to the carrier to set Enzo free. Quinn wants to give him the good news. It's been too quiet back there since the bridge crossing. I sense trouble.

When I throw open the solar cover, Enzo is obscured behind a thick paste of watermelon pulp. There are chunks in his hair, rivulets running the length of his shirtless chest. As a playmate, Enzo leaves something to be desired. The watermelon has been decimated. So much for safety harnesses. It looks like one of those Martha Stewart craft projects gone horribly wrong, a high-class melon boat stolen by frat boys for a weekend vodka blowout.

The best I can tell, Enzo began digging into the top and didn't stop until he hit rind at the other end. I'm reminded of Piggy from *Lord of the Flies*.

"It's 7-Eleven, Enzo, and Dad said *anything we want*."

Enzo stays put, a hefty chunk of melon in each hand.

"None for me," he says, letting fly a massive burp. "I'm good."

30

"Night swimming deserves a quiet night."
—R.E.M.

August 10   2,470 MILES
Jefferson City, Missouri

Besides the symmetry of Jefferson City as the halfway point across Missouri, we're beaching ourselves in the capital so that I can write and send off the first half of our magazine article. Since we'll be here for the next 48 hours, picking the proper hotel is crucial. Our needs differ from many tourists.

The boys require two things; a bed not being one of them.

1. A pool

2. The Cartoon Network

I need Wi-Fi, air conditioning, buffet meals that don't limit one's portions and a hotel staff with an open mind regarding bicycles inside the room.

I'd like to take credit for finding the lodging experience of the summer, but we ended up in The Ramada Inn parking lot because I couldn't pedal another revolution. In fact, I had to push our rig the last hundred yards up to the lobby.

"Ah, you'll be wanting our Katy Trail rate?" asks the towering desk clerk. His smile says be our guest, but the cynic in me worries that it's a roundabout way to overcharge cyclists, while making them feel special.

"Next time, ring our shuttle driver. We have a free pick-up from the trailhead," he adds.

Had I known this nugget of information a few hours ago, the

bridge of terror and gauntlet of hills between the river and the Ramada could have been avoided. On second thought, where's the fun in that?

"At checkout, will you be needing the shuttle back out to the trail?"

"Definitely."

I've had enough Jefferson City hill climbing fun to last a lifetime.

The Katy Trail rate was so low it has to be underwritten by the Make-A-Wish Foundation. By the time you factor in the free buffet breakfasts, drink coupons by the pool, and free movie tickets each evening at an adjacent first-run theater called the Ramada Four, someone's paying us to stay there.

I allow the boys to view *Cinderella Man* on the big screen by rationalizing the violence as sports violence on one level, and metaphors for the pain and struggle of Depression-era characters on another. That and because the theater has the coldest air conditioning in Missouri. The boys were so entertained by this *Rocky*-style story set to nice suits and stylish hats that they beg me for an encore visit to the big screen the next night. This time we're treated to a film with a target audience of prepubescent girls.

Not five minutes into *The Sisterhood of the Traveling Pants,* Quinn asks if anyone is going to stop talking and do something. Enzo's overjoyed with his complimentary popcorn and a cameo appearance by a donkey that one of the characters rides in on. When the popcorn and gummi worms run out, he pulls at my shirtsleeve in the dark.

"Dad," he whispers. "When is the goat coming back?"

Quinn leans in close, sighing like a tired parent. "It was a donkey, Enzo . . . and, and it's never coming back."

We decide to swim off the effects of their first chick flick. A radio lays down country music just the way I like it, low enough so I can't make out the lyrics, just the tune, while floating around the deep end.

"Hi, Dad."

Quinn is by my side, dog paddling around the eight-foot mark. I'm stupid with surprise. Though he'd gained the ability to stay afloat back in Colorado, we've been waiting on his confidence to catch up. Let him get in over his head on his own terms.

Hot damn! This is a "that" moment; one of those milestones that, unlike learning to walk or talk or free himself from the confinement of diapers, Quinn will actually remember. As will I.

Now we have a shared memory of night swimming . . . of taking lap after lap alongside one another, Quinn's grin unending while Enzo tries to bounce a ball off our heads from the shallow end. It's seamless and ours to keep—like a class portrait that freezes all your childhood friends and fiends in that instant forever.

When I outlive my usefulness in this world and my ability to pedal from one ocean to another, I will still have this moment, and the feeling of our limbs moving with silent grace through water. It will remind me that the world will always hold beauty and power and mystery, even as it promises to break our hearts.

I float on my back and stare up at the stars.

"Listen," Enzo says, "The karaoke song."

We stand in the shallow end and perk our ears.

"Achy Breaky Heart, My Achy Breaky Heart . . ."

And just like that I'm reminded that life is also filled with mullets, white guys with suspect rhythm, and a craze that had the audacity to wed break-dancing and line dancing together in one song.

If there is a merciful God, don't let this melody be the pervasive memory that loops endlessly during my Golden Girls Village years. Best to retire to a state with permissive assisted suicide laws, just to be on the safe side.

"It's catchy," Quinn says.

"Makes me want to dance," adds Enzo.

And that's precisely how things like the Macarena and "YMCA" got started. I throw in the towel and teach them what I remember of a goofy two-step in three feet of water under a Missouri moon. We clap and line dance and kick up water like the Rockettes until the song comes too quickly to a close.

Now *that* I'll proudly put on loop: the three of us laughing and moving our bodies through wet space on a summer evening. File it under my Greatest Hits of Fatherhood collection and relive the moment until they come to take what's left of me away.

31

"We are healed of a suffering only by expressing it to the full."
—Proust

August 12   2,490 MILES
Jefferson City, Missouri

"Let's get the little ones some chocolate milk for the road," Kelly says, wheeling the hotel shuttle van into 7-Eleven's parking lot. The very 7-Eleven where we'd gorged ourselves on the way into town.

From the moment Kelly met us in the lobby, I was struck by the way he carried himself; an outgoing, rather put-together gent about my age with deep-seated compassion in his eyes. That or he'd found a way to achieve the perfect buzz before 9 A.M. Alert but laid back—gotta get me some of that.

Rail-thin from years of cigarettes, Kelly showed extreme caution in his driving but a disregard for formalities in conversation. By the time we arrive at the 7-Eleven for supplies we're chatting away like old high school buds. He keeps saying how much he's always wanted to hit the road, and once upon a time he'd even thought about doing it by bike. A lot of people say this when they meet our rolling party, but only a few of them actually mean it. Most of them are just caught up in the moment, seduced by the idea, not the actual doing of it.

"You take extra care with these boys out there on the road," he says. He's repeated this enough times now that it borders on a mantra.

I nod again. "You have any kids, Kelly?"

He looks down at the wheel for a moment. When my van driver surfaces again, that "Up with People" gleam in his eyes has been edged over by a world-weary haze of melancholy.

"Almost?" he says.

I wait him out.

"We'll be passing by where it happened in a minute."

What happened was a carload of drunks sideswiped his fiancee's car one summer evening in 1988. She died when the door handle punctured her heart.

"I know it's messed up, but one reason I took this shuttle job is so I can pass by that spot every day."

I don't know what to say to that. We do things in life that fill voids. We do things that fulfill needs.

"She was five months pregnant with my son at the time, celebrating her baby shower. Her girlfriend was driving home with her."

This explains why he's so protective of my boys.

It went from an unfortunate accident to something else in a hurry. The driver of the other car was a teenage girl. Her older brothers were the passengers. When they realized that Kelly's fiancee was dead and it would be on their baby sister's head, they surmised the best course of action would be to beat the injured passenger to death with a tire iron and flee the scene.

She came out of her coma weeks later, broken up something fierce but with her recollections fully intact. Everyone went to jail for a long time. But Kelly's been driving Bad Memory Lane longer.

"I tell myself if I hadn't gone on vacation to Colorado for three days, they might be here today."

I've moved my hand onto Enzo's knee almost unconsciously during Kelly's horrific tale.

"Man, I've been driving folks on this loop forever, and I've never told anybody that story before."

I put my other hand on his shoulder.

"It must have given you something you needed at the time," I say.

He nods. We drive in silence. His smile returns for a moment.

"There it is." Kelly points to a pair of crosses: a bright, well-kept roadside shrine, just like the man who maintains it. Enzo waves, though at what I don't think he really knows. Maybe he's hoping we'll stop so he can play with the toys and trinkets.

Kelly pulls up to the Katy Trail drop-off lot. We sit in the van with the AC roaring.

"Whatever it helped me with once, man, has been gone a long time. I just don't know how to move beyond it. I want to . . ."

He helps me unload the rig. I've spent my loose bills on chocolate milk. When I tell Kelly the boys drank up his tip, he laughs. Then he hands me a twenty-dollar bill. I refuse it.

"As much chocolate milk as they want the rest of the way to the coast." His face says it all. "Take it for me, please." I tuck it away.

Kelly keeps kicking the bike tires and testing my handlebar grips.

"Why don't you give it a try if you want. See how much weight I'm carrying."

Kelly is Christmas-morning excited by this suggestion.

He takes right to it. Unlike most of the curious who hit me up for a test ride, Kelly's actually comfortable in the saddle, finds his balance on the second pedal stroke and rolls down the trail with purpose. He's gone long enough for my heart to stutter a few beats.

There's no LoJack or tracking device on my rig, or on my children. If he were to decide to keep going, I'm just a guy in tight clothes and a funny hat by the side of the trail.

When Kelly pulls back into the parking lot his face is that of a boy—one who hasn't lost the love of his life yet or been scrambled but good by the days going by. It's the face of hope when hope is still new.

"Whatta you know about that?" he says. "I realized something just now. I drive cyclists here all the time, but I've never ridden a bike on the Katy."

"Until now," I say.

This gives me an idea.

"What's keeping you in Jefferson City, Kelly? You gotta girl here, but you said it's nothing serious. Driving a shuttle bus is honest work, but if you want more . . . if this isn't healthy anymore, maybe it's time to stage a breakaway."

His face is a mask of pain.

"I'm not saying it isn't . . . I guess I worry they'll be forgotten."

We look at each other.

"I know I need to move on. I've even loaded up the car a few times . . ."

I steer Kelly into the shade.

"Boys, jam some sticks into the handle of that drinking fountain, make yourselves a poor man's water park. I need to sit down with Kelly for a minute."

We huddle in close.

"Quid pro quo, Kelly. Here's something I've kept to myself about this little cross-country trek. Course a magazine's covering some of the expenses, this is what I write about and all that, but the truth is, I haven't bit off something like this . . . something on the edge of insanity . . . since before the boys were born and here's why . . ."

We look over at the pair, dancing under an arching stream of water. They'll push and splash and laugh at each other all morning if I let them.

"Kelly, I'll lie like a senator if asked about this under oath, but after the boys were born I think I lost most of my edge. I know I did. Aside from book tours and weekend rides, press junkets and two-wheeled personal appearances at festivals, I stayed in my own little loop. I must have thought it was the safe and responsible thing to do; the grown-up thing. Then Stacy had to start blowing through the intersection at the end of my block."

Kelly needed to hear Stacy's story, and I couldn't do that without Benny's story sharing the bill. Stacy's this middle-aged dwarf who, like half the ambulatory population of Portland, used the bluff overlooking the Willamette River as her preferred place to walk or ride. It's a fitness freeway of sorts. Stacy's one of our regulars. She's been marching or pedaling by my door every day for years; rain, heat, hail balls, it didn't matter. Seeing her go by on her child's-size pink bike became part of my daily routine. Talking to her did not.

Say this for Stacy, she's always been cautious: helmet, looking both ways, a poster child for bicycle safety. So when I witnessed her shooting the intersection without so much as a head fake, it freaked me out. Remember, I've never actually said more than hello, even when she sat down next to me at the neighborhood Christmas party last year. I don't have a defense. I just didn't know what to say. "Were any of your relatives in the Wizard of Oz?" seemed both absurd *and* tactless, but it was the only thing that came to mind. So I smiled and went for some more eggnog.

When she pulled the same stunt for three days in a row, I'd had enough. Bright and early on the fourth morning, I stormed into the street, effectively blocking her way.

"Look, Sal . . ." I couldn't place her name.

"Stacy," she informed me.

"Look, usually I mind my own business, and you're a big girl (bad choice of words), so do what you want, but if you keep blowing through that intersection you're gonna be a statistic in no time."

Her smile was as tight as it was brief.

"I know what I'm doing," Stacy said. And with that she ran the intersection again.

Weeks go by; she must know what she's doing because I forget about it and she keeps passing the house right on schedule. Halloween weekend finds us driving home from the ZooBoo party. It's one of those perfect fall afternoons; you get about three or four of them each year, crisp with all the fall colors, and the angle of the light carries with it something extra. I'm hopped up on chocolate already and the boys are decked out in a Harry Potter costume and a ghoul face, respectively.

I watch a white car pass me going the other direction before I swing through the intersection and onto my street. An instant later brakes screech, followed by an awful thud. Stacy's down, the bike's in the grass twenty-five yards away and a stunned father wearing a tie of smiling pumpkins stumbles from behind the wheel of the white car.

"She came out of nowhere." The man's cry-talking as he wanders around his car.

Beth takes the boys inside. I pull my fleece off and add it to the coat someone else has already put under Stacy's bloody head. She's broken up all over the place, but somehow she's still with us.

"It's gonna be okay," I tell her, which is not what I'm thinking.

Sirens howl in the distance.

Her smile is loose and permanent this time.

"It's going to be okay," I tell her again.

Stacy looks right at me.

"I know," she manages.

And that's it. She lived long enough for her family to have their goodbyes at the hospital.

I talked to her sister at the wake, telling her about the intersection issues. I learned that Stacy's daredevil behavior coincided with the loss of some of her closest friends and a job that gave her life its center.

"She was a devoted Catholic and knew the deal with suicide. I've been thinking that maybe this was her way of giving up without breaking the rules. I knew she had gone inside herself, but I didn't know how far."

The other person I reached out to at the wake drove a white car.

"Nothing's gonna change what happened, but telling me what you've just told me, well it takes a little weight off."

Only this confessing of Stacy's death-wish plans wasn't moving any weight off me. Maybe if more people (me) had tried to connect with her when she was around . . .

A few weeks later I'm taking out the trash when Benny, our resident Italian cyclist, pedals by on a clunky three-speed for all he's worth. He's a diminutive man who every day comes to the stop sign that Stacy blew, and turns around. It's his routine. I offered him a wave. It all felt too familiar. He's not a dwarf, but so petite I doubt he'd have been taller than Stacy back-to-back. The bike he rides is disproportionately large for his frail little frame. So much so that I always fear he's gonna go ass-over-teakettle at the turnaround.

I was overcome by this fear that letting him go past me that day without some more meaningful contact would validate what a crappy person I'd become—sleepwalking through my "welcome-to-middle-age" script.

"Benny," I called, which startled him into an awkward, jerky stopping motion.

With nothing else planned, I launched into a caffeine-fueled list of questions about his life and cycling, and the fact that I'm married to an Italian woman. (I failed to impress him with that one.) Floundering, I offered up a cup of coffee.

He's still there when I come back with the java. I take this as an encouraging sign. We stand around for a minute.

"So what's this about? You in one of those programs where you have to do a bunch of steps to help you feel better about yourself?"

I learned in a hurry that Benny is a bust-your-balls, no-nonsense retiree. In other words, he's from New York. I know there's gotta be a hint of good-natured ribbing in there. I choose to take his attitude as a challenge. Also, I've got some cousins from New York. I can hold my own.

It's now or never to hit him with the Stacy story. Both guns blazing, a spectacle of metaphors and symbolism fill the air. When I'm through I feel exhausted but all he does is shake his head. I lean in for some Zen-like wisdom.

"Quitter."

I don't know what to say, but my body clearly does. It's racked with laughter. Benny's a butcher cutting through the fog and bullshit of our existence so everyone can see its bones. Everyone needs one professional meat cutter in his life. I still think Stacy had a hard road, but Benny makes a valid if not succinct case for personal responsibility.

Benny tells me my wife knows coffee. (As a tea drinker I know squat.) He also tells me a good Italian girl who doesn't serve old people Sanka is a keeper. What's implied here is that I married well and shouldn't forget it. Also, he says out loud that I married well and shouldn't forget it.

I say it's inspiring to see how much he loves to ride.

"I've been pedaling this road for fifteen years; started after my heart attack. The bike keeps me out of the ground."

Okay, so it's more need than love. I try a different tack.

"Bet you didn't know I make my living riding bikes around the world and writing about them."

Benny hands me the empty mug.

"Then why aren't you riding?" It's the first time a hint of a smile exposes what remains of his soft gooey center—if there ever was one.

"I got kids now. It's complicated."

His grin goes back into hiding.

"I got a heart attack. It's pretty simple."

Now we get together in my driveway a couple of times a month. He's the human equivalent of diesel fuel; a little Benny goes further than my conventional friendships. He sets me right when I'm feeling sorry for myself or the world. I set him up with quality coffee. We connect, after a fashion.

"So Kelly, that's what got me back out here. Not magazine articles or book deals, or even the romantic notion of a parenting-life-less-ordinary. It comes down to a dead dwarf I couldn't help and a live New Yorker who didn't need any."

Kelly rubs the stubble on his cheek. "That bike did feel good."

We stand up. "I don't know about signs, Kelly or even half the stuff I tell myself I should believe, but I came back out on the road for something . . . maybe it was this."

That's how, on the outskirts of Missouri's overlooked capital, I ended up in an extended shoulder-patting man-hug before 9 A.M.

32

"Anything more than the truth would be too much."
—Robert Frost

August 13   2,550 MILES
Rhineland, Missouri

Rhineland, Missouri keeps moving itself to higher ground, but each time the river floods it loses a little more—buildings, people, hope. Forget about a finger in the dike; we rolled up to an old-school all-metal playground, slides and swings too hot to play on at high noon, only to discover a man holding back the demise of his little town with hand-me-downs, fresh fruit, and Gordon Lightfoot on eight-track tape.

I park under a pavilion next to the playground. Three dozen picnic tables are crowded with stuffed animals, laundry baskets of books and some of the finest gourd specimens this side of Hermiston, Oregon. I don't know if my boys have ever had zucchini. They might tonight.

Scanning the open-air building for some sign of life, I settle on a sturdy old farmer: straw hat, cut-off jeans shorts and beer belly. He's the only one manning his booth; probably served in Korea without so much as a complaint. Clearly, the heat and humidity have chased his fellow operators indoors.

"Some fine fruit and vegetables for the taking," he tells me.

I poke, pinch and smell them for a few minutes, buy a sack of peaches, then move a couple tables down to the Robin Williams DVDs, Neil Diamond records, and Best of Bread eight track tapes. Up pops the old farmer. He's wearing a ball cap now.

"Hello, again." I say. He acts as if we haven't just talked fruit for ten minutes.

After an in-depth discussion about which of Eastwood's Josey Wales films was the best, I join my boys in a three-picnic-table library on the far side of the pavilion. We're greeted a minute later by the old farmer. This time he's sporting bifocals and a librarian's name tag that reads MARY.

"So what gives?" I ask.

He's not ready to acknowledge his charade. I look around one more time just to be certain.

"You're running the entire flea market, aren't you? Nobody's blind here."

"Mommy says you are sometimes." I know Enzo's just trying to be helpful, so I let it slide. He goes back to a pop-up book.

"It doesn't matter to me, really, but I gotta know what's up with all the different hats and badges? It's quite theatrical. Maybe I could get dinner with this show?"

The old farmer removes the bifocals and rubs his eyes a few times before he comes clean.

"It used to be a big party twice a week out here. I got this thing off the ground years ago. We had it good. Then everybody started getting sick and dying on me; mostly cancer. The state came out to check the water, but they think it's just coincidence."

He doesn't look like he buys that one.

"The dead ones willed all this stuff to me, and for my friends too ill to come out most days, I sell their books and dresses and give 'em the money."

Jesus, it's a Dead Man's Bazaar, as imagined by Tim Burton.

"Sometimes I think I'll stop coming out. But then it's something to do."

I tell him not to give up on the props and hats.

"I wasn't trying to give you a hard time. In fact, it's a nice touch."

He smiles for a photo. His name tag still says Mary.

"I think it helps me sell their stuff better," he confesses. "I know the histories of everything out here. Whose nephews and grand-children read those books your boys want. And which field them carrots came from."

We linger. I buy more stuff than we need. It's worth every penny.

33

"We are all travelers in the wilderness of this world, and
the best we can find in our travels is an honest friend."
—Robert Louis Stevenson

August 14   2,725 MILES
Near St. Louis, Missouri

Many friends threatened to join me, but Peter Weiss makes good
on it outside St. Louis. An ad man with mad people skills and a

thick, rich vein of authenticity underneath, Big Pete is everything Willy Loman wasn't. With nearly ten years on me, Pete feels like an older brother. Moving through a number of transitions in his life that summer, out of all my pals Peter has legitimate excuses for begging off, but of all my pals, he doesn't. At the tail of the Katy Trail he rides up like the cavalry, carrying supplies such as ice cream sandwiches, a new Kings of Leon CD and word from back home.

He steps onto the limestone trail, and takes a long incredulous look at us.

"Man oh man, the updates in *The Oregonian* don't even scratch the surface. You're something carved out of granite or diamonds now, Buddy Boy. Freakish, really."

We embrace, which causes him to be instantly covered in a patented Gatorade/water blend of sweat, complemented by a sunscreen wax chaser.

"Good to see you, too," he says, "but handshakes from here on in."

Reasons I like Peter:

1. He firmly believes in the adage "90 percent of life is just showing up."

2. He straddles excess and austerity, but rejects nihilism outright.

3. He never knows when to fold, even when I tell him I have the cards.

4. Like me, he loved and lost his Dad too soon. His was a rabbi who outwitted, outplayed, and outlasted the Nazi bastards who wanted to grind his bones.

5. We can talk music until the universe folds in on itself and still leave whole genres untouched.

6. My kids adore him. (For the record, my kids don't like everybody, and when they don't like someone, they don't hide it well.)

We burn across the southern tips of Illinois and Indiana to the prize that is Kentucky. Neither of us smoke tobacco or endorse the practices of tobacco companies (though Peter once crafted a marketing campaign for one, which brought in fresh recruits and made buckets of money, thus earning him a front-row box in hell; he's fond of telling me he'll be sure to save me a seat), nor do we have anything against states that begin with the letter I, but Kentucky seems like the prize. We base this on nothing more than that rolling hills and bluegrass sound cooler than busted gravel, tornados and cornfields.

Pete's melding in well with our caravan of spokes, grease and gears, breathing new life into the operation, if the truth be told. We're trying to show him the best that the road has to offer; off-kilter roadside attractions and our favorite food offerings—translation: We're eating to the edge of capacity at Hometown Buffets and breakfast bars. I'm carrying some of Peter's gear because his borrowed bike doesn't have proper racks.

"Here's the deal," Peter says. "If I can handicap you with one more kid and convince you to carry all my gear, I think I might be able to keep up with you for the length of the next cross-country ride."

He speeds up a little just to see if I can match him. I can't.

At the next rest stop, I ride off on Peter's lightweight performance bike, laughing like the bully kid on "The Simpsons."

"Ha-ha!" echoes off the rolling hills and across the horse farms of Western Kentucky.

Nothing says humility like carting someone else's kids and a few hundred pounds of gear for even a couple miles.

"This is not right, man," Peter marvels between labor pains. "On so many levels, this load you are carrying is not right."

I take pity on him and take back my burden, but not before doing a few victory laps around my friend for good measure.

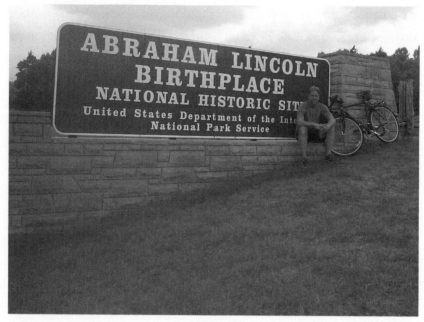

34

"I like to see a man proud of the place in which he lives.
I like to see a man live so that his place will be proud of him."
—Abraham Lincoln

August 16   2,930 MILES
Hodgenville, Kentucky

As we close in on Lincoln's birthplace, Hodgenville, Kentucky,
Peter points out the marketing genius of overkill. Every laundromat, convenience store, clothing outlet, even the churches, has a
Lincoln theme. Kentucky is damn proud of their native son, a little too proud, in fact, as we would soon discover.

"Let's take the ten-dollar tour, boys."

It's actually free, but I like saying that to my sons so they know we'll be staying awhile. The park that houses Lincoln's family cabin is gorgeous. Quinn and Enzo use their bodies to stage rolling races down grassy hills on either side of a marble-columned monument. A colony of velvet ants anchors them around a dirt patch for the better part of an hour. State and federal dollars have built a fortress of climate-controlled granite over the sixteenth president's boyhood hovel. Peter and I marvel at the grandeur.

We enter the structure with the reverence reserved for cathedrals and museums. Velvet ropes separate us from the log cabin. Expensive graphics round out the story of Lincoln's early years. I think about all those hours spent with the Lincoln Logs of my childhood. And here I am, finally, at the source. He died youngish and violently, but to get to be president, end slavery, and have a Hasbro toy phenomenon named after you, seems like a fair trade-off.

Signs everywhere advise us to refrain from flash photography because it could damage the integrity of the building, a fragile but lasting symbol of the birthplace of freedom from slavery. The roof is not constructed of green plastic and it's short on yellow doorway connectors; still, it's quite exciting.

The interior is blackened by cooking fires. I fantasize Lincoln eating too much bacon as a boy. Peter strikes up a conversation with a visibly bored ranger, asking him all sorts of questions about the photography restrictions and carbon dating for authenticity. Maybe what happens next is because it's the end of his shift, he's been drinking, someone pissed him off proper, or because we're all alone in the mausoleum. Maybe it's just the way Peter has with people, but the ranger calls us in for a huddle.

"Here's the thing. A bunch of history geeks and researchers from the university came out a few years ago. They ran a battery of tests on the soot and the wood and the mud and everything else. They're pretty much certain that this wasn't Lincoln's childhood home. It's typical of the cabin he lived in and comes from the same area, but they feel his home burned to the ground about twenty miles from here."

"It's no Roswell Incident we've stumbled upon," I say to Peter, "but if you can't trust Lincoln, who's next? The man took a bullet for us. The word 'trust' floats right over his head on the penny."

"It's generally agreed that the penny has outlived its usefulness," Peter notes.

I'd forgotten how lively conversations with another twisted adult can help stave off the insanity that roots in the hearts and heads of every primary caregiving parent. Even more so when said parent is alone on a bike for four thousand miles of daddy duties.

With that, Peter begins whirling off shots of the impostor cabin, each flash a dare to Lincoln's Judas in government greens. Just try and stop me, Ranger Rick, just try.

I'm left to explain the subtle differences between hypocrisy, pageantry, sham, national monuments and symbolic re-creations to my boys.

Frankly, I'm not up for the task. Instead, I give them some copper Lincolns to toss in the little spring where our stovepipe-hat trendsetter supposedly bathed as an infant.

35

"Everything has been figured out, except how to live."
—Jean-Paul Sartre

August 17   3,050 MILES
Central Kentucky

On occasion, the creative powers of the universe look after the most foolish among us. It has something to do with a pure heart I think, or dumb luck. It's one of those two. Whatever the reason, when the unseen tailwinds of fate pushed us over another long climb and onto the road where Gethsemani Monastery is headquartered, I believe I heard a few cosmic cogs click into place. It could be the chain, though. I hadn't lubed it in days.

Incidentally, by high school we'd decided as siblings to nickname my parents "cosmic." This term covered all behavior that could not be explained away by modern science. It's a common survival mechanism most teenagers use to avoid death by embarrassment. I'm sure you had pet names for your parents too. At least ours we could say in public. It will be interesting to see what my boys come up with for us.

One summer the cosmic duo took off on pilgrimages to Kentucky, leaving my sister in charge for a full week. We had no relatives in Kentucky, but that didn't stop the enigmatic couple. Mom's destination was spiritual renewal in the pastoral setting of this very monastery, home court of pacifist and philosopher Thomas Merton. It's ground zero for meditation, early mornings of devotion, and the art of fruitcake preparation. My dad dropped her at the gate and floored it for his own promised land: a lazy loop tour of Kentucky's distilleries.

And now I'd come full circle. I explained the significance to Peter, who, being Jewish, knew from pilgrimages.

"Lead on, Buddy Boy."

Fruitcake is an acquired taste. One I hope I never acquire. As luck would have it, preparation of the holiday hobbit food had ended for the day. It was 9 A.M. Guess that's what happens when you're a monk greeting the morning at 3 A.M.

We stood over Merton's grave site. For a pacifist his death was surprisingly violent. It involved an electrical fan, standing water in a shower and a moment of forgetfulness. Because he was shaping up to be an outspoken activist in the vein of Mr. King and Robert Kennedy, conspiracy theories abound. What is certain: in an ironic twist, he's buried beside the abbot who argued, battled, and made his life a lively misery in a world generally given over to silence.

"We put them together for all of eternity. So they might work out their differences," says the cleric at reception. Hand it to those monks, theirs is a bone-dry wit, but a wit all the same.

Roaming the grounds brings a measure of peace I haven't felt as deeply since trying to outrun the wild mustangs of Montana.

In a world of technology as mother, teacher, and savior, these plain-spoken pilgrims wandering about in their brown robes have refused to saddle up and ride in the rat race. Right or wrong, their commitment to a simple way of life is as rare as those bareback thoroughbreds.

"Dad," Quinn whispers as we lounge in the last row of the chapel during midday services. "It smells good in here. Is that the famous fruitcake?"

"Incense," I say.

"Let's have some of that for lunch."

Booker Noe's barrel-shaped family is our next stop. In the film we watch and in framed photos around the plant, four generations of bourbon makers share an uncanny resemblance to the barrels they put their product inside. The distillery is deceptively close to the monastery on the map, but hills don't tend to show up on cheap Chamber of Commerce giveaway maps.

The Jim Beam distillery is, in so many regards, a mirror operation to the monastery. Not even factoring in that the bourbon baked into those fruitcakes comes directly from the distillery's remainders, Beam's operation is a tranquil refuge where serious people focus on their work and celebrate the divine through the gifts of nature—just not in the same ways.

The boys climb over a playground of stout bourbon barrels, then come inside to sample homemade fudge. The silver-blue coloring on each storage building is like no other I've ever seen. It bathes the surrounding woods in an ethereal cobalt-blue light.

"Gentlemen, if we make it to the Kentucky Derby by sundown we could pull off a Bible Belt hat trick, bagging three forms of Kentucky religion in one day."

I recognize shot glasses, visors, bottles of Knob Creek Select, and golf shirts; my dad collected these on his pilgrimage the way others bring back crosses and candles and statues of the Virgin Mary.

That's when I have my answer. Holy crap, it's been here all along.

"Peter, could you watch the boys for a few minutes?"

His is a happy nod brought on by clean country air and several shots of Booker's finest. I grab my bike and head for the woods. The land behind the distillery is roped with single track and wooded foot trails, braided creeks and lush hollows.

A few hundred yards back of beyond I dump the bike, grab out a bag and meander over to the water's edge, as a chorus of cicada songs rise and fall from the high branches. It's my favorite time of day, an effortless shift from the incendiary heat of afternoon to the open promise of a summer evening. I break the seal on a road-worn bag of ashes one last time, take a deep breath, and set the past free.

Goodbye, Dad. It's been a good ride.

36

"The best car safety device is a rear-view mirror with a cop in it."
—Dudley Moore

August 17   3,125 MILES
Bowling Green, Kentucky

"Riddle me this, Buddy Boy." Peter's talking to me from outside the bathroom door of a hotel room in Bowling Green, Kentucky. Like a high roller in Vegas, I've played my luck one too many times at the all-you-can-eat buffets. The hot browns (turkey, pork, mystery meats of all denominations) at a country-time eatery have bound me up tighter than that ball of twine back in Kansas.

"What does Bowling Green, Kentucky have that Bowling Green, Ohio doesn't?" Peter asks. Clearly, he knows the answer. Normally I like to be left alone in the bathroom, but his conversation is taking me outside my pain.

We'd established at dinner that our reference points are all screwed up. This is not the epicenter of Kentucky, let alone the south. We'd thought Bowling Green was a destination; but only if you're looking for strip malls and restaurants with two sections: smoking and heavy smoking.

When we asked our waitress what's in Bowling Green, she offered a refreshingly honest answer.

"Not me, as soon as I raise traveling money."

Back to the bathroom for Peter's game-show questions. "Here's a hint." He slips a four-color brochure under the door: THE CORVETTE MUSEUM. "It doesn't get much more Americana than that," Peter says before slipping something else under the sizable gap.

My gut feels as if I swallowed a boa constrictor, but I have to grin between spasms of teeth-clenching pain. He's delivered two single-serving bottles of margaritas.

"Here's what I don't get, Joe. You're home to the wet dream of sports cars. Your claim to fame is the ultimate muscle toy, the factory turning these things out 24/7 for years, but no one argues this car is all front end and damned easy to get away from you. The Achilles heel of most muscle cars. Hell, just ask James Dean.

So what do you do? Put in more walk-up and drive-through liquor stores than churches. There must be three dozen places between here and the highway to buy the hard stuff from the convenience of your bucket seat."

He isn't kidding. The last time I saw a single-serve bottle of margarita outside a hotel resort minibar or airplane was at a Florida drive-through liquor barn.

"Corvette conventioneers and caravans of Stingray believers should not have such easy access to alcohol, that's all I'm saying."

I grunt in agreement.

"Drink up, Buddy Boy. It couldn't hurt. While you're at it, give thanks you're driving that porcelain bucket tonight and not one of those death bullets. Nice paint jobs, though. I'm gonna find the boys something on the Disney Channel. Try not to fall asleep in there."

37

"Reality is merely an illusion, albeit a very persistent one."
—Albert Einstein

August 18   3,250 MILES
Cincinnati, Ohio

We get within a stone's throw of Cincinnati when a storm of biblical proportions sends us for cover. Nature has made several admirable attempts to end our lives this summer, but this go-round she seems downright hell-bent on finishing the job. We realize too late that we can't outrun the weather but manage, through dumb luck, to sniff out a bike shop. Not just any bike shop, but one that features "bike trees." I'm not talking about those metal repair stands bolted in the repair bay—the ones tech geeks refer to as trees. These are the living, breathing cherry and maple variety out front. Neon green, cotton candy pink and Orange Julius-painted kids' bicycles hang from limbs like peaches.

Enzo breaks into song; a verse I recognize from "Big Rock Candy Mountain." It's the part about gumdrops and cigarettes growing on trees.

"It's what we do with the bikes that people never come back for," says Scooter.

He's a bearded, wild-eyed radical who never gave up the good fight begun thirty years earlier. The shop barely feeds him, but Scooter has held onto a remarkably upbeat attitude through it all. We bash the current administration mercilessly, discuss the folly of our species, and contemplate the fluid poetry to be found in a world where only bikes would coast along roadways.

"Every rig deserves a proper resting place." He nods to a few Schwinn single-speeds in the upper canopy. "This way, on the worst days I can peek out my front door and still make myself laugh. Reminds me not to give a shit what people think and keep looking at things from different angles. Hell, reminds me what's possible."

Broader philosophical statements notwithstanding, the boys can't get enough of this conceptual art installation. If the world made any sense at all, trees from here to DC would be filled with an array of items limited only by the imagination. Each tree a different theme: musical instruments, tropical fish, fruit pies . . . Enzo is especially partial to the notion of spaghetti loops and saucy meatballs hanging low enough for him to fork at on the fly.

They sit back on the front porch, rain coming down in sheets, breathing deep of the steaming sidewalk aroma while one-upping the other over what their trees would showcase: dinosaurs, trolls with funny hair, Baby Ruth bars.

It isn't until I wander into the depths of the store that I realize where I am. Déjà vu, all over again. Two decades peel away when I see "The Wall." Covered from floor to ceiling with signatures, dates and drawings, it's where touring cyclists sign in, where they leave their mark—like this nineteen-year-old kid named Joe, on his first flight of fancy from Maine to Florida.

So much has changed, but not my signature. During hours upon hours of mind-numbing institutionalized education, I would perfect the big loop on the J and attempt variations on a Zorro-style slash for the K—just in case someone ever published my stories and, even more absurd, someone else wanted to read them.

"Quinn and Enzo, see if Scooter can find you a Sharpie."

This time I add my Metal Cowboy moniker to the end of my latest signature. The boys scribble their Hancocks on the wall next to it.

We anchor it in place with a date. Pleased enough with our handiwork, we have Peter snap a photo.

I've always longed for a riveting family history worthy of a Discovery Channel special. Until there's an outcry for "WASPS on Wonder Bread" in America, I fear ours will remain unfilmed. Marrying into a big Italian family has helped fill in the gaps and given me traditions dating back further than the invention of Jell-O squares and pool parties. But these are hijacked memories. I never completely shake the feeling that I'm party-crashing.

Stumbling onto "The Wall" again gives me a sense of what it means to be the source of a tradition. Maybe the boys will roll their kids up to sign "The Wall" in twenty years' time. Maybe it will be a field covered in flowers by then. Either way, I like feeling part of something bigger than myself for a while.

"Can we hang my trailabike from the plum tree when we get home?" Quinn asks.

It's not the worst idea floated today.

"Let's start with the bike hook in the garage, son."

38

"A hot dog at the ball park is better than steak at the Ritz."
—Humphrey Bogart

August 19   3,340 MILES
Cincinnati, Ohio

"The trick to any successful ticket scalping purchase is to establish the going rate, then find the one guy selling short. He's usually a few blocks from the front gate, pacing on a side street with a look of desperation in his eyes."

Peter's done this before.

"That, or hope I get lucky. What's our ceiling?" Peter asks.

It's my sons' first major league baseball game. Can one put a price on that?

"Twenty-five dollars a ticket," I announce. Evidently I can.

I wait with the boys and bikes at the entrance of Great American Ballpark. Cincinnati takes its national pastime seriously. The rain of earlier has done nothing to dampen attendance. The Giants are playing the Reds in what I hope will be an orgy of hot dogs, red ropes, grand slams, and ice cream gobbled out of little plastic batter's helmets.

Whether it's our rig or too much Lycra, we turn heads. Some classic looks, double-takes from guys sporting gorilla mullets, no less, and sunburned families on vacation. It's not every day Joe six-pack sees a grown man in Lycra locking up a boat masquerading as a bicycle. We answer a few questions from stunned spectators, but before we can launch into our best stories, Peter is back.

This can't be good news. If we were going to The Show he'd have been gone longer.

"Sold out?!" I say.

He fans a fistful of tickets. "Twenty dollars for lower-deck seats sold me."

It's Peter's last night with us. We're going to do it up right after all. A bottom-of-the-ninth homer from Ken Griffey, Jr. is the highlight of my sons' first foray into professional baseball. We howl, high-five, and celebrate the continued existence of Middle America as much as anything else.

39

"Gimme back that wheel," says God,
"I don't think you're quite ready yet."
—Shel Silverstein

August 20   3,420 MILES
Leesburg, Ohio

Eighty miles east of Cincinnati, the roads deteriorate to such an extent that I'm convinced many haven't seen improvement since a CCC crew laid Depression-era asphalt and called it good. Peter punches out as planned. We're certainly going to miss his spirit, but it's up to me alone to fight our way across the Buckeye State.

He has no idea how much energy I drew from his presence.

There's no karaoke, harpists or engineers to help me over my emotional hump this time. I feel like a one-man breakaway leaving the peloton far too soon. That's the rider known as the rabbit, and it's the rarest of occasions when he is anything more than a sacrifice. But I'm not going down like that.

It's still a long way to the Atlantic, sure, but with more behind me than ahead, momentum is most assuredly our friend. The same can't be said for these blind curves, shoulderless stretches and constant rollers. It's doesn't get really dicey until after lunch, which we don't indulge in due to a complete lack of eateries along State Road 28.

If I were by myself I wouldn't give it a second thought. I'd chance the corners and blind spots with my catlike reflexes and mad skills on two wheels, but I have to think for the next generation. We're getting off this road as soon as we hit a town of any kind. When we do find civilization, it's of the one-light variety: Leesburg. I offer up a silent prayer of thanks, and roll in the direction of something called Fat Boy's Pizza. It's after 3 P.M. If they've closed the lunch menu down we'll camp out on their front stoop like Pearl Jam fans awaiting the summer tour, at least until dinner.

Leesburg doesn't look big enough to support a pizza joint, but when we push against the door it gives, and a blast of arctic air greets us. This slice of climate-controlled heaven comes compliments of Shane, pie-maker extraordinaire and unofficial concierge of Leesburg, Ohio. At thirty-one years old he chose to semi-retire from the position of chief of police to feed hungry farmers in the tri-county area.

"I'm still a cop, but there's a lot more action in pizza than crime in these parts."

That's a good thing, Shane. Hold tight to your little slice of Mayberry as long as you can.

We kick around the particulars of our adventure for a few minutes. Shane leans over the counter.

"I saw you working the road on my drive in. Hats off to you, brother; all the way in from Cincy today?!"

I mull over the menu for a few seconds longer than Shane's willing to wait.

"I'm not sure why you're weighing that decision, 'cause I would have to be a soulless bastard to charge a father hauling his sons by bike from the other side of the world up to my little snack shack."

I wave him off the idea of comping our meal, but it's too late. We're family now.

"It's my honor," Shane says. I've known the man ten minutes, but even I can surmise that honor is not something Shane tosses around lightly.

When he comes over the other side of the counter it reminds me of those famed rum runners during Prohibition turning a quiet diner into a rowdy juke joint with the pull of a few levers and the spin of a hidden wall compartment. In our case, Shane ditches the cable news network for cartoons on the big screen, keys a secret reset button on his old-school Donkey Kong game so that it rains free replays in Quinn's direction, and loads me down with bread sticks. I munch on doughy goodness while I wait for our free pizza. Each boy has a liter of soda in hand quicker than you can say "childhood diabetes."

Shane looks around to see if he's missed anything. Wait for it . . . he positions a chair so that the formidable AC blows steady and strong, then offers it to me with two quick dusting swipes and a theatrical flourish.

I can't help myself. "This wasn't by any chance called Sargent's Pizza Emporium at one time?" I ask. I had to ask.

Shane puzzles this one for a moment.

"Before my time, maybe, but it doesn't ring a bell."

I take my seat. "Don't worry about it," I tell him. It might as well

be. My dad couldn't have dreamed up a better spot. "This place is absolutely perfect."

He looks around, wondering if perhaps I've let the heatstroke confuse his humble little pizza joint with the Ritz Carlton.

After the fourth piece of pie, but right before the air conditioner freezes over the sweat on my upper lip, I know we aren't going any farther today.

"You can set up in the city park a few hundred yards from here. No one will mess with you. I'll have the squad car swing by throughout the evening anyway, just to give 'em something to do."

We stumble onto a still-water creek behind the gazebo, score worms in the soft mud and fish it until sunset. A full moon rises behind me right before bedtime. Of his own volition, Quinn snaps a photo of his old man bathed in moonshadow. I can't remember being more tired or happier in all my days. Later, we'll label this shot "La Luna è la Lunatic." I'm running on fumes and feeling just fine.

40

"I have always depended on the kindness of strangers."
—Blanche DuBois, *A Streetcar Named Desire*

August 21   3,510 MILES
Greenfield, Ohio

The road flattens out for twenty miles before turning unrideable outside Greenfield. We pick our way into the parking lot of a McDonald's. The boys enjoy their first plates of Mickey D's hotcakes ever while I grope around for a lifeline. It's the first time in 3,000 miles I don't have an escape clause. Sure, we could catch a ride out of Ohio, but that would be tantamount to quitting.

And what would Benny think of me then? I can see him inside my head, a disgusted look on his tight little Italian face. "Quitter!" he'd say in that clipped New Yorker accent.

After riding three different east-west roads with the same result—fear and loathing in Ohio—I'm gonna have to reach deep into the collective knowledge of the locals for safe passage. Even more frustrating are the north-south routes; paved in this century, they're wider than a swollen river in flood. If I stayed on those it would be smooth sailing, but akin to tacking the boat back and forth at the mouth of the bay, never getting any closer to shore.

I ask around but no one has an easy answer.

"Could you have cuter kids if you tried?"

A pair of robust ladies in Curves T-shirts and Lycra shorts are dispatching a few plates of hotcakes in the back booth, balancing the morning workout with a couple thousand calories of carbo loading. I share our predicament. They smile and nod. We make our way out to the rig again. I want to keep my chin up, but it's starting to drag along the pavement. Maybe the boys won't notice.

"We didn't mention the bike path that runs all the way to Chillicothe, since it's about twenty miles north and a hair west of here." The Curves gals are back. I learn that the older, less curvaceous one fighting sixty—and winning—is Cricket. She's a long-haul trucker for Walmart.

"Done that Portland to Arkansas loop up from the dirty side so many times I feel like a cat chasing his tail."

Cricket's the real deal. All that's missing is a CB in her right hand and an 84-ounce jug of coffee in her left. Our truck-driving momma's taller, wider sidekick, who looks as though she stacks bricks all day in the summer sun for the fun of it, is Cricket's daughter. She's not what you would call chatty, a full-grown woman, and Cricket refers to her only as Daughter. I wait for more, but that's it. Daughter it is. They remind me of an inverted version of the magician duo of Penn and Teller, only the short one does all the talking with this crew.

"Truth is we have a few trucks at the homestead. If you wait here we'll be back in no time." We wait.

Enzo walks the curb while Quinn practices flicking bottle caps, a new trick one of the regulars at Treloar Grill taught him back in Missouri. We wait some more.

Proving that he's let the harder edges of the road seep in just a little, Quinn turns to me, shaking his head, and says, "You think they're coming back?"

Hold the phone, son. I'm supposed to be the cynic of the group. It's a valid question though, with a lot riding on it.

"There they are!" Enzo points at a decrepit Chevy swinging into the lot.

And that's how Enzo ended up learning how to drive stick.

While Quinn and I watch miles of corn fields roll by from the back of the bed, Enzo sits on the bench seat between Cricket and Daughter, belted in, his little hand on the shifter under Daughter's sturdy mitt.

"Shift," Daughter hollers. It's the first word, and nearly the last, we'll hear out of her. Enzo giggles, pushing the lever around as if it's attached to something heavy.

Quinn leans against his sleeping bag. I can't help thinking of seasoned hobos riding the rails. "I love it when a plan comes together," he says.

And I love it (usually) when my pet phrases echo out of my son's mouth. Enzo waves at us through the back window before dropping it into fourth. I'm ruining these boys in the best way I know how.

Cricket's bike path is everything we could ask for and more; woods on one side and water on the other. A few hours in we overtake a golf cart with an official VOLUNTEER magnet sign plastered across its boot. She jerks the wheel wildly in startled fear when we pull along side for a quick hello.

"I'm guessing ten miles to Chillicothe?" I wait for her to concur or correct me.

"Chillicothe?"

I'm not sure this retiree knows who she is, let alone where. That's a Vicodin smile if I've ever seen one. The Eskimos put their elders onto ice floats in a cold-shoulder (some would argue humane) send-off to the other side. In Central Ohio it appears the electric cart stands in for the traditional ice float.

Maybe it's hearing loss.

"CHILLICOTHE?" I scream.

She nods. I might as well be asking about jelly beans.

"HOW FAR?"

"A hundred miles?" She delivers this in the form of a tentative question. It's less than a hundred miles to the West Virginia border. Even I know that.

When she sees I'm not buying it, our convoluted trail volunteer, bless her heart, tries again. "Twenty-five?"

I bring out my cell phone. "Is there someone I can call to come get you?"

This spooks her. She breaks into a nervous laugh that sounds like a helium balloon being tortured. Then, without warning, she turns into a wind-up toy the dog might have damaged during fetch. Next thing we know she's hollering out random distances while wheeling away from us, and Chillicothe, as fast as her cart will go . . . which, thankfully, is about five miles per hour.

"That lady's crazy." Quinn says. "Someone oughta stop her."

Damn it.

"I noticed she had a sack lunch on board," I say. It's a pitiful form of rationalizing. I shake my head. If there's one thing a touring cyclist hates to do, it's head back over ground he's already covered.

Still, that woman was in no shape to be driving anything faster than a couch. I really should go after her. Where's my humanity?

"We could leave a note about her at the end of the trail," Quinn suggests.

I mull it over. There are so many reasons to keep going. Not the least of which, we have seven hundred more miles to cover to the nation's capital. If there wasn't a water hazard running the length of the trail I could almost ride away with a clear conscience. That, and if I didn't have a mother of my own . . .

"We could just let Cricket pick her up," Enzo says.

From the mouths of babes. I'm shamefaced as I turn our rig around.

"We have to be someone's Cricket this time, Enzo," I say. He likes that.

With that, we go after an electric-powered ice float in 100-degree heat. It carries one bike trail volunteer on an extended senior moment. Quinn starts really pedaling now.

"Maybe she'll let us drive that cool golf cart."

The rescue is anticlimactic. We find her above waterline, at an information depot bench, rocking gently. A phone call to trail maintenance secures her health and welfare for another day. We don't deserve a medal, but like flexing a muscle so it doesn't atrophy, the act of making your moments little experiments in kindness is enough.

41

"I fell in to a burning ring of fire
I went down, down, down
and the flames went higher."
—Johnny Cash

August 22   3,540 MILES
Chillicothe, Ohio

We spring for a decent hotel with deluxe pool in Chillicothe. One thunder-boomer of a summer storm almost clips us on the way in. I could take the shallow way out and blame the ice float rescue for our brush with bad weather, but I'm still feeling peacock proud of my behavior—even though it was foisted on me by my children. I've decided it takes a village to raise most forty-year-old men.

The pool is under a glass dome, which keeps me in close contact with the cigarette smoke and robust beer-fueled conversations of a family reunion two patio tables over. I now know why the parking lot is crowded with Camaros and El Caminos.

I want to say something caustic, but their girls seem to have hit it off with my sons, exchanging snorkels for floaties with the ease of stock traders swapping after-hour tips at the bar.

No one's really being that obnoxious. In fact, it's even a subdued affair, considering their numbers and beer consumption. I just hate cigarette smoke. Someone offers me a tallboy.

"Is that your bike locked under the stairwell?" Bobby asks. He has a roofer's tan and a blond ponytail that runs halfway down his back when it's wet.

"For thirty-five hundred miles now," I say.

Bobby wants all the details. It's half an hour later when I find my manners and ask what everyone's celebrating on a Wednesday afternoon. Trish looks over to her girls, then back at me.

"They don't know yet, so keep this under your hat. Bobby, show him the article."

Lottery winners? The family of some American Idol hopeful, maybe? Someone's getting a new step-daddy?

The headline doesn't register for a moment. I look around the page for another story. I sit way back in the lounge chair when I'm done reading.

"Burned to the ground? A total loss?"

Trish bites her lower lip. It's her house we're talking about; *was* her house. Bobby and the rest are brothers, cousins and girlfriends circling the wagons for moral support and making suggestions about a problem with no easy answers.

"Trish and the girls were away on vacation when it happened," Bobby notes. "I was able to cut them off at the pass."

We all take long pulls from our tallboys. It feels like a macabre drinking game at this point.

"My daughter doesn't know yet."

Enzo's locked in an all-out splash contest with her. She's in heaven.

"I wanted to give her a little more fun before her world changes so much. Plus we needed a place to stay and regroup."

Trish looks as if she's going to cry. Judging by the mascara marks it's been a Wednesday of waterworks.

"I really want to be thankful that no one was hurt. I do. Everyone keeps telling me it's not about things, but come on now, they were my things."

Bobby takes her hand. I take another drink.

"We're going back over there tomorrow to see if anything can be saved," he says. "What the fire didn't get, though, I'm thinking the water did."

Trish sucks it up. Her voice is stronger when she speaks again.

"Our photos. All her stuffed animals."

Bobby decides to lighten the mood.

"We're gonna rebuild for her; lots of handymen in this family when they aren't on the sauce."

He punches his brother and hands me a camera.

"And we're gonna take a lot more pictures."

I'm blinded by broken smiles and beer cans raised in brave defiance at what the world has thrown at them. And here I wanted to tell these people to grow up only minutes earlier.

None of us could know that in a few days the entire Gulf Coast region will be wiped clean by Katrina; a lot of people losing their things and much more.

"It's not the end of the world," Trish adds. "It just feels like it."

42

"We are not retreating—we are advancing in another direction."
—General Douglas MacArthur

August 23   3,610 MILES
Outside Wheeling, West Virginia

A rookie mistake is to underestimate the Appalachians. For a guy who has six Continental Divide crossings and more than a handful of ten-thousand-foot-plus climbs in his back pocket on this ride alone, I've earned the right to scoff at the relatively puny peaks of the East. I don't. Instead, I quake and shake in my toe clips. And here's why. You ask any math geek with his regional Science Bowl ribbon—it always comes down to angles, grades and the devastatingly short distance between two points—in this case peaks and valleys. Where the West is thick with 3- and 4-percent government-approved grades that switchback gently into the heavens, West Virginia is a minefield of 7- and 8-percent grades, crazy shit sketched out by Dr. Seuss that shoots straight up for a mile or two at a time, down for another three miles, then it's rinse, puke, and repeat; a contiguous series of rollers without end or straightaways reaching out to the horizon.

I speak from personal experience. I've tangled with this old mountain chain before and it wasn't pretty; took up the challenge by bike in 1985. On any cross-country bike tour the Appalachians can be deal-breakers. It's a poorly kept secret in the industry. These mountains have ended many a tandem dream and even a few marriages. They've sent college dropouts bolting back to class and soul-searching would-be Kerouacs right "off the road."

As we edge closer and closer to Wheeling, West Virginia, I have a decision to make: take the more direct route into the mountains or shank it to the left through Pittsburgh. It'll add a hundred and fifty miles or more onto my bar tab, but I get physically ill every time I replay the heart-stopping inclines and over-too-soon drops which paid miserly dividends. As a ripped twenty-year-old carrying a trifling of my current rolling weight it almost ended me then. Most people bring their inner child along on a cross-country adventure, but when you haul actual kids along, it has repercussions. A few hundred extra pounds of repercussions, in this case. I smell insult to injury. I can hear the water cooler talk now . . .

"He pulled them through fifteen states, over eleven mountain passes in hundred-degree heat, but I hear the Virginias were too much for him."

"Who we talking about again?"

Exactly! I could've been a contender. That's why I turn us north without another thought and take dead aim on Pittsburgh, the place of my birth.

"Dad, what the hell is that?" Quinn screams from his Brooks rumble seat atop the trailabike.

I'm a nanosecond away from my "Where'd you learn to talk like that, Mister" speech (we all know good and damn well where) when I spot what he's talking about.

"What the hell is it?" I repeat.

We watch the creature waddle across the pavement. It's dark and gray, long and furry.

I channel George Colony's bemused astonishment from the Coen brothers' masterpiece, *O Brother, Where Art Thou?*

"Beaver?"

No, that's not right.

"Marmot?"

Can't be.

"Badger?"

Ridiculous.

And then it hits me. Only one animal owns that waddle.

"Otter!"

"That's it!" Quinn concurs. There's much rejoicing, for no particular reason beyond our rudimentary grasp of animal husbandry. We see it shuffle back and forth before ducking into a marsh of cattails.

"Quinn said 'hell,'" Enzo says gleefully. He knows he's succeeded in saying the same word under a cloak of complete immunity.

It's out there now, like someone taking off dirty old shoes in church. I have to say something to Quinn. He shoots first.

"You said 'hell' after me."

Kid's gonna make a good lawyer.

"And that's the last time I want to hear you, me, any of us using such language." It won't be—we all know this—but saying it keeps the boundaries of our father-sons relationship intact.

"How 'bout that river otter, though? Wanna double back and see if he comes out again?"

We're sitting in Primanti Brothers Deli, a Pittsburgh institution for as long as anyone can remember. Lunch is over, but we find it difficult to move after consuming the best sandwich my boys would have created if it hadn't already been on the menu: hand-cut fries and heaps of coleslaw stuffed right in with meat, melted cheese, and tomatoes. It's the deli's second most popular item. The house favorite? Beer. I make the boys order milk.

Our tour guide is one of my best and longest-running friends in the world, Albert Pantone. Except for a five-year stint camp directing in Central Florida, a six-month film shoot on the island of Antigua (as a pirate in Michael Caine's *The Island*—it ended with a laughable misunderstanding, what some might call an international incident, and an extended vacation to photograph Costa Rica's tree frogs), Al's another of Pittsburgh's institutions, staying put to raise his daughter, Alice Rose, in the Steel City he loves and loathes—depending on what day you talk to him.

Al's hosting our visit in style. He's loaded the fridge with watermelon, taken us to the amusement park of my childhood, Kennywood, and rented the boys the final *Star Wars* prequel installment. Sweet weeping Jesus, this means I won't have to answer any more questions about the empire, the Alliance, or Clone Wars.

I'd made the grievous mistake of attending a 9 A.M. showing of the movie based solely on the fact that we were experiencing a rare Portland heat wave. Fate handed me a few hours to kill before noon, and sitting in air conditioned darkness on a Tuesday morning had a decadent ring to it. That itself wasn't the mistake. Telling my son was.

If I'd known there was going to be a full-on final exam administered daily for two months by a seven-year-old sitting right behind me, I might have watched the movie with an eye for details. Or even with my eyes open for more than ten minutes at a time. I blamed George Lucas and his stilted character development for my troubles.

It's amazing how much a young boy can know about a film he has yet to see. I wised up somewhere in Idaho and began regurgitating the very information he was using to correct my mistakes and knowledge gaps. By the end of the summer I'd created the illusion that I was the resident Star Wars film authority again. Al's rental should put that lie to bed once and for all. But it gives us a chance to catch up.

"What in God's name are these, Joe?" Al's holding the worst souvenir purchases of the tour so far. After letting the boys rummage through Big Mike's Rock Shop, I actually paid someone to let me add rocks to our rolling weight. I'm the first to admit that questionable decisions have been made on this adventure—some would argue the adventure itself should top that list—but there's no doubt about the buying of three-pound rocks. That was just plain wrong.

Al brings out the battered Speak & Spell toy. "Here's something educational," he says, trying to make me feel better about the rocks.

"Not exactly."

We have a good laugh listening to the toy stumble over its words like the corner bar drunk. He fingers the universal remote he finds in the left pannier.

"Can I have this?"

43

"With the possible exception of the equator,
everything begins somewhere."
—Peter Robert Fleming

August 24   3,755 MILES
Pittsburgh, Pennsylvania

Unlike other times when I've come back to the town of my childhood—and I've come back enough as an adult to know that I must
be looking for something—this summer there's no distance
between myself and everything I once thought of as my second

skin: all the sidewalks I rode Big Wheels down, and the porches I played hours of Crazy Eights and Hungry, Hungry Hippo on. It's been a subtle but real disconnect from the zoo, the pool, the parks and bridges we gave secret names to and my return to them as an adult. It's the same melancholy feeling that being at school after-hours as a kid for teacher conferences or to retrieve a lost coat used to give me. Familiar, but wrong.

It takes seeing my sons swing in the Highland Park playground, roll recklessly down the lawns of Squirrel Hill and wait for their eyes to adjust to the twilight of the nocturnal zoo to fully understand.

I start to explain myself to the boys, but there's no need. For the only time on the trip I'm all kid for one day. We stay in the city pool long after the afternoon crowd thins and our skin prunes, then we play round after round of freeze tag and hide-and-seek on hallowed ground. It's a rare moment in our relationship when Quinn or Enzo calls it quits before me.

To locate home I needed to return as a child. And while that shouldn't be possible, my sons have made it so. For this reason alone, I pedal us back to Al's house feeling like I could pull them anywhere, feeling no weight behind me at all.

The countryside east of Pittsburgh hasn't changed that much since my childhood. The suburbs have done the usual slow creep into agricultural zones, but you still find yourself on the farm in short order. It taps into memories of school field trips and a Sunday drive my Dad managed with us each summer.

Could this be it? The improbable source of my cycling affliction. It was right around here that I was first bitten. You never know where or when your future will make a guest appearance.

It felt as though my father had been navigating the family car, a 1965 navy blue Mustang with too many coffee stains across its dash and more than a few deferred dreams in its driver's seat, for untold eons and through distant galaxies. In point of fact, the Harveys' farm couldn't have been more than a breezy hour drive outside of Pittsburgh. But from the sticky upholstered recesses of the back seat I rattled about with the restlessness of a prisoner in Sing Sing doing the full knock on a life sentence.

My siblings, far from representatives of church-choir propriety, seemed to be holding up better. A hazy twinkle in my brother's eyes indicated a candy-coated daydream or the approach of a full-fledged nap. Lucky bastard.

Jen was all about the Crayolas. We could have been hurtling down a waterfall and her concentration would not have faltered from the connect-the-dots page she was suturing together. To no one's surprise, Jen would become a physician. I suspect my window-seat view of Pennsylvania's rolling hill country—at the height of the season—was only adding to my pain.

Clearly, life was greener on the other side of the glass. I could see it for myself. Summer's distinct look and feel—the hum of insects from the sawgrass, tractors turning warm, rich earth and the mystery patchworks of lush woods so thick and full as to be capable of insinuating the hint of themselves into a car at sixty miles per hour.

As we came to a stop the gravel pinged about and made a satisfying crunch under the weight of the Mustang's racing tires. I could taste freedom, but it was a ruse—Dad stopping for ice, Pabst and directions. I strained to see beyond my prison, and though I didn't have the slightest inkling of its importance, I caught a glimpse of my future. Blinding Lycra fashion was still years away. His wardrobe consisted of Converse Chucks and wide, white tube socks with a band of green stripes circling the top, cut-off jeans, and a T-shirt advertising some dirigible company named Led Zeppelin.

She was bent over his bicycle, an awkwardly loaded contraption.

She was adeptly working a menagerie of gear into place—jugs of water and impulse purchases. Her gypsy-style dress made popular the world over by Stevie Nicks only a few years later seemed incredibly exotic at the time, the calling card of a dancer on break from the bustling bazaar of Zanzibar.

And to be so out-of-bounds as to wear a camouflage T-shirt tied into a halter, with tennis shoes poking out from under that dress. Who were these people?

Having learned the float and glide of two-wheeled travel only the summer before, I'd already managed to snap a limb and sustain a slight concussion in my excitement, my need for speed and a self-imposed slow learning curve regarding the laws of gravity. Cycling already had a fierce hold on me, and now this: moving from the happy-hour appetizer buffet of biking to the full dinner menu. All those gears, lines and angles—the thin spokes, devoid of playing cards; these were bikes, not toys to tool around the neighborhood on and jump plywood ramps until Mom yelled something about medical insurance and gray hair. With their narrow, sleek saddles and tight drop handlebars, these machines could eat up miles and take you from Amish country to points . . . well, points I hadn't even names for yet.

She hiked the gypsy high, exposing acres of leg as she climbed onto her rig. At six or seven, I did not connect this directly to anything sexual, but certainly it indicated the end of civilization as I knew it . . . and it couldn't have come soon enough for my restless heart.

Now, how to stage a prison break or get word to them somehow. I had to know where these rare species came from, and if they could leave some bread crumbs for me to find my way back there at a later date. The pair was casting off and all I had to return to was a car full of coffee stains, the contemptuous familiarity of siblings, and an afternoon featuring the promise of rolling down hay piles, chickens to feed, and goats in need of petting. This had all been well and good, desirable, until this couple and their bikes had appeared.

I felt a fuzzy rush come to a point at the top of my forehead. I was emerging from a sleepy dream state into a stuffy room filled with too many people and not enough air.

"Damn it," my father whispered from the front seat. I thought he'd spilled his beverage again. Mom looked concerned, but it turned out to be a declaration ending some internal discussion he'd been having with a person I'd never met.

Dad took quick, deliberate steps to cut off the pair. Not a small man, it could end in violence. But why? Had they so upset his New England sense of tradition, his view of what people did and did not do with their time and energy, that he felt compelled to confront them with it?

Fear and a giddy excitement bum-rushed my veins. Maybe I was to witness the end of an exotic species, but at least something was going to happen. The air was going to enter back into my room. I couldn't hear what they were talking about, but if Dad planned to rough them up he was using charm and a disarming level of friendliness to lull them into the ambush. We waited. Dad brought out his fist, but it contained a six of Pabst. They stood together drinking and talking and laughing.

Then Dad got out a pen and wrote something down. I was confused. He'd been decorated in the Coast Guard, choosing from there to make his living in white shirts and dark suits purchasing parts of nuclear reactors for a multinational corporation. On more than one occasion he'd muttered to my Mom that the neighbor's kids, who exhibited more than a passing resemblance to that pair on the bikes, had parked their damn hippie van in front of our house again.

Dad was moving into enigma territory—cozying up with people his world view demanded he fantasize turning a hose on. Come on now, we flew an American flag from our porch at even the whisper of a national holiday. We owned pesticides; we certainly weren't trying to find our way "back to the garden."

Years later I'd unearth a collection of photographs Dad had taken on a relatively tame walkabout between the Coast Guard years and his citizen career of not-so-quiet desperation. Shots of old gas stations at dusk, a homeless New York City guy holding a door open for a mother and her kids, grapes ripening in the shadow of a power plant. While not the scandalous images of, say, a Mapplethorpe, they went some distance in explaining why he invited those cyclists back to the Harveys' farm.

At the height of my own bike odysseys, somewhere on New Zealand's South Island, word reached me that Dad felt he had nothing to do with my interest in bikes (aside from making a mess of the brake system on my first ten-speed—which, after an afternoon of cursing and pinched skin and still more cursing, he'd admitted defeat and took it to the local bike shop), nor my wanderlust. Had I not been on the other side of the world, I'd have argued him on both points. My defense would have been short and sweet. Exhibit A: Zeppelin shirt. Exhibit B: gypsy dress and legs that went on forever.

After dinner the couple regaled us with road tales that succeeded in making North Dakota sound like a heartland poem and the Canadian border a stargate to another realm. My eyes ping-pong from them to the bikes while their stories unfurled.

At some point my head caved in, becoming a road map as far as the synapses could fire. All I needed to excavate was a strong pair of legs and the memory of them—the immediacy of their nomadic lives and the playful sense of peace on their faces as they set up sleeping bags in a quiet corner of the barn.

Maybe they're still out there—using Social Security checks to pedal roads they coasted together years before. Maybe they went their separate ways before those wheels even touched the salt water of the Jersey shore. It doesn't matter, because the Gypsy and Zeppelin take to the road every time I settle into the saddle. And when I'm trapped in traffic, caged in a steel frame of combustion engine and shock-jock rhetoric, when I sit there resembling my dad but for the Pabst Blue Ribbon and the chances not taken, I hold onto this knowledge—the knowledge that my other vehicle is a flashback to the summer of 1971.

It never fails to carry me over until my next long ride.

44

"What you see before you, my friend, is the result of a
lifetime of chocolate." —Katharine Hepburn

August 26   3,920 MILES
Hershey, Pennsylvania

Pennsylvania's hill country was the right call. We may be north
of the nation's capital, but we're going to get there right on time, if
not ahead of schedule. I shudder to think which ditch we'd be lying
in along the Appalachians of West Virginia.

My original plan, cooked up at Al's kitchen table, was to pick up
the Towpath Trail as soon as possible. It's Pennsylvania and
Maryland's version of Missouri's Katy Trail, a mostly contiguous
series of relatively flat bike paths—the Great Allegheny Passage and
the C&O Canal if you're looking for its official name—that will get
you from east of Pittsburgh to Washington in style. With only a few

interruptions, it would usher us all the way to our terminus.

That's when the sweetest place on Earth intervened.

Of course, Hershey, Pennsylvania, always deserves serious consideration—it's the closest place on Earth to a live-action Willie Wonka's Chocolate Factory. Given a choice between regular heaven and chocolate heaven, I'll always pick chocolate heaven. It could be a trick, but if it isn't, hmm boy, look out . . .

Hershey's a study in opposites coexisting within the same ZIP code. To reach Hershey World you must enter or exit through Amish country. Lancaster County is the epicenter of horse-and-buggy transportation, very serious people, and some of the finest handmade basket crafts you'll ever come across.

Tourists travel the world over to partake in the hedonistic pleasures of chocolate in every possible shape, state and form. Then, still spinning from all those amusement rides, with milk chocolate dripping down some of their faces, they scoot right over to see how people live without electricity. In this way, the Amish are like our conscience. Comic Steven Wright pointed out that a conscience is what hurts when all your other parts feel really good.

After an employee dressed in a bulbous aluminum-foil Kiss costume hands us our fifth candy bar sample in so many minutes, most of our parts are feeling damn fine. I've decided to save the barn-raising attraction of the Amish for tomorrow. I base this on the maxim that life is short, so eat dessert first. If it's not apparent by now, I'm a weak, little man.

This is brought into sharp focus when I agree to a quick stop in the Hershey gift shop. Avoiding the Appalachians has made me cocky. Perhaps it's why I forget I'm still pedaling a weighty rig with several hundred miles to go. What else would explain the twenty pounds of chocolate I purchase? I realize my mistake outside Lancaster.

It's ten o'clock in the morning, and the humidity allows me to learn what breathing through cotton would be like. I'm a few pounds over my pulling capacity; twenty pounds, I believe.

I pull over. So it's come to this. I rip open four family-size bags of assorted Hershey products and smile lovingly at my sons. The boys can't believe it. Daddy has finally shaken loose the last remnants of his mind, and it looks as if it's falling in our direction. What are the odds? I create two generous piles in the shade before delivering my edict.

"Boys, what happens in Hershey, stays in Hershey." The last of my resolve escaping on the damp currents of a deep sigh. "Your mother never needs to know about this." I look around, in case she's listening. Halloween is about to arrive a few months early.

"Come closer, boys, because you will not hear me say this again in your lifetime, but today I need you to eat chocolate like your very existence depends on it."

By lunchtime they've had enough. Reese's Peanut Butter Cup wrappers litter the trailer. Quinn's face is a Picasso of chocolate and nougat. Enzo, of the steel-trap stomach clan, complains of a slight tummyache.

We come to a stop under a billboard for tours of an Amish Village. The thirty-foot-wide stoic face of an elder in black hat and prodigious beard scowls down at us.

"You think the Amish might enjoy some York peppermint patties?" Enzo asks.

It's taken nearly four thousand miles and twenty pounds of chocolate, but they seem to have mastered the art of sharing.

45

We skip rocks along the Potomac before pedaling the last few miles of the C&O Canal towpath that leads right onto the Mall. Statuesque blue herons dot the shoreline of this famous waterway.

The last two days have been unusually tranquil. The downhill run in muggy heat has taken the talk out of us, but it's a good silence, a comfortable one.

Photographers and friends join for the final morning. It's no presidential escort, but since when did the Rebel Alliance ever require one? Element of surprise, brothers and sisters, element of surprise.

Champagne flows in front of the Washington Monument. I douse myself with bottles of water and take a victory lap, but the truth is I resemble Forrest Gump when he'd had enough running and turns to his followers, all those folks looking for a guru in track shoes. With the monument towering behind me, I turn to no one in particular and echo Gump's words.

"I'm pretty tired. I think I'll go home now," I say.

Bone-tired, really, but as complete as I'll ever hope to be. At the steps of the Capitol, I face west and really savor our victory for the first time. Miles and the accompanying experiences have chiseled my body into performance art and cleared my head. Maybe it's the endorphins, but the idea of racing in the forty-and-over class this fall doesn't seem like crazy talk. The pull of mid-life, with all its second-guessing and settling for what will be, was left sucking wind somewhere back in Idaho.

When I think no one is looking, I extend my middle finger and smile.

Epilogue

You have to give it up for those Russian gymnasts. If there's one thing I've learned since rolling away from the nation's capital, it's that it's not easy to stick the landing. Our flight home, scheduled to connect in Atlanta, was rerouted through Salt Lake City because of a little weather disturbance by the name of Katrina.

I snuck the boys back into Oregon one day before the new school year. Standing with them as the morning bell rings, they look like the rest of the students, but we know better. Despite RV Roy's warning not to let anything happen to my sons, something has, and I couldn't be happier about that. Nothing meteoric; they did not come home speaking four languages, able to see in the dark, or pilot a stealth bomber. But little miracles are where it's at, anyway. We share a secret, the three of us; one permanent summer in our hearts now, where we're never apart.

As for sticking my own landing, it's been touch-and-go, but I've taken to heart the advice of my favorite bumper sticker of the summer: QUIT YOUR BITCHIN' AND BE YOUR OWN REVOLUTION. (I'll grant you it's a questionable place to turn for life-altering answers, but why not? I mean, do you really think Dr. Phil is a highly trained professional? I'm guessing he just speed-reads a helluva lot of bumpers on the way in to work.)

To this end, I've opted out of middle age, choosing to return to my early twenties, not so I'll be at my sexual peak, or because it was easier to eat everything *and* retain my six-pack abs, (or the four I started with, anyway), but for the goofy, pissed-off, inflamed passion I felt about things I thought mattered back then.

At forty, with the poison in my gonads reigned in enough to think clearly for more than five minutes, I see that the best of what mattered back then to me still matters now; even more so as a husband and father of *three* sons.

That's right, regarding the poison in my gonads, a few slipped by the doorman when no one was looking. Blame it on both boys being in school full-time for the first time. That's too many hours for parents to be left unsupervised. Now I'm wondering what we'll look like in years to come on a bicycle built for five.

But about that revolution. We're an imperfect work in progress, but we've chucked our TVs, taken our bike travel, education advocacy, and humor program to schools, business groups, anywhere that will have us, converted a car to run on cooking oil and stopped buying a lot of crap. The GNP will have to grow without us. I cycle the boys to school on the rig (that turns a few heads), and we're knee-deep in the founding and organizing of Camp Creative, an outdoor arts and activism summer camp and year-round experiential education expedition school.

I'm not trying to save the world (well, maybe a little piece of it), but the truth is we just can't blend in with the mess anymore and respect ourselves in the morning. I'm done calculating the costs/benefits of unchecked national appetites and making concessions for myself and my fellow man. I still love this claptrap of a species, but I've made my way out of the conga line into a lifeboat, and I'm begging you to put down the reality TV and come with me.

We may have lost the republic while our backs and ballots were turned, but people, the world still awaits tomorrow's choices. Idealism isn't a dirty word. Doing something noble isn't naiveté best left on college campuses and the stages of charity concerts; it's the only road worth taking if we want to give our children a crack at safe passage, and I know from roads.

Apathy isn't hip, and if I can pull two boys, three generations, and two hundred and fifty pounds of back-fat from one ocean to the other on a bicycle, then there's no reason you should go down without a fight. Heads up: Superman ain't coming. Besides, it would be a pretty lame third act if he did. What we need now is what we've always needed: a few more Clark Kents with imagination.

And just for the record, it was probably the fungus water talking to me out there in Kansas, but Pittsburgh won the Super Bowl.

Acknowledgements and author's note

I owe a debt of gratitude to everyone who made our coast to coast outing a reality. Foremost, my wife, Beth. I've said it before and I'll say it again for the Congressional Record: the most understanding woman in the world. Thanks for playing along, my love. And to the rest of my family, immediate and extended, you make my life that much richer for being in it, and my e-mail inbox not so lonely. But stop with the Viagra spam.

Dave and Mark at River City Bicycles for stepping up with gear and encouragement. My Canadian bros, eh, at Arkel Panniers, for making a killer line of bags. And my other top-flight sponsors; Chariot, Adidas (for those shoes), Mountain Hardwear and Clif.

On the literary side, *Men's Journal* editor Peter "you're really going through with this?" Frank for green lighting the ride and cover story. Joel Weber for tactical as well as spiritual assistance. *MJ* photographer Julien Capmeil for making me look better on the page than I could ever hope to by day. All the talented editors at the helm where my syndicated columns run each month, including Claire Bonin at *The Bicycle Paper* in Seattle, Becky Roberts at *Bike Midwest,* and Matt Nelson and Mark Flint at *Tailwinds.* All my peers who gave early drafts a good wash and spin, and my literary pals in positions of gainful employment at   Literary Arts Inc.—Elizabeth Burnett and John Morrison; and Community of Writers—Larry Colton—who keep allowing me and paying me to work the next generation of Northwest writers into a lather before handing them back to their regularly scheduled teachers.

Michelle Bergkamp for that wonderful cover shot of her son,

Brysen. My regular Friday night poker mates for their wisecracks and money. It's a cash only table, boys. Chris Andon for volunteering his sleeping bag last minute. I still have no idea who has mine.

For your faith in this project, and for editing, design, layout, and general in-the-trenches, roll-up-those-sleeves-and-get-muddy-with-words work, Breakaway Books publisher Garth Battista, and proofer Jim Moore.

And finally, for all the people we met, heard about and learned of along the way who are trying to make a positive difference through their actions, you humble me.

Author's note

If you would like to help make a difference connected to work I am doing through the founding of an arts, expedition and activism program; Camp Creative go to www.metalcowboy.com to learn more, donate and get involved.